THE FORGOTTEN SONGS OF THE UPPER THAMES

The Forgotten Songs of the Upper Thames

FOLK SONGS
FROM THE ALFRED WILLIAMS COLLECTION

Edited by
MARTIN GRAEBE

LONDON
THE BALLAD PARTNERS
in association with the Traditional Song Forum
2021

Published by
The Ballad Partners
19 Bedford Road
London N2 9DB
theballadpartners.co.uk
in association with the Traditional Song Forum
tradsong.org

ISBN 978-1-9161424-3-5

Printed and bound by Biddles Books Ltd, Castle House, East Winch Road, Blackborough End, King's Lynn, Norfolk PE32 1SF.

The Ballad Partners is a not-for-profit cooperative venture established with the aims of:

• publishing, or facilitating the publication of, monographs, essays, peer-reviewed papers, and other materials in the fields of folk and traditional song, music, dance, and custom (the folk arts), street literature, and related areas

• raising awareness and encouraging the study of the folk arts by the timely and affordable publication of suitable materials and their subsequent sale and distribution.

The Ballad Partners may also organize or support other activities, such as conferences, meetings, exhibitions, and displays, the purpose of which is to encourage research or to disseminate information in the subject areas listed above.

To become a subscriber please contact: info@theballadpartners.co.uk.

Cover illustration by Christine Molan, based on a photograph of Alfred Williams with Elijah Iles at his home in Inglesham (p. 305).

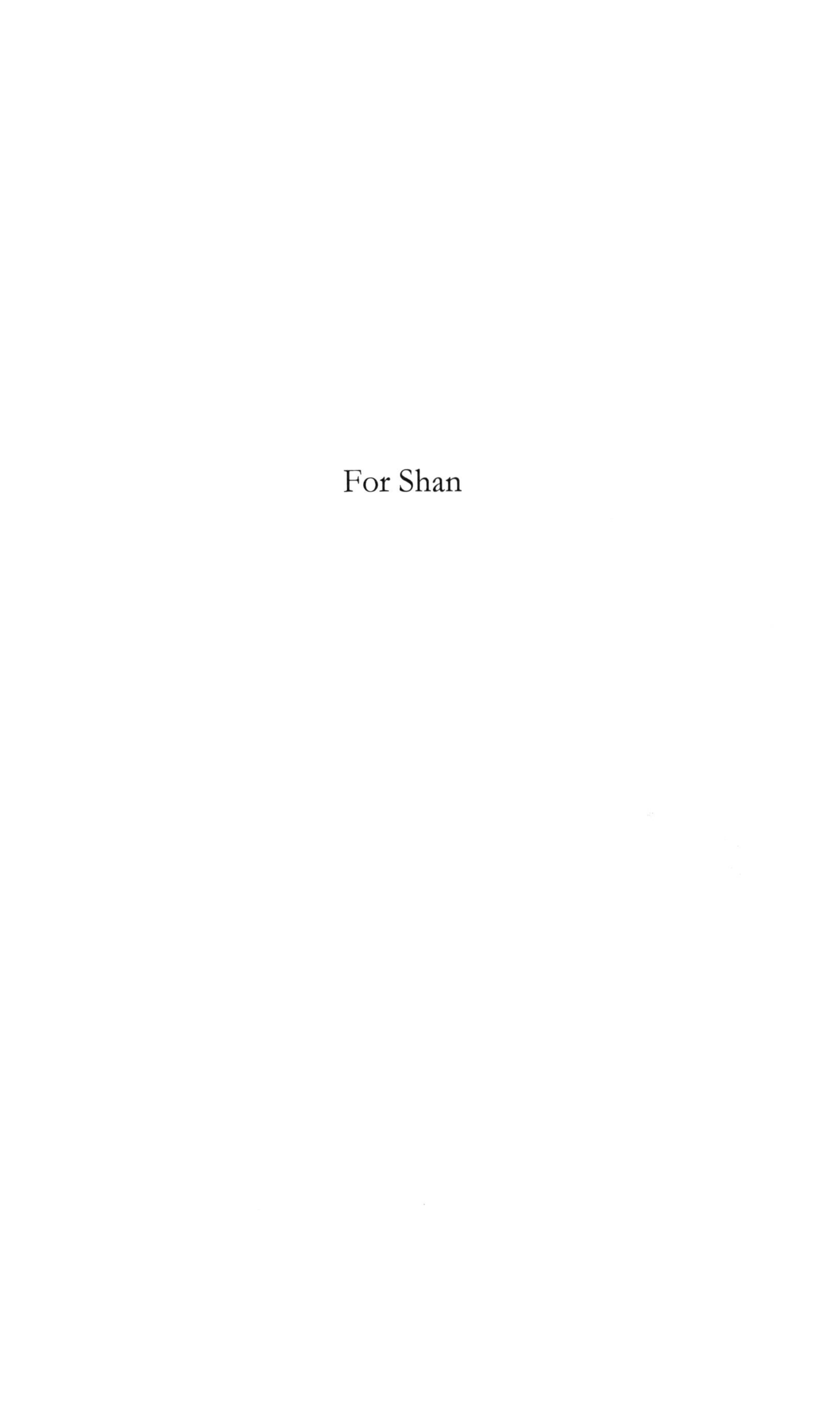

For Shan

Contents

Acknowledgements

A number of people have helped in the creation of this book and I would particularly like to thank:

- Chris Wildridge for creating the essential Williams Archive on the Wiltshire Community Website, for unselfishly offering the use of his original files, and for his unfailing patience in answering my questions.
- Steve Roud for many useful conversations and for his tolerance of my challenges to the amazing Roud Index, without which the project could not have been completed.
- David Atkinson who is invariably a patient source of advice on the technicalities of writing books and articles on folk song, as well as being an outstanding and sympathetic editor.
- Steve Gardham whose knowledge of the origins of songs and early street literature has proved of enormous value.
- John Baxter for help with finding sources some of the songs written later in the nineteenth century.
- The staff of the Vaughan Williams Memorial Library at Cecil Sharp House, London, for help with many enquiries and for their wonderful online database and archive without which, in a plague year, this work would not have been possible.
- The staff at Wiltshire and Swindon History Centre who helped me find those bits of the Williams archive that I needed to understand Williams's collection better.
- The staff at the Central Library, Swindon, for access to the early biographies of Williams, and to ephemera in their collection.
- The staff at the Bingham Library, Cirencester, for access to newspapers, including the *Wilts and Gloucestershire Standard*, and other local resources.
- Pam Debenham at Cricklade Museum for identifying Henry 'Wassail' Harvey and showing me his photograph.
- And Shan Graebe has put up with me being even more locked away than Covid-19 required, and provided support and sustenance as well as valuable editorial advice and proof-reading.

Thank you all.

Martin Graebe
May 2021

Alfred Williams, from a cabinet card produced by Viner and Shilk of Swindon and Highworth, 1905–1910. Courtesy of Paul Williams.

Preface

> At the end – though not yet at the end – I am happy, and happiest when I am on the road, having found, or hoping presently to find, another old song to add to our collection, at the same time not forgetting matters of graver import – the tragedies of life, the prolonged agonies and privations of this terrific war, and the greater and more glorious future that is most certainly before us. Perhaps then our songs may be treasured with tenderness, and our labours kindly remembered.
>
> Alfred Williams, 1916

Alfred Williams was very different from most folk song collectors in respect of his background and in his approach to collecting songs. He was born in Wiltshire in 1877 and had little formal education, having left school at the age of eleven to work on a farm. When he was fifteen he went to the Great Western Railway Works at Swindon where he became a skilled operator of the big steam drop-hammers that forged parts for railway carriages. All this time he was educating himself, reading English literature and teaching himself to read Latin and Greek so as to study the classics. He wrote poetry, and he also wrote about the people and the area in which he lived in books such as *A Wiltshire Village* and *Round About the Upper Thames*. The area that he designated as the 'Upper Thames' is shown on the map on page xiv.

After being forced by ill-health to leave the railway works in 1914, he eked out a living by supplementing the modest income from his writing by market gardening. He also began to collect folk songs, though his motives for doing so were not those of the other folk song collectors of his day. Williams sought them out as another part of his record of the language and preoccupations of the people of the Upper Thames. He made no attempt to record the tunes he heard. That was not part of his plan, though it should be said that he did not have the skill to do it in any case.

Between 1914 and 1916, when his health had improved enough for him to join the army, he cycled more than 13,000 miles around the Thames Valley and parts of the Cotswolds and heard nearly 800 songs.[1] Many of these were published in the *Wilts and Gloucestershire Standard* and later in his book *Folk-Songs of the Upper Thames* (*FSUT*). He never got the recognition that he felt he deserved – but he could be a difficult man, and his views were not

[1] Although it is generally believed that Williams started collecting songs in 1914, he says in the Preface to *Folk Songs of the Upper Thames* that he began his collection in 1913. There is also some evidence that suggests he added to his collection after his return from military service in 1919.

conventional. Sadly, he died in a state of poverty in 1930 at the age of fifty-three.

While the book, *Folk Songs of the Upper Thames*, published in 1923, is relatively well known (though still undervalued and misunderstood) the newspaper series that preceded it is not. The *Wilts and Gloucestershire Standard* published 439 songs collected by Williams in a 44-part series between October 1915 and September 1916. Only 234 of these songs were carried forward into the book.

This book presents the 205 songs that were published in the *Wilts and Gloucestershire Standard* but were not used in the 1923 publication. They are a mixed bunch; many are old favourites, though wearing unfamiliar clothes, while others are welcome strangers, only found in this collection. My mission has been to present the songs and Williams's comments on them as they appeared in the newspaper. I have added brief notes about the songs which amplify or correct comments made by the collector. Williams frequently recorded his view of the age of a song. This was, unsurprisingly, a matter of opinion rather than of evidence. The only instances where a date can be given with certainty are where the writer is known and a date of publication can be established. The collection includes a number of such songs and I have identified these in my notes.

For other songs all we can give is the date when they were first printed. In most cases their earliest appearance was in one of the forms of cheap literature – broadsides, chapbooks, or songsters. As databases of broadsides become more comprehensive we are able more frequently to find early versions of songs in print. Where the printer is known, we may know when they were in business and thus be able to date the printed item. This, though, only tells us that a song was in existence at that time; it may have been in circulation before it was published. Neither does it, except in rare cases, tell us who wrote a song.

Many of the song texts conform closely to broadside versions. Williams mentions singers who said they had learned songs from broadsides. Some of them were able to show him the broadsides. Williams himself owned a number of broadsides, though these are no longer with his papers. He was well aware of the role that print played in the dissemination of songs, as you will read in his Introduction which forms part of this book.

I have provided Roud numbers for each of the songs and I have also included Bathe-Clissold references. This is a system devised by Colin Bathe and Ivor Clissold when they worked extensively on the Alfred Williams song manuscripts in the 1960s. The system was constructed with advice from Frank Purslow and is similar to the one he used when working on the Hammond and Gardiner collections. The songs are organized into alphabetical order, by county, location, singer, and finally song. The complete collection was then numbered from top to bottom, and a prefix assigned to denote the county. So, for example, Gl.145 is 'British Man-o'-War', sung by James Mills of South Cerney in Gloucestershire, and is the 145th song in the collection. This corresponds with the way in which the Williams folk song manuscripts are organized in the Wiltshire and Swindon History Centre. Bathe and Clissold also created a section designated 'Mi.', for Miscellaneous, for the 234 songs for which neither singer nor location is specified. They also included a list of songs that were known to have been collected by Williams but for which no manuscript survived. When preparing his online database for the Wiltshire Community History website Chris Wildridge assigned these songs an 'X' number. Six of these songs were among those printed in the newspaper series and are included in this volume.

Initially, I intended to follow Bathe and Clissold's lead and to present the songs by county. I soon discovered, however, that it was a better plan to present them in the order in which Williams published them in the *Wilts and Gloucestershire Standard*, as his headnotes often refer to another song that preceded the one he is describing. As a reference, I have given the part number and publication date for each song. I have also adopted the system devised by Chris Wildridge which assigns to each song a consecutive number within each part.

It is often lamented that Williams did not collect tunes for his songs. He explains the reasons for this in his Introduction and even more clearly in notes that he made for a lecture on folk song, where he says:

> I should like to point out that my purpose in getting the songs was not identical with that of most collectors. I did not know anything about the Folk Song Society, or its members. And I was not looking for music. I didn't wish therefore to make any additions to existing collections of folk songs, but only to complete the work I had undertaken (or which I thought I had undertaken) in my prose books towards depicting the life of the Upper Thames District. I never pretend to be scholarly, and I don't pose to you as a critic, or an expert. I was rather an enthusiast. I like the people and I like to know about their amusements; what they said, thought, and believed, and I thought that we ought to have a record of their songs, as far as we could get them.[2]

He was in any case not musically literate and could not have noted the tunes without involving someone else, which would have reduced his ability to range the area freely on his bicycle. It is unlikely, too, that he would have found anyone with the stamina that he displayed, which was remarkable considering the relatively poor state of his health.

In the passage quoted above Williams asserts that when he started to collect folk songs he had no knowledge of the Folk-Song Society or its members. In his Introduction to the *Wilts and Gloucestershire Standard* series he wrote: 'To safeguard myself in this particular work I have purposely isolated myself from all others engaged in the indiscriminate collection of folksongs. I have neither communicated with them nor seen any of their books. I did not require their assistance.' He certainly never met them in person, but he does appear to have been aware of the work done by Cecil Sharp in Somerset, and

[2] See the passage 'My purpose in collecting' in the lecture notes in the Alfred Williams Manuscript collection (VWML Digital Archive, AW/1/31).

one of his biographers reported that he admired Sharp.[3] We do not know if he deliberately targeted two of Sharp's singers in Bampton, Shadrach Haydon and Charles Tanner, but he did collect some of the songs that Sharp had heard from the two men.[4]

The only contact he had with a fellow collector was with Frank Kidson, with whom he exchanged a series of letters to the Editor of the *Wilts and Gloucestershire Standard.* These are reproduced in *Appendix A* and resulted from Kidson having provided unsolicited comments on the songs Williams had published. A particular bone of contention was that Kidson took Williams to task for publishing songs that were not 'folk songs'. Williams did not take kindly to Kidson's intervention. He did, though, go as far as to read Kidson's book, *Traditional Tunes*, which Kidson had casually mentioned in his letters to the *Standard*, in his notes to two songs.[5]

Williams wrote about the difficulty of defining folk song in a newspaper article, 'The Evolution of the Local Folk Song', written in 1926:

> There is a good deal of misconception, not to say disagreement concerning the origin and the definition of the folk song. It is not this, and it is not that. Really, it is difficult to say exactly what it is and what it is not. According to the accepted canon of the experts hardly any of the pieces figuring in collections are true folk songs. That is, if they insist upon the folk origin. I, for one, do not believe it. The folk were uneducated. They could not even read much less compose songs and poems. The farther we go back the more ignorant the people were, and yet the songs were superior in quality. Later, the folk composed rhymes, but they had no artistic or literary merits. We have only to compare 'The Seeds of Love', or 'Lord Thomas and Fair Eleanor' with such a piece as 'The Wiltshire Labourers', or 'On Compton Downs', both of which were written by uneducated people, in order to be assured of this. The difference is startling. I think the folk song was adopted by the people, not produced by them. It is due, I imagine to the collective efforts of generations of singers and minstrels, and not to individuals who, out of a small original stock, by arbitrary methods, produced an almost endless mass of new and ever-changing versions.[6]

Many would now agree with him on the key point that the 'folk' did not actually create the songs, though they might be a little less condescending in their language. In any case, his goal, as stated in his Introduction, was different from that of the other collectors. He aimed to record what the people actually sang in the area he was studying, not just the folk songs. In his Introduction to the series he wrote:

---

[3] Leonard Clark, *Alfred Williams: His Life and Work* (Bristol: William George's Sons and Basil Blackwell, 1945), p. 93.

[4] See more about this in 'The Singers' below.

[5] 'The Indian Lass' (no. 117) and 'The Bold Privateer' (no. 118).

[6] Alfred Williams, 'The Evolution of the Local Folk Song', *Wiltshire Times*, 1 May 1926, p. 5.

> I make no apologies for the musical tastes of the people; I cannot help what they liked. That is no business of mine, and I have nothing to do with it. I want to show not what they might have sung, nor what they ought to have sung, but what, in fact, they did sing. And what right have I, or anyone else, to condemn the taste exhibited in, or the imperfections of the old songs, and mutilate, patch, polish, or correct them in deference to the wishes of those trained exclusively according to the modern ideas of poetry and music, and who are unable to appreciate simple measures.

Had Kidson, and Williams's other critics, read more carefully what he had written perhaps they might not have responded as they did.

There is much talk nowadays of cultural appropriation (or, rather, misappropriation) of folk songs. Williams had strong views about this, as will be found in his Introduction. He suggests that many folk song collectors believed that the people from whom they heard songs could not really appreciate them, and so carried them off as intellectual curiosities to be shared within their own circle. So they were lost to the ordinary people. He wrote:

> I always think it radically wrong to take from many thousands in order to give to several hundreds, and probably less than that. And folk songs never belonged to the intellectuals, they were the property of the people. And if they stand any chance of being remembered and held as cherished possessions it will be by the simple peasant folks, those who have not been educated out of their nature. We are all ready and eager to give a man that which belongs to another. But who will ever be so simple and ingenuous as to think of rendering him his own?'[7]

He goes on to suggest that the songs should be given back to the people: 'If it were in my power I would see that there were not a cottage in the land but possessed a book of the ancient national folk songs and ballads.'

He returned to this theme again in his Conclusion, published at the end of the series. He explained that the objective of printing the songs in the *Wilts and Gloucestershire Standard* was to make them more widely known in the localities where he had heard them. As a result:

> They have become common property, and some of the pleasure I have taken in collecting and preserving them has been shared by numerous others. That is my satisfaction and my chief reward. I hold it one of the most meritorious of things to have done, something worthy of serious public interest, and every good act requites itself.

He wrote that it was his intention at some point after the war to publish a book of the songs, but that it might not matter if the newspaper's readers did not buy a copy since they had already had an opportunity to see the songs.

---

[7] This section of Williams's Introduction was not carried forward to that for *Folk Songs of the Upper Thames.*

Preface

I suspect that some readers of this Preface may at some time have asked themselves, 'What is it about folk song that draws me to it?' Williams gives us his own answer to that question:

> What we love most of all about the folksongs, is not their beauty, which may be conditional, and dependent upon a cultivated taste in the individual, but their old-fashionedness. They are like the quaint figures and ornaments we find on the mantelpieces in the cottages, that were bought centuries ago and handed on from generation to generation, dear and delightful by reason of their association with the time that is past, and the memories they awake in us.

The 205 songs in this book are a diverse and interesting collection, many of which are not found in those of the Victorian and Edwardian collectors. In many cases this is because they would not have met their criteria as folk songs. Songs like 'The Emigrant Ship' (no. 105) commemorate events that took place during the lifetime of some of the early collectors, so they would not have thought to include them. And Kidson correctly identifies a number of songs written for stage or parlour in the mid-nineteenth century. But in other cases Williams has found a song that is unarguably 'folk' but which is found nowhere else. 'The Shepherd on the Plain' (no. 3), for example, is unique to Williams and does not appear to have been printed on any broadsides. As a whole, the selection is representative of the English traditional canon.

I have transcribed the songs from the newspaper articles as closely as I could manage, bearing in mind that the punctuation is sometimes idiosyncratic or difficult to read. Chris Wildridge kindly gave me copies of his transcriptions of all of the songs, but his text is often taken from the manuscripts rather than the newspaper articles, which results in occasional small differences.

The names of the singers I have given are, in the majority of cases, those given by Alfred Williams in his headnotes to the songs. He did not always record names accurately – not a surprise, given that he was dealing with elderly men and women who might not have had their full complement of teeth, even though he had the advantage of being familiar with the accent. I have leaned heavily on the work on the singers' personal histories done by Chris Wildridge and have used the corrections or additional names that he has found through his work with the census and other sources. Williams, like others of his time, referred to his singers, particularly the women, using the appropriate title. I have opted, as is the way nowadays, to give their first names. This is not intended to be disrespectful, rather the reverse.

The section on 'The Singers' describes four of the principal singers, but many of the others are also of interest and deserve a more detailed account. Williams's Introduction, and some of the headnotes, give a good idea of the kind of people from whom he heard the songs, and I hope that for the time being this will suffice. More can be gleaned from his books.

Andrew Bathe investigated the background of many of the singers for his doctoral thesis and, though carried out in the days before digital sources made it easier to find information about our ancestors, this has provided a valuable starting point for such work.[8] Research by Chris Wildridge and Christopher Bearman added to our knowledge of many of the singers, and a substantial body of census data and other personal information is to be found on the Wiltshire Community History Database which was compiled by Wildridge.

While admitting to what I have *not* done, I should also say that I have chosen not to provide a biography of Alfred Williams beyond the few words that opened this Preface. There are some short biographical essays on Williams to be discovered on the internet.[9] You can also refer to Andrew Bathe's thesis for more on Williams's life and his folk song collecting. I have included some bibliographical notes that identify the currently available biographies. There is still a need for a good biographical study that focuses on his work with folk song.

I should add that I have not, in this book, looked at the way in which Williams edited the songs. It is clear that he combined versions from different singers, as he tells us this in a number of instances. Nearly all of the manuscripts that remain are, though, fair copies and give few indications of how he did this. Other writers, notably Clissold, have taken a stern view of his rearrangement of stanzas and insertion of words to improve the sense.[10] This is a matter that requires further study, and a key part of this will be to look carefully at the one surviving field notebook.

On the question of what he described as 'rough' songs, he followed the mores of his time, often to the puzzlement of his singers who saw nothing wrong in what they sang. He deals with this issue at length in his Introduction, concluding, 'They were morally immoral, if I may say so, and not cunningly suggestive and damnably hypocritical, as are some of the modern music hall pieces.'

Williams's Introduction also sets out his view of the importance of integrity in recording the songs. He makes it clear that he has not improved them by importing stanzas from songs not heard in the Upper Thames area. He regarded that as a deceit, and wrote that 'literature is a fine art, and true art cannot admit of deception [. . .] To be valuable it must be trustworthy.' He laid such emphasis on this point that we should take it that he truly believed he was creating a faithful record.

---

8 Andrew Lee Bathe, 'Pedalling in the Dark: The Folk Song Collecting of Alfred Williams in the Upper Thames Valley, 1914–16' (unpublished PhD thesis, University of Sheffield, 2007) https://etheses.whiterose.ac.uk/14510/.

9 The best such essay, 'A Different Drummer: Alfred Williams and the Edwardian Folk Song Revival', by Mike Yates, ceased to be available with the demise of the Alfred Williams Heritage Society website. It is to be hoped that a new home will be found for it.

10 Ivor Clissold, 'Alfred Williams, Song Collector', *Folk Music Journal*, 1.5 (1969), 293–300 (p. 296).

Working through these texts has been an interesting and rewarding experience. Talking to friends about it, I have described looking at one of these songs for the first time as being like opening a birthday present. Many have been a delight, a few have been the box of hankies that your auntie gave you, and there is only one song that I really dislike and wish that Williams had not included. I hope that you will enjoy reading through them.

Martin Graebe
May 2021

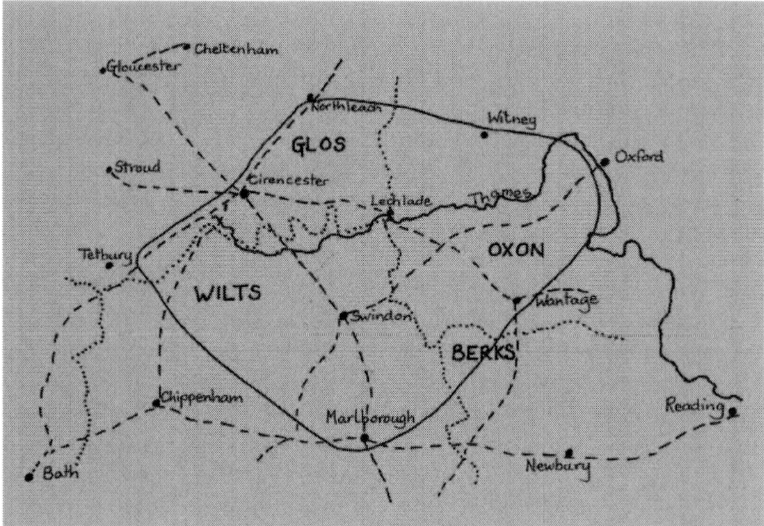

Alfred Williams's 'Upper Thames'

The Singers

The 205 songs in this book were collected by Alfred Williams from 104 named singers. The singers who supplied six or more songs are listed in the following table. The figure in brackets is the number of songs each singer contributed to the whole of Williams's collection:

David Sawyer	Stratton St Margaret, Wiltshire	18 songs (50)
Elijah Iles	Inglesham, Wiltshire	12 songs (53)
Charles Tanner,	Bampton, Oxfordshire	7 songs (24)
Henry Harvey	Cricklade, Wiltshire	6 songs (26)
Shadrach Haydon	Bampton, Oxfordshire	6 songs (11)
James Mills	South Cerney, Gloucestershire	6 songs (6)

It can be seen that David Sawyer and Elijah Iles contributed the most songs not only to this subset but also to the collection overall (albeit in reverse order). The distribution of the 104 singers between the counties is:

Berkshire	5 singers	8 songs
Gloucestershire	45 singers	72 songs
Oxfordshire	29 singers	55 songs
Wiltshire	25 singers	87 songs

Some of the 205 songs were noted from more than one singer. Williams quotes 222 instances of collecting a song within the set of 205, but he did not always identify all of the additional singers, so the total would have been greater. The fact that Wiltshire provided the top two singers and was also the most productive county, based on the number of songs per singer, is not really surprising. Wiltshire covers roughly one third of the area that Williams described as the Upper Thames and it was also his home county.

I do not propose to write in detail about all of the singers but have chosen to describe four of the principal singers, who will serve to give an impression of the people Williams sought out. You can find biographical details of many of the other singers on the Wiltshire Community History website. This information is based on work with the census and other sources by Chris Wildridge and the late Christopher Bearman. As might be expected, their work has thrown up some differences between the official documents and the names Williams gave to the singers. There are also differences between the places where Williams says he heard the singers and where they actually lived. In these cases I have prioritized the information from Wildridge and Bearman's studies.

David Sawyer

An example of the difficulties concerning location is found with the principal singer in this group, David Sawyer. Williams usually associates him with Ogbourne. Although he was born there, Sawyer moved several times in the course of his life and at the time Williams met him he was living at Stratton St Margaret, less than three miles from Williams's own home in South Marston, which ensured his ready access to this interesting man and his large repertoire of songs. There are eighteen of Sawyer's songs in this book:

6	In High Germany	Roud 904
22	The Mantle of Green	Roud 714
35	Down in Moorfields	Roud 578
47	In the Lowlands of Holland	Roud 484
53	The Disconsolate Lover	Roud 602
80	The Wild Rover	Roud 1173
82	Remember, Love, Remember	Roud 2674
86	The Gay Ploughboy	Roud 1639
93	Creeping Jane	Roud 1012
115	The Shannon Side	Roud 1453
116	The Rioting Blade	Roud 21216
121	It's Forty Long Miles I've Travelled this Day	Roud 608
124	Canada-I-O	Roud 309
135	Bonny Blue Handkerchief Tucked under her Chin	Roud 378
138	William and Harriet	Roud 536
152	The Lady and her Apprentice Boy	Roud 903
154	The New Garden Fields	Roud 1054
162	The Highwayman	Roud 2638

In the note to 'New Garden Fields (no. 154) Williams describes David Sawyer's life:

> He and Granny, who is aged eighty nine, live in a little cottage by the road side. David does all the work. He gets Granny's breakfast, cleans up, makes the bed, puts on the pot, cooks the dinner, washes the clothes once a week, and sees to everything else. He has travelled far in his time and is possessed of much useful knowledge, in addition to his songs, which are numerous. 'You never seed a better songbook than I be, I warn,' says David. And I admit that I never did.

This picture of domestic bliss is in sharp contrast to reports of the couple's earlier life in the pages of the local newspapers. In 1868 Sawyer moved to Bishopstone, the village where his wife, Eleanor, had been born and where he made a living by market gardening and growing watercress and withies. A newspaper report of a court case in December 1874, headed 'A Rebellious Spouse', records that Sawyer's wife had called the police after he had beaten her. The couple had taken produce to the market and he was annoyed that she only gave him 3*d.* from the day's takings. They visited several public houses before returning home, where Sawyer assaulted his wife, broke up the furniture, and accidentally set the chimney on fire. The police attended and he was bound over by magistrates to keep the peace with his wife for six months. Shortly afterwards he put a notice in the paper saying that he would not be answerable for any of Eleanor's debts.

Four years later a further instance of his threatening behaviour towards his wife came to court, but this was followed shortly by another case in which Eleanor was charged with using threatening language. The report in the *North Wilts Herald* records Sawyer telling his wife,

> It would be a great deal better for both of them if she helped him reap in the fields instead of continually 'nagging' him when he came home to meals. Upon this, defendant picked up a table-knife and swore she would slit her husband's face down if he spoke another word. Complainant assured the Bench he was afraid his wife – towards whom he is bound over to keep the peace – would do him some serious injury. – Defendant asserted that her husband's statement was 'a abominable story'; but the Bench bound her over to keep the peace towards her husband in £5, for six months, and administered a well-deserved caution. – Complainant (to the bench): I should like to ask, sir, if she is supposed to look after me and act as a wife should? – The chairman: That is a point upon which I cannot offer advice, but I would remind you that you took her 'for better, for worse' (loud laughter).[1]

The watercress business was the cause of several other court cases, some involving violent behaviour, culminating in 'The Swindon Watercress Case' which occupied several column inches in 1879. Sawyer had left the area owing two years rent on the watercress beds, saying he was going to America. He returned several months later to find that the beds had been let to someone else and sued, unsuccessfully, for their return.

He then moved to Somerset where he worked as a gardener for several years before returning to Wiltshire, where Williams found him at Stratton St Margaret in 1914. By then the couple had been married for over sixty years and produced three children. 'Granny', as Williams knew Eleanor, was by then infirm, but cared for by her husband. It is likely that David's repertoire was enhanced by considerable time spent in public houses. He was, indeed, a living songbook. As Sabine Baring-Gould wrote, 'The singing birds are not, I am sorry to say, a very respectable lot.'

Elijah Iles

Only twelve of Elijah Iles's songs from the *Wilts and Gloucestershire Standard* series remained unpublished, though his overall total of fifty-three songs beat David Sawyer's score by a small margin. The twelve songs included in this book are:

---

[1] 'Matrimonial Felicity', *North Wilts Herald*, 17 September 1877, p. 5.

17	John Barleycorn	Roud 164
63	I Courted a Bonny Lass	Roud 154
69	Phoebe and her Dark Eyed Sailor	Roud 265
83	Caroline and her Young Sailor Bold	Roud 553
88	The Rover	Roud 1112
110	If You Will Walk With Me	Roud 573
125	The Banks of Sweet Primroses	Roud 586
126	You Ask Me to Sing	Roud 2479
147	Sweet Peggy O	Roud 545
150	The Shepherd and the Hermit	Roud 2449
156	The Green Bushes	Roud 1040
202	Down in the Lowlands There Grew a Tree	Roud 129

Iles – or 'Gramps', as Williams called him – first appeared in a series of articles entitled 'Round About the Upper Thames' in the *Wilts and Gloucestershire Standard* in 1915, published shortly before the series of articles on 'Folk Songs of the Upper Thames'.[2] Iles was then nearly ninety-five and rather frail, though still capable of singing and reciting the local version of the mummers' play.[3] His daughter told Williams that he was 'dull of understanding', but Williams wrote:

> There was no need of the apology. A man of ninety-five, and a rustic, of no school education, who can talk intelligently for hours about the farm, the passing of laws and acts, electioneering, historical events, and great national monuments, who can explain many of the phenomena of the heavens and describe the equinox, discuss local topics, from the old Priory of St. John to the British village on Badbury Hill and the Hannington "Liberty", and finish up with singing a score of songs remembered for 60 or 70 years, is not dull of understanding.

For thirty years Iles had driven teams of oxen and when that became too demanding he scraped a living by weaving baskets and chair bottoms from rushes gathered near the Thames. He talked of old men he had known who had fought at Trafalgar and Waterloo. It is no wonder that Williams treated such a man with respect and valued what he learned from him.

Henry Harvey

In the Cricklade Museum there is a photograph recorded in the catalogue as 'Three Men, a Woman, and a Pig'. The man standing on the right in the photo is Henry Harvey, another of Williams's favourite singers, known to

---

[2] These articles were published in book form as *Round About the Upper Thames* (London: Duckworth, 1922).

[3] Williams devotes most of the final chapter of *Round about the Upper Thames* to a description of a gathering of family and friends at Elijah Iles's house for an evening of eating, drinking, and singing, the culmination of which was Elijah reciting the whole of the play of 'Robin Hood and Little John'.

him as 'Wassail Harvey'. He was born in Cricklade in 1826 and as a boy helped with the boats carrying goods on the Thames. He worked all his life as a labourer and met his wife, Mary, while both were working on a farm at Lushill, near Castle Eaton. He earned his nickname because he was the last of the men who performed the wassail at Cricklade, a tradition that his father and grandfather had kept before him. Williams described him as 'a dear, gentle old man, of great simplicity, but a fine singer'.

'Three Men, a Woman, and a Pig'.
Courtesy of the Cricklade Historical Society and the Cricklade Museum.
Henry Harvey is the man standing on the right.

Henry Harvey contributed twenty-six songs in total to Williams's collection, and six of them are included in this book:

7	Down Covent Garden	Roud 490
45	Chesapeake and Shannon	Roud 1583
87	The Gipsy Girl	Roud 229
109	Aaron's Lovely Home	Roud 1427
158	The Pitcher of Water	Roud 2671
159	Down Ratcliffe Highway	Roud 598

In his note to 'Down Ratcliffe Highway' (no. 159) Williams wrote of Harvey:

> He died recently in his ninetieth year. I was a long time securing any of his songs; he appeared to have forgotten them and was very infirm. Happening to look in upon him in his tiny cottage one wet night in mid-winter, I found him possessed of a very severe cold, and gasping for breath. Thereupon I went to the inn, fetched a little rum and insisted upon his taking a glass hot

> immediately. The result was magical. After expressing gratitude he commenced to sing in a wonderfully deep tone of voice, that surprised me and quite startled his wife: she said he had not sung like it for fifty years. After that I saw the old man frequently till the time of his death, and we had many musical afternoons and evenings together. He was also possessed of much quaint lore and useful knowledge.

Charles Tanner

I will say a little about one more singer, Charles Tanner, who had the distinction of singing for both Alfred Williams (in 1914–15) and Cecil Sharp (in September 1909). Tanner was seventy when he met Williams and, like so many of his singers, had worked as an agricultural labourer. Tanner had followed his father into morris dancing in the long-lived Bampton tradition. He also learned many of his songs from his father. He lived at Weald, near Bampton, near the home of another well-known singer, Shadrach Haydon, who also sang for both Sharp and Williams. He sang a total of twenty-four songs for Williams, seven of which are printed in this book:

49	The Transport	Roud 3913
52	Sarah Gale	Roud 22074
61	The Copy Boy	Roud 1030
62	Yonder Sits a Pretty Little Creature	Roud 146
71	The Shepherd on the Mountain	Roud 1433
72	At Seventeen Years I Was Young	Roud 1479
113	The Chain of Gold	Roud 1417

Two of these songs, 'Sarah Gale' and 'The Shepherd on the Mountain', have only ever been collected from Charles Tanner.

Sharp collected six songs from Tanner. One of them, 'William and Dinah', is not recorded in Williams's manuscripts as collected from Tanner, but he does give a version and notes that he had heard it from several singers.[4] Sharp noted only the tune, possibly because it was overly familiar. The songs in this book that both Sharp and Williams collected from Tanner are 'The Shepherd on the Mountain', 'At Seventeen Years I Was Too Young', and 'The Chain of Gold'. These three songs provide an opportunity to compare the two collectors' transcriptions of the words, and I comment on the example of 'The Shepherd on the Mountain' in my note on that song.

Two other songs that were also collected by Sharp, 'Poor Old Horse' (Roud 513) and 'The Maltman and the Highwayman' (Roud 1309), were published in *Folk-Songs of the Upper Thames.* The latter, which Sharp called 'The Maltman and the Miller', is unique to Tanner and does not appear to have originated on broadsides. It is an eleven-stanza song and there are some

---

[4] The version of 'William and Dinah' that Williams collected elsewhere is no. 155 below.

small differences between the two collected versions, but it is a good story and it is surprising that it has not been found more widely.

Charles Tanner, photograph by Cecil Sharp.
Courtesy of the Vaughan Williams Memorial Library.

Sharp also recorded details of morris dancing at Bampton from Tanner and other men, and both Sharp and Williams noted some of the jingles sung during the dancing. Some of these were used to fill in small spaces in the *Wilts and Gloucestershire Standard* series, including:

Oh, once they said my lip was red
But now is the scarlet pale
And I myself a poor silly girl
To notice their flattering tale

But he swore he'd never deceive me
And so fondly I believed thee
While the stars and the moon so sweetly
Shone over the willow tree.

Alfred and Mary Williams in their garden at South Marston in 1924.
Courtesy of the Wiltshire and Swindon History Centre.

Folk Songs of the Upper Thames
Introduction

This is Alfred Williams's Introduction to the series published in the *Wilts and Gloucestershire Standard* between October 1915 and September 1916. It was published in two parts, the first on 2 October 1915 (Part 1) and the second on 9 October (Part 2).

Let it at once be understood that my intention never was merely to gather folk songs for the purpose of adding to the more or less undigested mass of materials in the collections already existing. That is not my business. There are others who can do that, and do it very well. There is really but little trouble experienced in obtaining old songs and ballads. You have usually but to ask for them to receive them. Of course, one meets with difficulties, but with none that are very considerable. You have to know your people. One also requires a certain amount of patience and enthusiasm. In addition he must have tact, and, what is most important of all, taste. And, having got the pieces, one necessarily must have some means or disposing of them to the best advantage. They should not be looked upon merely as so many crown pieces scraped up here and there for profit's sake, afterwards to be stuffed in bags and boxes and hoarded up for the selfish pleasure of one or two individuals. Money is meant to be circulated. While it is in use it remains bright and begets interest; hoarded it has no value but rusts and moulders away. Songs also need circulation. Given that, they retain their brightness and beget other songs; denied publicity, they waste and wither, and soon vanish into the dust of things. Such circulation they had formerly. I shall show the reasons of its discontinuance presently.

I should like to be thought of not merely as the reaper, but the cultivator of a field. I mean I do not want to take away but to develop and establish what is already there. I would at all times rather give than receive. It is the virtue of the good painter to show, in his picture, not what everyone could see but what they could not, or did not, see before. And that brings us to the point I wish to elucidate. It is far easier to reap a field than to cultivate it. And it strikes me as being far easier to collect the literature of any field, or region, and make off with it, than, having discovered it, to fix it in its local habitat.

Why should this be? I think the reason is obvious. It is a matter of courage, strength, and opportunity. For you need courage. For the past century the people of England have been befooled in much of their literature, and especially in their lyrical poetry and songs. They have been fed on blown nonsense, and have lost the taste for the simple and original. The poets have got away from the people. That is equivalent to saying they have got away from nature; while the educated classes stand for art, real or so-called. The plain old songs and lyrics have been forgotten, or, if they have not been forgotten, they have been allowed to fall into disuse, and even into disrepute. This was for Art's sake. Scores of fine old songs and ballads have been allowed to perish under the eyes and nose of superfluous Art. They were born beautiful and continued to be beautiful, but they were become old. That should have been recommendation, but it served, and still serves, as an objection. People will not sing them merely because they are old. Of course, the taste is perverted one, but it was inevitable, under the circumstances. The children have been taught to be smart and modern, and I agree that such of course is highly necessary, up to a certain point. But it has its penalties. One thing it brought about was the fatuous condemnation, for all practical purposes, of such things as old histories, philosophies, poems and songs. They are considered out of date and antiquated, and one has to be courageous nowadays to stand in their defence, or to insist upon their value and the advantages to be derived from a study of them.

For my part, I must confess that I am old-fashioned, and have an affection for simple and elemental things. I am not ashamed to say this. For the simple things are the great things, and the elemental are also the fundamental things, and they remain when every other part of the superstructure has been swept away. And it has always happened that when Art, in literature and poetry, as well as in sculpture and painting, has become corrupt, obscured or debased by a diversion from its true course the process adopted for its recovery has been a total and unconditional surrender and repudiation of the means and a return to and re-employment of the original and elemental forms. That is what needs to be done just now with much of our literature, and especially with our poetry, both lyric and epic. We want not to kill the new spirit, nor suppress it, but to chasten and purify it. We want to new blood in the old veins, not old blood in the new veins. Things dead are dead, the good as well as the bad. But be sure a thing is dead before you heap oblivion's dust upon it. I claim that the spirit of the old poetry, and even that which animated the ballads and folk songs, is not, and cannot be dead, and that it might, in part, at least, be revived to advantage, not in the form, nor in the absolute spirit, but as a basis for future work.

I have said that strength, as well as courage, is needed in the attempt to deal justly and squarely with the common literature of a locality or region. That is, the strength to grasp it in its entirety, and to understand its relations and functions comprehensively; to fit it in with the life from which it sprang and of which it continues to be that the faithful reflection and representation. There are certain errors to be avoided. A common one is that of imagining that the people of the locality are incapable of appreciating their ballads and songs. Consequently, the average collector, when he has obtained any pieces, never thinks of restoring them to the peasantry, to whom they belong, but carries them off into a new atmosphere, exhibits them to a few intellectuals and is satisfied with that. In reality, the pieces are lost about as completely as they were before, and perhaps, relatively speaking, more so, since he who communicated them to the collector feels weakened by having parted with them, and, thinking them safe, is himself now inclined to neglect them.

I always think it radically wrong to take from many thousands in order to give to several hundreds, and probably less than that. And folk songs never belonged to the intellectuals, they were the property of the people. And if they stand any chance of being remembered and held as cherished possessions it will be by the simple peasant folks, those who have not been educated out of their nature. We are all ready and eager to give a man that which belongs to another. But who will ever be so simple and ingenuous as to think of rendering him his own? That is what we want to do in the matter of the folksongs. Give them back to the people. Schools and universities do not want them. They are lost amid our great towns and cities. They cannot live in the atmosphere. And the dwellers there have other compensations, poor ones though they be. It is in the villages and small country towns where they would be welcomed. If it were in my power I would see that there were not a cottage in the land but possessed a book of the ancient national folk songs and ballads, together with examples and summaries of other choice and useful literature. People would read them if they had them. One of the things most to be deplored, in my view, is the fact that so much that is good, beautiful, and *vital* should be kept locked up in books and libraries out of the site and reach of all but privileged few, while millions are languishing daily for the want of it.

We come next to the matter of opportunity. I mean the opportunity of developing or establishing the relics of any literature of a locality. Few people, perhaps – if I may be permitted to say so – ever get the opportunity of doing this successfully. In the first place, they have not the necessary qualifications. They may be deficient in taste, literary skill, judgement and critical ability. Or they may have plenty of materials and yet be unable to arrange and dispose of them to the best advantage. I do not mean the matter of classification, because to classify it is generally inartistic; we want a book and not a catalogue of songs. At the same time, some kind of arrangement is indispensable, and the amateur is apt to lessen the charm and effect, and also the value of his work, by careless and injudicious display of it.

Another is handicapped by reason of his comparative obscurity and the slightness of his achievements in other walks of life and literature. He is not well known, and lacks authority and prestige. He has nothing with which his efforts and labours may be associated. Consequently, though he toils hard and long he fails to obtain adequate recognition. It is possible that his work lacks design. He has been induced to do a little here and little there, to glean in many fields far remote, and in no wise connected with each other. In such a case the result must be that his work, when completed, will be scrappy and incoherent, unsatisfactory because it has not definite object. He has no field or locality of his own, for the simple reason that he has not been able to make himself master of one. He is like a painter with good colours, and a fair scene in his eye, but who wants a canvas, and his work is in the same position as the ship that is doomed to be lost because she has nothing to which she may be moored or anchored. In spite of all his efforts, then, he has not the opportunity of establishing his literature upon a permanent basis.

I am hoping that I am more favourably situated than is such a one. In the first place, I can lay claim to a ground. In the second place, I have not attempted to do too much, and, finally, it is possible that the publicity my work has already obtained may serve to attract the necessary attention and stand as a guarantee of its merits and value. At least, I hope that it will be so. I said that I did not wish merely to add to existing collections of folk songs. What I wanted to do was, as nearly as I could, to complete the work I have undertaken in my prose volumes and to leave a permanent record of the language and activities of the district in which I find myself.

I have set out with the intention of depicting some portion of the life of the Upper Thames Valley. That is my field, or canvas – call it what you will. The ground is limited. It should rather be called the 'Upperest' or 'Most Upper Thames Valley.' Some people would drop the idea of the Thames altogether and say the Valley of the Isis; but I do not like the word Isis. Some particular definition is necessary, however, since the Upper Thames Valley may be considered as extending as far as to Wallingford or Reading. What I mean by the Upper Thames Valley is that part between Oxford, Abingdon, and Wantage on the one hand, and Swindon, Purton and Cirencester on the other. This includes the Vale of White Horse, which, strictly speaking, is the tract lying between the slopes of the chalk downs of Wiltshire and Berkshire from Swindon to Wantage, and the stone ridge running from Blundsdon past Highworth and Faringdon to Cumnor.

I have not yet covered all the ground, though I hope to do so in the future, if circumstances permit. For the sake of making myself understood, and having my design clear, I will briefly show what I have done to date. First however I will take the opportunity of mapping out the area. Generally speaking, for the purpose of the folk songs, I might draw a line from Cirencester to Tetbury, turning thence by Malmesbury and Wootton Bassett to Marlborough, and continue eastwards, encircling Aldbourne and Lambourn, to Wantage. From Wantage the line would run east of Hanney to Abingdon, touching Oxford, and, veering round, include Witney, Burford, Lechlade and Fairford, and so back to Cirencester. I am situated about in the centre of this region. My book, *A Wiltshire Village*, deals with South Marston and its surroundings. *Villages of the White Horse* comprehends the whole of the downside between Hay Lane and Kingston Lisle, east of the White Horse, and treats of some twenty villages. *Life in a Railway Factory* deals with the town of Swindon, and *Round About the Upper Thames* covers the north-western portion of the inner area, and especially that part through which the Thames flows from Campbell to Eaton Weir. The eastern part of the field remains to be done. If the war had not broken out it would have been completed by now. As I have said, I hope to do it by and by. The things I have had in view have been: Nature, Work and Life. I have tried to depict the beautiful and the actual. Above all, I wanted to describe how the people spent their days and nights, in what employments, recreations, and amusements. In a word, I wished to show how they lived.

It is impossible to do this without treating of the folk songs. A passing reference to them, or even a few examples thrown in, would be insufficient. Nothing less than a representative collection will suffice. I did not realise this at first. For one thing the existence of the songs is not obvious. You may pass through hundreds of villages, with eyes wide open and wits alert, without finding one. They are not on the main routes; they are hidden in the nooks and crannies. Consequently they escape the observation of the ordinary traveller. It is only when you have pored over a scene, or a village, and become thoroughly intimate with its people that you can discover them. A countryman never sings to a stranger. First win his heart and confidence before you can expect a song from him. And this requires time and effort on your part that is why, as I have said, the folksongs escape attention. They are there, although their presence was unsuspected. The knowledge that many of them still existed dawned upon me gradually. At first I noted speech and story, local lore, and rhymes. And while I confined my attention to these matters I got nothing else. A villager seldom, if ever, offers you a song. You must ask him for it. You will be sure to get a negative reply at the outset. And blunt questions and imperative requests will never succeed. The manner of asking needs to be cultivated to such a point as to be of the nature of fine art. I have sometimes been forced to spend several hours of clever manoeuvring with people before I succeeded in tapping their store of folksongs. I have talked subtly on almost every conceivable subject, enticing and suggesting, and artfully working round to the crucial point. And sometimes I have had to entreat, and almost to implore; but I have never once absolutely failed to obtain a song from an individual after I had learned that he was possessed of some. Once or twice I've had to buy a song outright, as though it had been a saucepan or kettle. Such as require you to do this usually have a highly exaggerated idea as to the value of their pieces. The great majority, however, when once you have crept into favour with them, give you the songs freely, with profuse apologies for their rudeness. They are mostly surprised that you should discover yourself to be interested in such a thing as a country ballad, and I have more than once been reminded that 'only fools and fiddlers learn old songs.'

It will be seen that what I hope for is that my collection of folk songs and ballads may be accepted as a corporate part of my general work undertaken towards depicting the life of the Upper Thames Valley. That has been my aim throughout, and not, as I have said, to swell the collections of others. It is possible, indeed, that the whole of those I have obtained figure in other compilations. It is certain that very many of them do. For, hardly any of them are local. Songs are often claimed for this or that locality, but if you should make careful enquiries you would find that the evidence upon which the claim is based is invalid. The mention of a place name in a song or ballad is by some taken as a certain sign that it is a local piece. But very often the evidence is absolutely untrustworthy. The song will usually admit of almost any name being used. The professional ballad singers, passing from town to town, substituted a fresh name to fit in with the locality. It helped the song to 'catch on,' and served to sell their sheets. And even though the printed sheet showed the original place name, the local singers substituted one well known to them. And since one has, at this time, to depend entirely upon oral recitations, what he obtains will be, not the song as it originally stood on the ballad-sheet, but as it has been altered and fitted into the local requirement.

As I have pointed out, very few of the folksongs are, or appear to be, local. Out of the four hundred I have obtained I do not think there are above three or four which were composed in the Thames Valley. There were local rhymes. There are also several inferior songs composed on local events, such as the one on Watkins, the Purton Stoke murderer, and 'The Poor Tradesmen's Lamentation,' printed at Wotton-under-Edge. But there is this interesting fact to record: many ballad sheets were printed at Cirencester. I have in my possession four broadsides bearing the imprint *Clift, Cirencester*, and one bearing the name *J. Ricketts, Highworth*. At the same time, I am certain the pieces were not composed in the locality. The ballads were probably out of print and unprotected by copyright. I also have sheets that were printed at Wotton-under-Edge, Bristol, Newport, Birmingham, Winchester, and London. The majority of the songs and ballads, in my opinion, are written in London and other large towns and cities. There appears to have been a school of such ballad writers, very well trained to their work, and admirably informed as to the best means of captivating the ear of the public. No doubt the work was remunerative. We know that enormous quantities of the sheets were sold up and down the countryside; hundreds, if not thousands, were commonly disposed of at a single fair time.

A friend of mine, who is deeply interested in folk songs and the literature of the people, asked me a few days ago, how many of the songs which I had obtained were in dialect, and was surprised to hear that hardly any were in that form. He thought that country songs would necessarily be in dialect. Many people make that mistake. As a matter of fact it is difficult to meet with one genuine piece of composition in the vernacular, in the south, at any rate. Dialect writing is a species of composition of a rather recent introduction. What they commonly called dialect in the old writers approximated to their natural language. Written dialect today is an artificial and very often vulgar get-up. It is usually a fraud, meant for the deception of the ignorant. People who write it appear to think that anything will do. But anything will *not* do. Approximations are useless. You may deceive the eye but not the ear. It is by that true or false dialect is discovered. The writing of true dialect chiefly depends upon a perfect skill in the science of phonetics. It is a matter of sound, and of the ability of the writer to translated into articulate language. But they seldom – if we except 'George Ridler's Oven,' the finest dialect peace with which I am acquainted – date back further than about the middle of the Nineteenth Century. And they are never very good specimens. They are invariably comic, and have for their subject the doings of clownish countrymen, farmers' daughters, and dairymaids. 'Dick of Taunton Deane' and 'Zarey Zikes' are examples. One of the best-known dialect songs around these parts is 'The Vly be on the Turmut.' This, too is practically modern, and is claimed by several counties – Wiltshire, Somersetshire, and Gloucestershire. They are welcome to it; it has little to boast of. As dialect it is a fraud; as a song it is negligible. There is no suggestion of art in it. It is the favourite, not of the rustics, but of the townsmen. The villagers will not sing it. That is a certain proof of its inferiority. The villagers speak dialect but do not care to read it. They are shocked and offended when they see their own language written. The townspeople do not speak dialect, but like to read it. There is the difference. Clearly, then, our dialect as we know it, was written by outsiders, not by those who spoke it. And that is why so very few of the regular folksongs survive in the dialect form.

It is evident that if I wished my folk songs merely to help elucidate the life of a particular locality it was imperative that I should set myself certain limitations, and, above all, that I should be strictly conscientious in my claims to any single piece. And here let me say that there are temptations. One would sometimes like, on hearing a good folksong outside his district, to be able to incorporate it with his own. It would enrich his store and no one might be the wiser. But the fraud would be nonetheless shameful. And no one should practice deceit in literature. For literature is a fine art, and true art cannot admit of deception. And though one should write never so well, and do sterling work, if he has committed fraud and interpenetrated the substance of his labour with lies, it will rest upon rotten foundations. Especially is this true in regard to such work is that upon which I am here engaged. To be valuable it must be trustworthy. There must be no question of its authenticity. Both the author and the book must be above suspicion. All temptations to purloin and deceive must be resisted. It will be better not to be confronted with them. That, at least, is my view. To safeguard myself in this particular work I have purposely isolated myself from all others engaged in the indiscriminate collection of folksongs. I have neither communicated with them nor seen any of their books. I did not require their assistance. My plan was first to collect and then to collate – if that were necessary. That is the safe method. And from the beginning I laid down this rule – never by any means to admit a piece into my collection unless I had definite and personal proofs that it was actually sung in the neighbourhood and within the area I have mapped out. That plan I have carefully and scrupulously followed, and shall follow. My pieces may have been sung in Somersetshire, Cornwall, Surrey, Warwickshire, Lancashire, Yorkshire, or Aberdeenshire, if you will. But as long as I have proof that they were also popular in the Thames Valley I am satisfied. That fact alone answers my purpose. And though infinitely better songs and ballads may belong to the counties I have mentioned, unless I have certain proofs of their having been sung here I shall not admit them to a place in my collection.

The age of many of the pieces is astonishing; some of them date back three or four hundred years. It is to be noted also that the oldest are the best, whether they be purely ballads, folk songs proper, or comic or humorous pieces. In support of this it will be necessary to mention but a few compositions, such as 'Captain Barniwell,' 'The Bold Dragoon,' 'The Maid's Wager,' 'The Banks of Green Willow,' 'The Seeds of Love,' 'Lord Lovel,' 'Old Moll,' 'Gossip Joan,' 'Georgie Barnell,' or 'The Bugle Played for Me,' as against 'Brennan on the Moor,' 'The Lincolnshire Poachers,' ' The Cottage by the Sea,' 'Willie, we have missed you,' 'The Banks of Sweet Dundee,' 'Smiling Tom,' 'Joe in the Copper,' and others. Since few, if any of these, figure in the literature of their time, we must conclude that they were unknown to the educated and were perpetuated by means of the common broadside or passed on from one generation to another by the process of oral tuition.

It must not be forgotten that very few of the agricultural labourers of a hundred years ago could read or write. They consequently could not have learned the songs from the ballad sheets. But though they could not read they had remarkable acquisitive faculties. If they chanced to hear a song sung several times they had it. I have heard many old labourers say that if they could hear a song clearly once only they were able to remember it completely. And we must bear in mind the fact that they were not short pieces. One old labourer told me a song containing eight verses of eight lines each, and took his oath that he had only heard it sung once – at Highworth Fair. And knowing the man's keenness of wit and general honesty, I saw no reason at all for doubting him. But I think most people would admit that this could not be done today. Knowledge has been developed, though the memory has been terribly impaired. It was that which distinguished the village are in days past. If he had not learning he had wit. Though he was not educated he possessed much useful knowledge, and he was wise. Many a time after an old countryman has entertained me for several hours by telling me songs, and intelligently discussing a host of things connected with his life and work, he has apologetically explained that he was no scholar – he had never been to school and so could not read or write. And I have told him to stop talking such nonsense, and to think of himself as one of the best, as indeed he was, whether he considered himself as such or not.

The folk songs were exceedingly numerous. There must have been thousands, of one sort and another, in circulation. This is no exaggeration. I have frequently come into contact with those who have assured me that such and such a one knew from two hundred to three hundred pieces. And I myself have positive proof of the fact. It was common, years ago, during wet weather when labour out of doors was at a standstill, for the rustics to assemble at the inns and have singing matches, in order to see – not which could sing *best*, but which could sing *most*. There were seldom more than two competing upon any one day. And usually there was no chance for but one of them to sing. He commonly issued a challenge to the village, or the neighbourhood, and declared himself able and willing to sing continuously for twelve hours – from morning till night – and to have a fresh piece each time. It consequently took two days to decide the match. Of course, the inns were full of spectators. They were the daymen on the farms. Under the influence of Apollo they left their work, and had no thoughts of returning until their musical appetite had been satisfied. All the pieces were to be sung from memory. It was something of a treat for the audience. Many of them strained their ears for new pieces and went not away disappointed. Doubtless the singers got very tired, and the music grated, before the twelve hours were up but they were very strong and had voices like organs, while their throats were lubricated with frequent drafts of ale is. That they did the feat is beyond question. For such champions I myself knew and will mention their names: - John Pillinger, of Lechlade; David Sawyer, of Stratton St. Margaret; William Warren, of South Marston; and Gabriel Zillard, of Hannington. Of Zillard it is said that he would unbutton his shirt collar at six in the morning and sing for twelve or even eighteen hours, if necessary with the perspiration streaming down his chest. From what I have heard of his songs they were extraordinarily quaint and comical; unfortunately, by reason of his infirmity, I was unable to obtain possession of any of them.

The songs, as well as being numerous, were of infinite variety. Their range was positively amazing. They were upon every conceivable subject. No thing and no person escaped composition. The King, the nobleman, the knight, the admiral and general, the squire, the soldier and sailor, the farmer, the miller, the mower, the reaper, the waggoner, the dairymaid, the shepherd, ploughman, the cobbler, down to the barber, sweep, and ragman were honoured in song. Every event and occasion was celebrated. There were songs as sweet as the roses on the bush, or the dewdrops on the hedgerows. Others were as strong as brine or the cool northerly breeze. Some were of classic beauty. The song, 'Life let us cherish,' which I have on the broadside sheet, is equal in conception, language, phrase, and spirit, to much of the finest of the Greek lyrical poetry; Horace at his best could scarcely have surpassed it. These pieces were pure narrative; those were romantic or historical. Hundreds dealt with the imperishable theme of love. Some were concerned with pirates, outlaws, and highwayman; others told the delights of hunting, poaching, the occupations of the farm, of cattle, and sweet rustic joys. Many were most quaintly and cunningly humorous or satirical. In fact they left nothing untouched, and no part of life unreflected or unrepresented.

Besides the legitimate pieces there were many 'rough' songs in circulation. I make no apology for them. I do not know, indeed, that any is needed. They were rough but not altogether bad. Many of them were satirical. In fact, the most of that kind of which I have heard were so. They dealt chiefly with immorality; not to encourage or suggest it, but to satirise it. No doubt they served the purpose for which they were intended, in some cases at any rate, though we of our time should call them indelicate. And such, to us, they certainly are. Yet the simple, unspoiled rustic folks do not consider them out of place. They saw no harm in them. But they knew not shame, as we do. They were really very innocent compared with ourselves. We have had our eyes opened, but it what a price! I have more than once on being told an indelicate song, had great difficulty in persuading the rustic, my informant, that I really could not show the piece, and therefore I should not write it. 'But why not?' I have been asked. 'There was nothing wrong with that.'

Neither was there, really, though the eagerly apprehensive minds of most people today would soon read wrong into it. The unsophisticated villagers feel hurt at the decision and often discover considerable embarrassment, though if I were to tell the truth I should say that, upon such occasions, I myself have felt somewhat of a sneak and a hypocrite. Of a truth, the shame is on our side, and lies not with the rustics. And whether songs were professedly bad this much might be said of them – they were so honestly. That is to say, they were simple, open, and natural. They were morally immoral, if I may say so, and not cunningly suggestive and damnably hypocritical, as are some of the modern music hall pieces.

Other literature, in addition to folk songs and ballads proper, was disseminated at fairs and about the villages by means of the printed broadside or ballad sheet. This included poems on various subjects, hymns, carols, glees, and rude rhymes. Of the poems some were of a religious character, others were moral or didactic, and some were merely fables turned into verse. Of the religious poems the piece 'Death and the Lady' is a very good example. Other specimens are 'The Drunkards Catechism,' 'The Cat and the Fox,' 'The Shepherd and the Hermit,' and so on. We see accordingly, that the broadside played a very important part in the education of the people, and as well as keeping them informed as to new songs and recitations, brought to their knowledge matters of deeper and graver import, and afforded them other means of pleasant recreation.

What is the outstanding difference between the old and the new popular songs? There are really very many points of difference. The chief one, however, is that of simplicity. And the older the songs are, and the more nearly they touched the people, the simpler they were. But simplicity is not their sole virtue. A good many new pieces are simple. But their simplicity is of poverty and weakness, while that of the others is born of strength and riches. That is an elegant and artistic simplicity, rich and delightful with music and suggestion, and true to nature and life. Another difference is in their fragrance – I am speaking now of the best of the old folksongs, not the commoner sorts. We have plenty of chiselled songs and poems in our own time, but are they *sweet*? Unfortunately they are not. Sweetness proceeds from the heart, never from the head; and since the preponderating bulk of our poetry and songs is the result of brain-work the pieces have not sweetness. The natural thing is invariably sweet; the merely beautiful may never be so. It depends upon what we call beautiful. Many of the old-fashioned flowers our grandmothers planted and cherished have gone out of cultivation. They were simple and sweet, and therefore beautiful; but they were not gaudy. Now, however, our gardens are full of gaudy flowers, but they have no fragrance. They are materially beautiful; perfect in form and colour, but without souls. We have followed the same plan in regard to our gardens as to our literature. We have sacrificed the heart to the eye. What we love most of all about the folksongs, is not their beauty, which may be conditional, and dependent upon a cultivated taste in the individual, but their old-fashionedness. They are like the quaint figures and ornaments we find on the mantelpieces in the cottages, that were bought centuries ago and handed on from generation to generation, dear and delightful by reason of their association with the time that is past, and the memories they awake in us.

The rustic population – in spite of their illiteracy – discovered wonderful taste. This is evidenced by the kind of flowers they cultivated in their gardens, by their furniture and chinaware, and as we have seen, by the songs they sang. And the taste for good things still remains, at any rate, in the case of the old villagers yet surviving. They positively abhor the cheap, trashy, tawdry materials offered for sale nowadays. They dislike photographs. That fact alone is significant. They cling to the old coloured prints and woodcuts, to their antique tables and chairs, to their old clocks, watches, beds, pots, pans, and utensils. This they do not merely by reason of any stupid conservativeness, or unconquerable prejudice, but because they are convinced that the newer things generally are inferior. They cannot tell you their reasons for thinking this, if you should question them, but they feel sure that it is so. They are guided by the principle of taste. And I have never once known a rustic, or anyone else accustomed to singing the old folk songs, who would deign to learn any of the modern popular pieces. They speak of them with the utmost contempt, and feel insulted if you should ask them to sing you one. 'What! That stuff! That thing! Call that a song! Ther's nothin' in't master. Ther's no sense ner meanin' to't ner no harmony,' they will answer you. That their opinions are justified is realised and admitted by all who are qualified to speak with any degree of authority on the matter.

Different people sing different songs. I mean different types of songs. And that is natural, it is a matter of temperament. You would not expect a sprightly-minded individual to sing a doleful strain. And if all men were witty, or frivolous, what would become of the gravely beautiful in life? The one that is highly necessary as the other. Smiles and tears, too we want – the strong and the sweet, the stirring and the soothing. 'You can allus tell a man by the songs he sings.' This was said to me recently by an old man of ninety, who lived near Cirencester. And he was right. For the songs are a faithful reflex of the individual. As soon as I get into contact with a new singer I begin to be anxious to know what kind of songs he's about to discover to me. There is a real excitement in it. It is exactly like waiting for the development of a negative plate in the photographic dark room. *Will* it develop? And what will it be like? The uncertainty is tantalising. It is no use being impatient. As soon as the dark patches and outlines appear in the chemical bath you have an idea of what the photograph will be. And before a person has finished telling me his first song I have been able to estimate his nature and character and take a look into the recesses of his heart and soul. The songs of old Elijah Iles of Inglesham were gently humorous and witty, such as 'The Carrion Crow and the Tailor,' 'Sweet Peggy,' and 'The Old Woman Drinking her Tea.' The majority of the pieces sung by David Sawyer, the sheepshearer of Ogbourne, were rather sentimental. William Warren, the South Marston thatcher, sang the romantic-historical kind, such as 'Lord Bateman.' Shadrach Haydon, the old shepherd of Hatford, preferred the strong and formal order. Thomas

Smart, of Stratton St. Margaret, would sing none but what were moral and helpful. Those of Wassail Harvey, of Cricklade, were roughly hilarious, such as 'How I could ride if I had but a Saddle,' 'Dick Turpin,' Jarvis the Coachman,' and so on; and those of Mrs. Hancock, of Blunsdon, were of the *awful* sort, *i.e.* dealing with tragedies, lovers and blood, such as 'Johnny, the Ship's Carpenter,' 'The Gamekeeper,' and others.

It is charming to sit with many of these old rustics and to hear them singing their songs. They discover the most delightful natures and qualities. This one is sweetly shy; the voice of that one trembles and quivers with nervousness of a different order. Another receives you into his confidence straight away, and, with smiles and gentle simplicity, lavishes the wealth of his music and memory upon you. What a sweet disposition this one has, and how naive, heartless, and innocent is the behaviour of that one! They are all very primitive. They are fresh and unspoiled, born of the earth, beautiful children of nature, young all their lives, changeless under hardships, afflictions, and other adversities.

The majority of them cannot teach you their songs merely by speaking the verses. No; they must sing. At least, they must sing first. Then perhaps they may manage it. Even then it will be a difficult matter. Very often a line is wanting in the middle or at the end of the piece. No amount of pondering will suffice; the singer has never been trained to concentrate. Nothing will serve but to go back to the beginning and repeat the whole song through. Then the *habit* of singing will prevail, and the last line will appear naturally and take its place with the others. It is singular, also, that it is physically easier for the men to sing their songs than to recite or relate them. Wassail Harvey, aged ninety, was quite exhausted after reciting two or three songs, whereas he could continue to sing, in a deep and powerful tone of voice, for an hour or more without experiencing appreciable fatigue. Certain forms of words used imparted an additional charm to the singing; such as lov-yer for lover, air for are, breck for break, and coold for could. Many old singers invariably said chorius for chorus, and substituted v for w, saying ven, and Villiam, for when and William.

The women's songs were chiefly the sweetest of them all. This is as befits the feminine nature. They were rarely sung by the males. The women might sing some of the men's pieces, but the men seldom sang those of the women. They appreciated their sweetness but they felt that the songs did not belong to them. There can be no doubt but that many choice and rare old songs, comparatively unknown, still exist in the memories of the cottage dames. They are obviously more difficult to obtain than are those of the males. Most of the men sang at the inns, and their pieces were consequently more or less publicly known, while the women's songs were sung over the cradle and might not often have been heard out of doors. I have never omitted an opportunity of searching for the women's songs, where I suspected any to exist, and I was never disappointed with anything I obtained as the result of such inquiries. Examples of the kind and quality of song sung by women are discovered in such pieces as 'Maggie's Secret,' 'The Scarlet Flower,' 'The

Seeds of Love,' 'Lord Lovel stood at his Castle Gate,' 'If you will walk with me,' 'Cold Blows the Winter's Wind,' and so on.

I have spoken of songs being sung at the inns. It is well known that the inns had more to do than anything besides with the perpetuation of the folk songs. A few men never sang anywhere else. Their souls only expanded in society. It is sometimes sneeringly said that the men only sang when they were half-drunk. That is not true, or just. It was a matter of atmosphere. Lord Bacon observed that the mind of a man is more apt to receive impressions in company then when he is alone. That is so, as well of the poor and unlettered, as of the educated. But the songs were not sung at the inns alone. They might chiefly have been learned there but they were afterwards sung in many places, and under all sorts of conditions. The songs were mainly obtained at the fairs. These were attended by the ballad singers, who stood in the market-place and sang the new tunes and pieces, and at the same time sold the broadsides at a penny each. The most famous ballad singers of the Thames Valley, in recent times, were a man and woman, who travelled together, and each of whom had but one eye. They sang at all the local fairs, and the man sold the sheets, frequently wetting his thumb with his lips to detach a sheet from the bundle and hand it to a customer in the midst of the singing.

The pieces were afterwards sung on public and private occasions. A certain class was always popular at harvest-homes. They were usually such as dealt with, or referred to, the occupations of mowing and reaping, and often included the ballad of John Barleycorn. Others were sung at Seed-Cake, Shearing feasts, May and Morris games, Church feasts, at Christmas time, during Mumming, at Weddings, and so on. Let it always be remembered that we are speaking of the agricultural population; very few others, if we except stablemen at the inns, figured to any extent in the minstrelsy. Individuals had their favourite pieces. This one was popular with the ploughboys, who taught each other songs at the ploughtail, and in the stables. Another was the favourite of the women at work in the fields reaping, hoeing, or haymaking. This was commonly sung by the cowman to keep the cow quiet during milking; that was chanted by the shearers as they clipped the fleeces from the sheep in the spring-time. The husbands and wives, sitting at home weaving and straw-plaiting, whiled away the hours with song; the children learned the melodies and repeated them out of doors, or after they had gone to bed, and often sang themselves asleep. A few of the choicest songs were taught the children at school; this especially seems to have been the case at Lechlade. The servant girls and maids in the kitchen at the farms and country houses also regularly had musical evenings, and taught each other new melodies. In this manner the folksongs of different counties and localities became interfused. When the young women left their situations and returned home, or married, they remembered the songs sung by their companions, or, very often, by the farmer and his wife, and, in time, passed them on to their children, who treasured them for their mother's sake. A few men received nicknames by reason of the song they commonly sang. 'Froggy' Harvey, of

Cricklade, was so called because he always sang 'Froggy would a-wooing go', while David Sawyer, the old sheepshearer, was styled 'Phoebus' since, at harvest -home, he always sang the harvest song containing the line 'Bright Phoebus is sinking in the west'.

Not the most intelligent sang. For the most highly intelligent is not commonly the most musical. Often the reverse obtains. Otherwise all the singing would have been done by tradespeople and schoolmasters. Generally speaking, it was the middle class of the working people who were most musical. At the same time, very many of the best singers I knew were quite illiterate, and some were incapable of much interest in matters of more practical value. Still they were never stupid. The absolutely stupid person never sang. Yet he appreciated the music and provided an audience. And very often, when a villager who had been a singer left the farm and took up work of a more highly skilled nature, and mixed with other company, he felt ashamed of his songs and definitely relinquished the singing of them. The same thing happened in the case of the one who, fond of singing, and gifted with a good voice, was tempted to learn music and join a choir, or play an instrument in the band. Thereafter he, too neglected the purely folk song, and showed a preference for classical, or, at any rate, for standard pieces. He was under the impression that his taste had improved, whereas, in reality, the opposite had often taken place. Thus, the singing of the folk songs constantly and continually devolved upon the rank and file, the lower order, if you will, by which I merely mean the carters, waggoners, shepherds, cowmen, and other farmhands, and the stablemen at the inns.

As some individuals were more musical than others, so also were some families. Very often the entire members of the family, for generations, had been famed for singing, and their songs had usually belonged to a distinctive class or order. One of the most convincing illustrations of this is the case of the Kings, of Castle Eaton. They were a numerous family, and nearly all were good singers and possessed of fine voices. The entire choir at the church was composed of the Kings, male and female, and bands of them practised carol singing at the farm houses for miles around every Christmas time. Their songs were uniformly of the sweet and original kind, such as 'The Rifles,' and 'To Milk in the Valley Below'; they never sang comic, boisterous, or, in fact, any but quiet songs. Other well-known singing families were the Deans and Ricketts of Down Ampney; the Howses and Messengers, of Latton; the Barretts, of Marston Meysey; the Harveys, of Cricklade; the Ockwells, of Somerford Keynes; the Sparrows, of Crudwell; the Caswells, of Marlborough; the Leggs and Zillards, of Hannington; the Pillingers, of Lechlade; the Wheelers, of Buscot; the Jordans and Jefferies, of Longcot; the Tanners, of Bampton; and others too numerous to mention.

Certain villages, too, throughout the Upper Thames Valley, were celebrated above the rest for the number of their singers and the quality of their songs. In several of these about every other person you met with might have sung to you some piece. It is worthy of note that the most dull of all villages are those in which there is not and has not been and inn, and, consequently, no, or only very limited, means of association open to the inhabitants. The village reading-room is insufficient. The atmosphere of that has, and is meant to have, a certain curbing and correcting influence. The liberty of the members is restricted and that is detrimental to music; the folk song can live and thrive only in a state of perfect freedom and independence. The villages which have been most noted for the number of their singers and the reputation of their songs, in the locality with which we are dealing, are; - Down Ampney, Latton, Crudwell, Oaksey, Castle Eaton, Marston Meysey, Blunsdon, Purton, Ogbourne, Bishopstone, Longcot, Lechlade, Filkins, Southrop, Brize Norton, Bampton, Standlake, Kingstone Bagpuize, and Uffington. I am going partly by evidence I have gathered from the aged people still living in these villages, but chiefly from my own deductions, and from opinions formed on the spot after careful deliberations and an examination of all the materials available.

What, now, is the reason of the discontinuance and disappearance of the folk song? Of course, there are many reasons. The dearth, or, at any rate, the restricting of the fairs, and, consequently of the opportunities for disseminating the ballad sheets is one cause of its decline. The closing of many of the old village inns, the discontinuance of the harvest-home and other farm feasts, the suspension and decay of May games, morris dancing, church festivals, wassailing, and mumming are other obvious reasons. Another factor was the advent of the church organ and the breaking-up of the old village bands of musicians, that dealt a smashing blow at music in the villages. Previous to the arrival of the church organ every little village and family had its band, composed of a fiddle, base viol, piccolo, clarionet, cornet, the 'horse's leg',[1] and the trumpet, or 'serpent.' They were played every Sunday in church. But they did not solely belong to the Church. All the week they were freed to be used for the entertainment of the people. The musicians had to be continually practising, and much of it was done in public. As a matter of fact, the villages were never without music. And the *need* of the band kept the wits of the performers fully alive they laboured to make and keep themselves proficient, and the training they took both educated them and exerted an unmistakable influence upon the everyday life of their fellows. But when the organ came the village band was dismissed from the church; they were not wanted any more. Their music was despised. There was no further need of them, and the bands broken up. For a while the fiddle sounded at the inns and at the farm feast, and was soon heard no more. As to whether the substitution of the organ in church was uniformly an improvement, that may be a matter of taste. My own opinion is that it was not so. It is too mechanical and formal, and, to my mind, incompatible with the highest worship, for I cannot think of God as being pleased to be reverenced by machinery. The human breast, human skill, the direct cunning of the human hand, the absolutely and purely personal element seem to me the most fitting to be employed in the worship of the Divinity. If I could

[1] The 'horse's leg' was the vernacular name for the bassoon.

have my desire I would remove the greater part of the bellowing, groaning organs from our churches and chapels, and burn them.

Another reason for the disappearance of the folk song is that the life and condition of things in the villages and throughout the whole countryside, have vastly changed of late. Education has played its part. The instruction given to the children at village schools proved antagonistic to the old minstrelsy. Dialect and homely language were discountenanced. Teachers were imported from the towns, and they had little sympathy with village life and customs. The words and spirit of the songs were misunderstood, and the tunes were counted too simple. The construction of railways, the linking up at the villages with other districts, and contact with large towns and cities had an immediate and permanent effect upon the minstrelsy of the countryside. Many of the village labourers migrated to the towns, or to the colonies, and most of them no longer cared for the old ballads, or were too busily occupied to remember them. Before the middle of the 19th Century the writing of even moderately good folksongs had ceased; all that have been produced since then belong to another and an inferior order, approaching to what is commonly known as the popular song of today. At the same time, the singing of the old songs went on as long as the fairs and harvest-homes were held, and even after they were discontinued, till they began to be rigidly discountenanced, or altogether forbidden at the inns. This was the most unkind and fatal repulse of all. It was chiefly brought about, I am told, not by any desire of the landlord, but by the harsh and strict supervision of the police. They practically forbade singing. The houses at which it was held, i.e., those at which the poor labourers commonly gathered, were marked as disorderly places; police looked upon song-singing as a species of rowdyism. Their frequent complaints and threats to the landlords filled them with misgivings; the result was that they were forced, as a means of self-protection, to request their customers not to sing on the premises, or, at any rate, *not to allow themselves to be heard.* The songs, since they could no longer be sung in public were relegated to oblivion; hundreds have completely died out, and will be heard no more. The gramophone and the cinema have about completed the work of destruction, and finally sealed the doom of the folk song and ballad as they were commonly known.

I hope that I have not written or claimed too much on the half of the folk songs. And here I wish it to be distinctly understood that throughout this article I have had in view not the perfect unpolished composition, not even that one which is moderately correct in literary form, but that which was regularly recognised and sung by the people. I do not pretend to have a faultless collection. They are, emphatically, not a classic lot. Many of them are not as I should prefer to see them, but they were not my songs. I make no apologies for the musical tastes of the people; I cannot help what they liked. That is no business of mine, and I have nothing to do with it. I want to show not what they *might* have sung, nor what they *ought* to have sung, but what, in fact, they *did* sing. And what right have I, or anyone else, to condemn the taste exhibited in, or the imperfections of the old songs, and mutilate, patch, polish, or correct them in deference to the wishes of those trained exclusively according to the modern ideas of poetry and music, and who are unable to appreciate simple measures. I have been asked what the people sang, and I have told you what they sang. I, at any rate, I'm not ashamed of the pieces, and there is no reason why anyone else should be so. The words, verses, and rhyme of many of the songs are undoubtedly incorrect. What otherwise could one expect? Out of the four hundred I have all but two dozen were given me orally. I might, certainly, have gone to museums and libraries and examined those of other collections in order to verify my own, but I did not so. For one thing, I had not the time to spare. And I do not know that, if I had had the leisure, I was possessed of a sufficiently strong inclination. The versions of the songs differ widely in localities, and in searching out other copies and comparing my own with them – many of which have often been tampered with – I may have become confused, and, in trying to improve my pieces, have had them worse than before. At any rate, I hope I have acted honestly. If my readers grant me that I care but very little what may be their opinions of my general methods, or of the pieces themselves, and I shall not implore them to like a thing against their will, in deference to myself or anyone else.

As I have said, I did not want to write critically and abstractedly on the folk song or the Morris. Least of all did I intend to set out in search of the historical ballad and enter upon a tedious discussion of its metamorphosis in the hands of poetical and other quacks, and wear myself – and my readers – quite out with arguments that have no value beyond that of a purely dry-as-dust literary interest. Nothing of the kind! What I wanted to do was to show the songs, rough or smooth, in the exact relation to the life of the residents of the Upper Thames Valley, and, in some sort, to complete the purpose begun in my prose volumes before mentioned. I hope, therefore, if there be any disappointed at what I have *not* done, to bear this in mind, and not blame me for having failed to do more than I professed, or above what was my set intention. I considered the work to be fully worthy of my intentions and labourers, and I have no doubt that the materials I have gathered together will amuse and delight a few others, and provide a permanent record of not the least interesting side of the life of the former inhabitants of our villages. It is certain that if the work had not been done now it would not have been accomplished at all. In another ten years' time it would've been too late. The old villages are dying off very rapidly. About ten of my old singers have bidden farewell to this world during the last few months. What I have done, then, has been just in the nick of time. I have not saved everything in the district though I do not think that there is very much of value left behind in those villages which I have examined. I am surprised, not that I had failed to find more, but that I have succeeded in discovering so much. It has been a labour of love to me, and I trust that others will derive some amount of pleasure from perusal of the pieces.

The songs themselves, as far as singing goes, are practically defunct. There is no need to revive them. To do so, in fact, it would be impossible. It is also undesirable. We live in a new age, almost in a new world. Life has changed. There are other amusements. We move at a quicker pace. Time and custom decide what shall or shall not continue. Fashions in everything accept modifications. It is the same with morris dancing. Where a desire to sing or dance does not exist naturally, and is not spontaneous, no amount of artificial activity will suffice to restore the practice. Though you should resuscitate it for a time the life would not be permanent. You cannot graft a dead branch onto a living body. Let us, then, be content to say that the folksong is dead. But we want to preserve the words, not for their artistic or strictly literary value, but in order to have records of that which amused, cheered, consoled, and so profoundly affected the lives of the people of an age that has for ever passed away.

Alfred Williams

1. Meet Me by Moonlight Alone

Roud 767, Bathe-Clissold X.777
Unnamed singer, Southrop, Gloucestershire

Obtained at Southrop. A very old composition, possibly the original of another song possessing the same title.

O weep not, O weep not, dear mother,
O weep not, O weep not for me,
For I have a sweet story to tell you,
Must be told by the moonlight alone.
  Meet me, O meet me by moonlight,
  Meet me by moonlight alone,
  For I have a sweet story to tell you,
  Must be told by the moonlight alone.

O where and O where is my Willie?
O where, and O where can he be?
He's gone to the battle of freedom,
And when shall I see him again?
  Meet me, O meet me, etc.

There's a big ship out on the ocean,
It's loaded with silver and gold,
It belongs to a wealthy man's daughter,
And I'm sure my sweet Willie's on board.
  Meet me, O meet me, etc.

I wish I had wings like an angel,
I wish I had wings like a dove,
I would fly to the arms of my Willie,
To the arms of my bold sailor boy.
  Meet me, O meet me, etc.

Part 3, Number 7, 16 October 1915

An ancestor of this song, 'Meet Me by Moonlight', was written by Joseph Augustus Wade in 1824 and appeared in countless songsters and broadsides. Over the years, particularly in the USA, that song collided with a number of others to produce a range of songs not unlike this one, most notably Vernon Dalhart's 'Prisoner's Song'. Apart from the above, from an unnamed singer in Southrop, I have only found one other instance of the song in Britain. Baring-Gould heard 'If I Had Two Ships', which is similar to the last two stanzas of the Southrop version, from John Woodridge of Thrushelton, Devon, in 1893. Woodridge had heard this fragment repeated over and over by a drunken woman in a North Devon pub. Williams's original manuscript is missing.

2. The Blue Cockade

Roud 191, Bathe-Clissold Wt.517
Unnamed singer, Stratton St Margaret, Wiltshire

A very old favourite, now rarely met with anywhere. It was evidently written about 1750, during Lord Clive's war with the French in India. Obtained at Stratton St. Margaret.

'Twas on a Monday morning, as I was going to the fair,
I did not think of listing till the soldiers met me there;
Good company enticed me to drink their health all round,
The bounty that they gave me was ten guineas and a crown.

'Tis true my love has 'listed, and he wears a blue cockade,
He is a clever soldier, likewise a roving blade;
He is a clever soldier, and he's gone to serve the King,
Whilst my poor heart is aching all for the love of him.

'Tis true my love is gone, my love is gone from me,
He's gone to fight the French, my boys, in a foreign country,
But the ground that my love walks upon no grass will ever grow,
Since it's been his inclination, and my sorrow, grief and woe.

He took out his pocket-handkerchief to wipe her flowing eyes
And said – 'My dearest Nancy, leave off such mournful cries,
For when I return from India I'll have no girl but you
And I wish I'd never changed from the orange to the blue.'

Part 3, Number 11, 16 October 1915

This is a song that will be familiar to many because it has continued to feature regularly in the folk revival repertoire, though more often as 'The *White* Cockade'. The earliest version discovered so far is *The Light Blues*, printed on a slip by Evans of London in 1794. The song is close to more recent versions in structure and in many key phrases but differs in some interesting details. For example, in Evans, the young man says he was 'going to mass', which becomes 'I walked o'er the moss' in some later versions. His cockade is black, and he says 'fare ye well sweet Limerick', suggesting an Irish origin for the song. A later chapbook, *Queen Mary's Lamentation*, printed in Glasgow in 1823, has a six-stanza version, 'The Orange and the Blue', which is clearly set in Ireland. The colour of the cockade varies between the various versions of the song, most frequently either white, blue, or green. The colours had political, national, and military significance and are the subject of much discussion in relation to this song. The orange cockade mentioned in the final stanza is unusual, as that colour is often associated with the Netherlands.

3. The Shepherd on the Plain

Roud 32501, Bathe-Clissold Gl.83
Charles Sellars, Eastleach, Gloucestershire

A typical shepherd song. Obtained at Eastleach, of Charles Sellars.

It's of a gentle shepherd kept his sheep on yonder plain,
He was minding his sheep on a bright summer's morn;
A lady of honour he chanced for to find,
And on the young shepherd she fixed her mind.

He played on his pipe and his flock it drew near,
Which caused this young lady to stand still to hear;
She said – 'Gentle shepherd, pray where do you dwell?
I think in my heart I could love you right well.'

He says – 'Fair lady, you had better forbear,
You might have a man with a thousand a year;
You might have a man that is richer than me.'
'I am deeply in love,' this young lady said she.

Then straight to the tailor's shop she did go,
And ordered a suit from the head to the toe;
With a gold laced hat, and a holland shirt so fine,
She dressed her young shepherd, it was her design.

Down under the shady oak tree that was green,
She dressed this young shepherd like a squire to be seen;
A gold watch from her pocket she freely did give,
She says – 'Gentle shepherd! now can you believe?'

They went to the church and were married with speed,
And the shepherd he knew not his lady indeed;
A coach and attendants stood ready waiting there,
Now the shepherd's a squire worth a thousand a year.

Part 3, Number 12, 16 October 1915

This delightful male fantasy would, I am sure, have had special appeal for shepherds. This song, though, is unique to Williams's collection and has not appeared in print elsewhere.

4. Paul Jones

Roud 967, Bathe-Clissold Gl.109
John Pillinger, Down Ampney, Gloucestershire

Obtained of John Pillinger, the wooden legged veteran of Sevastopol and a native of Lechlade. Paul Jones was a Scotchman who went to sea and, during the American War with England, commanded various ships for the Colonists. He was a clever and a daring Captain and made many attacks upon British vessels. He died in Paris in 1792. The song is about one hundred and forty years old.

It's an American frigate, from New York she came,
She mounted guns forty, called *Massachusetts* by name,
A-crossing the channel of old England's fame
With her saucy commander – Paul Jones was his name.

We had not been sailing long before we spies
A large forty-four, and a twenty likewise;
'Come answer me quickly, I've hailed you before,
Or else a broadside into you I will pour.

We fought them four glasses, four glasses so hot,
Till fourteen bright seamen lay dead on the spot,
And twenty-five lay wounded, all covered with gore,
While the guns from proud Paul Jones like thunder did roar.

Our carpenter, being frightened to Paul Jones did say –
'Our ship she makes water since fighting today'
Then up spoke proud Paul Jones, in the height of his pride –
'If we cannot do better, boys, we'll sink alongside.'

And now, my brave fellows, we have taken a rich prize,
Here's a large forty four, and a twenty likewise;
God help every poor widow that has reason to weep,
For the loss of her dear sons in the ocean so deep.

Part 4, Number 8, 23 October 1915

Paul Jones was a Scotsman by birth but became one of the first and foremost captains of the American navy during the Revolutionary Wars. His ship USS *Bonhomme Richard* defeated HMS *Serapis* and the armed merchantman *Countess of Scarborough* at the Battle of Flamborough Head on 23 September 1779. The earliest known version of the song is on a broadside printed in Boston, Massachusetts, at the beginning of the nineteenth century which has thirteen stanzas. Despite its celebration of an American victory over the Royal Navy the song appeared on a number of British broadsides, though usually with fewer stanzas. It was heard by a number of the early collectors. Williams's version is similar to many of the broadsides and, as with several of them, the names of the ships involved are corrupted.

5. The North American Rebels

Roud 596, Bathe-Clissold Gl.107
John Pillinger, Down Ampney, Gloucestershire

This song, as the preceding ['Paul Jones'], *also relates to the American War of Independence. Obtained of John Pillinger.*

Our drums beat to arms, the thundering cannons roar,
Here's adieu unto old England, for we must leave the shore;
Our Captain has commanded us and we must all obey,
To face the proud rebels in the North America.

We marched out of Plymouth on the eleventh day of June,
When the trees were in blossom and the meadows in full bloom;
To see the pretty fair maids to the quay come running down,
To see our colours flying – to America we are bound.

Then up speaks lovely Nancy, these words she did say –
'You bold hearted captain, come take us all away,
Our captain answered with a frown – 'You all may stay on shore,
Our ship is over-loaded and we cannot carry more.'

By hearing of these words, it brought tears in every eye,
'You faint hearted Captain, you think we're afraid to die
We value not the broadsword, we'd cut and slash away
We'd show the rebels sport in the North America.

So, to conclude my ditty and finish off my song,
America is our delight, we'll take it before it's long;
Over lofty hills and valleys and many a seaport town,
And with our great strong army we'll tumble them all down.

Part 4, Number 9, 23 October 1915

A similar song, 'The Battle of King's Bridge', learned in Ireland in the early nineteenth century, refers to a battle fought at King's Bridge, near New York, in September 1776.[1] Sabine Baring-Gould heard a version, 'Farewell to Kingsbridge', localized to the Devon town of Kingsbridge, from Roger Huggins of Lydford. Recording it in his Personal Copy manuscript, Baring-Gould drew a comparison with 'The Highlander's March to America' in *Lord Anson's Garland* from the late eighteenth century, which gives the same date of 'the eleventh day of June' and contains many of the same phrases as Williams's version. Baring-Gould also quotes a later broadside, *North of America*, from his own collection. Both songs describe the soldiers' departure from Glasgow, but there is no mention of New York or King's Bridge, so the song may have been modified at a later date to include the battle.

[1] *Journal of the Folk-Song Society*, 2.2 (no. 7) (1905), 90–91.

6. In High Germany

Roud 904, Bathe-Clissold Wt.447
David Sawyer, Stratton St Margaret, Wiltshire

Obtained of David Sawyer. The song dates from the time of Marlborough's campaign in Germany in the year 1704. Unheard of in Gloucestershire and on the Thames banks.

'Oh Polly, love! Oh Polly, love! The route is now begun, [*rout*]
And we must march away to the beating of the drum.
Go, dress yourself all in your best and come along with me,
I'll take you to the wars, love, in High Germany.'

'Oh Willie, love! Oh Willie, love! You mark what I do say,
I am a feeble woman, I cannot march away.
Besides my dearest Willie, I'm not married yet to thee,
I'm not fitting for the wars, love, in High Germany.'

'Oh, I'll hire you a horse love, and on it you shall ride,
For all my delight is to march by your side.
We'll call at every ale house and drink when we are dry,
We'll sweetheart on the road, love, and get married by and by.'

'I wish the wars were over, or they never had begun,
For out of old England, they pressed many a bright son.
They pressed my Willie from me, likewise my brothers three,
And sent them to the wars, love, in High Germany.'

Part 4, Number 1, 23 October 1915

Over the years I have heard a lot of speculation about this song and about the two key issues: where is 'High Germany', and which war were they fighting in? There is no clear answer to either question, since modern Germany has been the geopolitical result of several wars, many of them involving British soldiery. An early version of the song is *Billy and Molly; or, The Constant Couple*, in the Madden Collection, which contains the key features of the story. There were sufficient European conflicts over the following 150 years to ensure that the ballad could be constantly recycled by later broadside printers. In many of these later versions, the young woman says she will not travel overseas because she is expecting her lover's child. Whether this detail was suppressed by Williams, Sawyer, or anyone else it is not possible to say.

7. Down Covent Garden

Roud 490, Bathe-Clissold Wt.352
Henry Harvey, Cricklade, Wiltshire

Obtained of Wassail Harvey of Cricklade. From the circumstances related it is of considerable age. The idea contained in the seventh and eighth stanzas is sufficiently naive.

In Norwich town I was bred and born,
I served my time and I died with scorn;
I served my time to the saddling trade,
And was always counted a roving blade.

At seventeen I took a wife,
I loved her dear as I loved my life,
And to maintain her both fine and gay
A-robbing I went on the highway.

My money being spent and my pocket low,
On the highway I was forced to go,
I robbed both lords and ladies bright,
And brought home the gold to my heart's delight.

I robbed Lord Gowan, I do declare,
And Lady Mansfield, of Covent Square,
I closed the shutters and bid them goodnight,
And went away to my heart's delight.

Down Covent Garden I took my way
With my blooming girl to see the play,
Till Fielding's Gang did me pursue,
And taken was I by that cursed crew.

My father said – 'I am undone,'
My mother cried for her darling son,
My wife she tore her golden hair –
'What shall I do in my despair?'

Oh, when I'm dead and brought to my grave
A decent funeral let me have;
Let six highwaymen carry me,
Give them broadswords and their liberty.

Six blooming girls to bear my pall,
And give them gloves and ribbons all;
And when I'm hanged may they tell the truth –
I was a wild and wicked youth.

Part 4, Number 11, 23 October 1915

Ballads about highwaymen were very popular among the old rural singers and were widely printed and collected. This song has acquired several different titles over the years but is best known as 'The Highwayman'. The first known printing of it is in a chapbook, *The Valiant Damsel*, where it is called 'The Dublin Baker'. It was printed several times more during the nineteenth century and has been widely collected in Britain, Ireland, and beyond. Cecil Sharp heard it in the USA as 'The Rambling Boy', with the opening line 'I robbed Saint James I do declare'. The song's popularity can be attributed to the strength of the story and the unrepentant hero who designs his own extravagant funeral. 'The Dublin Baker' ends:

When I am dead and in my grave
Six gallant whores let me have
Six gallant whores to bear my pall
Give them white ribbons all
Six jolly scamps on every side
Give them six swords and pistols bright
That they may say when I'm in grave
There lies a wild and rambling blade.

8. Johnny, the Ship's Carpenter

Roud 15, Bathe-Clissold Wt.318
Emma Hancock, Blunsdon, Wiltshire

Obtained of Mrs Hancock of Broad Blunsdon. Heard also at South Cerney. The song is of great age. This is evidenced by the reference in the ninth stanza, to the old superstition long held by sailors, that if a murder had been committed by any of the crew bad luck would attend the voyage and the ship would be doomed. Under such circumstances it was common to attempt a discovery of the culprit and if he should be found, to throw him overboard.

In Gosport Town a fair damsel did dwell,
For wit and for beauty none could her excel;
'Tis of a young man courted her for his dear,
And he was by trade a ship's carpenter.

The King wanted some sailors to go on the sea,
Which made this young damsel to sigh and to say –
'Oh Johnny, oh Johnny, pray don't go to sea!
Remember the vow that you made unto me.'

'Twas early one morning, before it was day,
He came to his Polly and thus he did say –
'Oh Polly, oh Polly, you must go with me,
Before we are married, my friends for to see.'

He led her through woods and valleys so deep,
He made this young damsel to sigh and to weep –
'Oh Johnny, Oh Johnny, you've led me astray,
Intending my life, my sweet life to destroy.'

'Oh Polly, oh Polly, true words you have said,
For all the last night I was digging your grave,
Oh Polly, oh Polly, there's no time to stand'
He took a long large knife in his hand.

'Oh Johnny, oh Johnny, oh pardon my life!
I'll never covet to be thy wedded wife;
I'll ramble the country and set thee quite free,
If thou wilt pardon my baby and me.'

'No pardon I give,' he replied, 'for my part.'
He stabbed her, he stabbed her, he stabbed her to the heart;
All from her left bosom the blood it did flow,
Then into the grave her fair body he throw.

He covered her up, so safe and secure,
That the murder could never be found he was sure;
He went on board ship to sail the world round,
Thinking this vile murder would never be found.

'Twas early one morning, before it was day,
Our captain came to us and thus he did say –
'A murder on board has lately been done;
Our ship is in mourning, we cannot sail on.'

Then up stepped the first seaman – 'Indeed it's not me.'
Then up spoke the second, the same he did say
Then up came young Johnny to stamp and to swear –
'Indeed it's not me sir, I vow and declare.'

But while he was turning from the captain with speed,
He met his dear Polly, and she made his heart bleed;
She ripped him, she stripped him, and tore him in three,
Because he had murdered her baby and she.

Part 4, Number 12, 23 October 1915

The earliest known version of this popular ballad is the 33-stanza epic, *The Gosport Tragedy; or, the Perjured Ship Carpenter*, which was printed before 1754 when it was listed in the catalogue of William and Cluer Dicey. David C. Fowler has argued at some length that the song was founded on an actual incident at sea.[2]

This is one of the relatively few ballads in the English tradition that invoke supernatural forces. The ship is prevented from moving by a mysterious force because, as the captain knows from maritime tradition,

[2] David C. Fowler, 'The Gosport Tragedy: Story of a Ballad', *Southern Folklore Quarterly*, 43 (1979), 157–96.

there is a murderer on board. In the final stanza the carpenter denies responsibility for the murder, at which point Polly appears and dismembers him. In another ballad from the Dicey print shop, *The Portsmouth Ghost*, a wronged lady sells her soul to the devil in order to win herself the right to visit her faithless lover on board his ship, from which she carries him off in a cloud of fire.

Many of the broadside ballads from this period tell complex tales which took longer to tell than was acceptable to later generations of singers. As a result, juicy sections of the narrative were spun off as new songs. In this case the early part, dealing with Polly's murder, became 'Pretty Polly' which is widespread in America and has been recorded by an astonishing array of leading names in American 'folk'.[3]

9. Jeanette

Roud 391, Bathe-Clissold Gl.163
Mrs Russell, Tetbury, Gloucestershire[4]

Obtained at Tetbury. Formerly popular alongside the Thames to Lechlade. The piece probably had its origin in the wars with France at the end of the eighteenth century.

You are going far away, far away from poor Jeanette,
There is no one left to love me now, and you too may forget;
But my heart will be with you, wherever you may go,
Can you look me in the face and say the same to Jeanette?

When you wear the jacket red and the beautiful cockade,
It's then I fear that you'll forget the promises you made;
With the gun upon your shoulder, and the dagger by your side,
You'll be taking some proud lady and be making her your bride.

O if I were the Queen of France, or, still better, Pope of Rome
I'd have no fighting men abroad, no weeping maids at home
All the world should be at peace, or, if kings must show their might,
Let them who make the quarrels be the only ones to fight.

Part 4, Number 13, 23 October 1915

[3] If you have the time to spare, I would suggest a search for 'Pretty Polly' on Spotify to see the number of recordings and hear the extraordinary range of treatments.
[4] Although Williams does not name the singer, Mrs Russell was the only performer that he met in Tetbury.

This was written by Charles Jefferys, with a tune composed by Charles Glover. Jefferys published it himself and there is a series of advertisements for it from late 1847 onwards, some of which cautioned potential buyers to ignore rumours that it was a reprint of an earlier song. Jefferys and Glover created *Songs of a Conscript* as a suite comprised of three songs – 'Jeannette's Song' ('You are going far away, far away, from poor Jeanette', Roud 391), 'Jeannot's Song' ('Cheer up, cheer up, my own Jeannette', Roud 13856), and 'Jeanette and Jeannot' ('From the field of fight returning', Roud V6807). The first two appeared in several songsters and on broadsides, but Roud records only a few instances of the third song.

Apart from this version heard by Williams from Mrs Russell, 'Jeanette's Song' was collected by Cecil Sharp in Devon and Somerset. It was also sung in the USA, notably by singers heard by Helen Hartness Flanders in New England. The earliest instance outside of the concert hall was found by Gale Huntington in a whaler's log from 1849. The other two songs have never been collected from singers, though 'Jeannot's Song' was listed in the biography of the Sussex singer Henry Burstow as one that he sang

10. Maggie's Secret; or, The Golden West

Roud 12886, Bathe-Clissold Ox.292
Mary Parrott, Standlake, Oxfordshire

Obtained of Mrs Parrot, Standlake, Oxfordshire. The song was formerly very popular throughout the whole of the Upper Thames valley.

There's many a time when I'm sad at heart,
And I haven't a word to say,
I'll keep from the lads and the lasses apart,
In the meadows a-making of hay;
My Willie shall bring me the first wild rose,
In my new bonnet to wear,
And the robin will wait at the keeper's gate,
For he follows me everywhere.
    Then I told them they need not come wooing to me,
    For my heart, for my heart was over the sea:
    Then I told them they need not come wooing to me,
    For my heart, for my heart was over the sea.

Two summers ago a brave ship sailed,
To the midst of the golden west,
And nobody knew that my heart beat true,
For the secret I never confessed;

A mother took leave of her boy that day,
And I heard her sob and cry,
As I followed her back to her dreary home,
But never a word said I.
    Then I told them, *etc.*

I sat by that mother one bright summer's day,
And she looked me through and through,
She spoke of her boy who was far away,
For she guessed that I loved him too;
She threw her arms round me and whispered low -
'You are worthy my sailor boy.'
My foolish tears began to flow,
But my heart beat high with joy.
    Then I told them, *etc.*

Part 4, Number 14, 23 October 1925

Written by 'Claribel' (Charlotte Pye) in 1858, this drawing-room song was successful enough for her to write a sequel, 'Maggie's Welcome'. Although the song appeared in several songsters and on broadsides, Williams is the only collector to have reported hearing it. This was one of the songs that Kidson told Williams should not be considered a folk song (*Appendix A*).

11. Come Tell Me When, Come Tell Me Where

Roud 13246, Bathe-Clissold Gl.146
James Mills, South Cerney, Gloucestershire

An old love duet. Obtained of Mr W. Mills, South Cerney.[5]

Youth
Come tell me when, come, tell me where,
Am I to meet with thee, my fair;
Come, tell me when, come tell me where.

Maiden
I'll meet thee in the secret night,
When stars are beaming soft and light,
Enough for love, but not too bright,
To tell our blushes there.

[5] The name is a typographical error; the manuscript makes it clear that the singer was James Mills.

Youth
You've told me when, now tell me where,
Am I to meet with thee, my fair?
You've told me when, but where?

Maiden
I'll meet thee in that lonely place,
Where flowerets dwell in sweet embrace,
And Zephyr comes to steal a grace,
All on the midnight air.

Youth
You've told me when, you've told me where,
But how shall I know that thou art there?
You've told me when and where.

Maiden
Thou'lt know when I shall sing a lay,
That wandering boys on organs play,
No lover, sure, can miss his way,
When led by the signal air.
With a fol lol lol, a fol lol lol,
The signal air, i-lay.

Part 5, Number 6, 30 October 1915

This song was written by the Irish composer Samuel Lover in the early part of the nineteenth century and was published in a number of songsters and on broadsheets. The structure that Williams has applied enhances the dialogue, but the original song was written in three six-line stanzas. The song was not reported by any of the other collectors, perhaps because they recognized that it was by a known composer.

12. Sheep Crook and Black Dog

Roud 948, Bathe-Clissold Gl.98
John Barrett, Long Doles, Lechlade, Gloucestershire

A quaint specimen of the old shepherd songs. Obtained of Shepherd Barret of Long Dolls, Lechlade, who learned it of an old woman, his neighbour.

'Come here, my dear Flora, and sit down by me,
And we will be married, if we can agree.'
'Oh no,' says dear Flora, 'my time is not come,
And to marry so early my age is too young.'

'We'll both go to service, and when I return,
We will be married all in the next town.'
'Will you go to service and leave me to cry?'
'Oh yes, loving shepherd, I'll tell you for why.'

It happened so to service she went,
To wait on a lady was Flora's intent;
To wait on a lady, and a rich lady gay,
It clothed fair Flora in costly array.

In a little time, after a letter was sent,
It was a few lines for to know her intent;
She wrote that she lived a contented life,
That she never intended to be a poor shepherd's wife.

The words that she wrote they pierced like a dart –
'I'll pluck up my spirits, I'll cheer up my heart,
In hoping fair Flora won't write so any more.'
But the answer she gave was the same as before.

'My ewes and my lambs I will bid them adieu,
My instruments of music I will leave them with you,
My sheep crook and black dog I will leave them behind,
Since Flora, fair Flora, has changed her mind.'

Part 5, Number 7, 30 October 1915

'Long Dolls' was actually Long Doles Farm, between Fairford and Lechlade, now lost to gravel working. In 1898 Frank Kidson wrote to Lucy Broadwood enclosing a transcription of a version of the song called 'The Constant Shepherd and the Inconstant Shepherdess' taken from a chapbook dated 1775. Gale Huntington found a very similar text in the logbook of the whaler *Vaughan*, of Essex, Massachusetts, which dates from 1767. There was probably an earlier song from which both are derived.

As well as this version from Gloucestershire, Williams also heard the song from an unnamed singer at Stanton Harcourt, Oxfordshire. It was also noted by several other collectors.

13. Adieu! My Lovely Nancy

Roud 165, Bathe-Clissold Wt.516
Unnamed singer, Stratton St Margaret, Wiltshire

Obtained at Stratton St. Margaret.

Adieu! my lovely Nancy, ten thousand times adieu!
I'm a going to cross the ocean, for to seek for something new,
Come, change a ring with me, dear girl, come, change a ring with me,
And that shall be a token when I am on the sea.

When I am on the sea, dear girl, and you know not where I am,
Letters I will send to you from every foreign land,
With the secrets of my heart, dear girl, and the best of my goodwill,
And let my body be where it may my heart is with you still.

And whilst we jolly sailors are fighting for the crown,
There's a heavy storm a-rising, see how it's gathering round.
The clouds are black as ink and the thundering cannons roar,
And we fear we'll never see old England any more.

Our officers command us, and it's them we must obey,
Expecting every moment for to be cast away;
But we stood to our guns and fought most manfully,
And the enemy's ships went sinking to the bottom of the sea.

Now yonder storm is over and we are safe ashore,
We'll drink healths to our sweethearts and the girls we do adore,
We'll call for liquor merrily and spend our money free,
And when that is all spent and gone, we'll boldly put to sea.

Part 5, Number 9, 30 October 1915

The first two stanzas of this song are similar to those in 'Molly's Lamentation,' one of the songs printed in *Cupid's Magazine, being a Choice Collection of New Songs Sung at Vauxhall, Ranelagh, the Theatres, and all Places of Public Amusement*, *c.*1800. Many songs in the folk canon were originally written to be performed in the pleasure gardens and theatres of London, from where they made their way to the countryside. Their travels were often facilitated by publication on broadsides which were then, as Williams describes in his Introduction, sold at markets and fairs. This is a good example of a popular song that achieved popularity through its appearance in cheap print and went on to be heard by many of the Victorian and Edwardian collectors in England.

14. Jeannie and Jamie

Roud 345, Bathe-Clissold Gl.160
Mrs Russell, Tetbury, Gloucestershire

An old Scotch piece that somehow or other became established at the western end of the Thames vale. From the references to Germany it would appear to have been written about the time of Marlborough's campaign in that country early in the eighteenth century. Obtained of Mrs Russell, Tetbury, late of Crudwell.

Jeannie
When ye gang awa', Jamie,
Far across the sea, laddie,
When ye gang to Germany,
What will ye send to me, laddie?

Jamie
I'll send ye a braw new gown, Jeannie,
I'll send ye a braw new gown, lassie,
And it shall be o' silk an' gowd,
With Valenciennes set round, lassie.

Jeannie
Tha's nae gift ava, Jamie,
That's nae gift ava, laddie;
There's not a gown in a' the town,
I like when ye're awa', laddie.

Jamie
When I come back again, Jeannie,
When I come back again, lassie,
I'll bring with me a gallant gay
To be your ain guidman, lassie.

Jeannie
Be my guidman yersel, Jamie,
Be my guidman yersel, laddie,
An' tak' me o'er to Germany,
With you at hame to dwell, laddie.

Jamie
I dinna ken how that would do, Jeannie,
I dinna ken how that can be, lassie,
For I've a wife and bairnies three,
An' I'm na sure how ye'd agree, lassie.

Jeannie
Ye should a telt me that in time, Jamie,
Ye should a telt me that lang syne, laddie,
For had I kent o' your false heart,
Ye'd ne'er hae gotten mine, laddie.

Jamie
Your e'en were like a spell, Jeannie,
Your e'en were like a spell, lassie,
That ilka day bewitched me sae,
I could na help myself, lassie.

Jeannie
Gae back to your wife an' hame, Jamie,
Gae back to your bairnies three, laddie.
And I will pray they ne'er may know,
A broken heart like me, laddie.

Jamie
Dry that tearful e'e, Jeannie,
Dry that tearful e'e, lassie,
For I've neither wife nor bairnies three,
And I'll wed none but thee, lassie.

Jeannie
Think weel for fear ye rue, Jamie,
Think weel for fear ye rue, laddie,
For I have neither gowd nor lands,
To be a match for you, laddie.

Jamie
Blair in Atholl's mine, Jeannie,
Little Dunkeld is mine, lassie,
St. Johnstone's bower and hunting tower,
An' a' tha's mine is thine, lassie.

Part 6, Number 4, 6 November 1915

This is better known as 'When Ye Gang Awa' Jamie', and was published as 'The Duke of Athol' in Kinloch's *Ancient Scottish Ballads* in 1827, 'as taken down from the recitation of an idiot boy in Wishaw'. It was also known as 'Huntingtower'. Francis James Child included it, along with Kinloch's note, as an appendix to 'Richie Story' (Child 232), from which it apparently derived.[6]

The song was set to music by Carolina, Lady Nairne, the writer of several well-known Scottish songs, who reworked the words and 'improved the *moral* of the composition'.[7] It was, unsurprisingly, collected more frequently in Scotland than in England.

---

[6] Francis J Child, *The English and Scottish Popular Ballads'*, Vol. 4 (Boston: Houghton Miflin, 1892), pp. 299-300.

[7] Rev. Charles Rogers, *The Modern Scottish Minstrel: The Songs of Scotland subsequent to Burns, with Memoirs of the Poets*, 2nd edn (London: William P. Nimmo, 1876) p. 62.

15. William Taylor

Roud 158, Bathe-Clissold Ox.308
Alice Rowles, Witney, Oxfordshire

Obtained of Mrs Rowles, Witney. Heard also at Cricklade and Marlborough.

William Taylor was a brisk young sailor,
Once he courted a lady gay,
But a little before they could get married,
Pressed he was and sent away.

Five long years she waited for him,
She thought him either dead or drowned,
'If he's alive I'll love him dearly,
And if he's dead for him I'll mourn.'

She dressed herself in man's apparel,
And boldly boarded a man of war,
With her lily white hands and her long small fingers,
Dabbling in the pitch and tar.

And when she reached the field of battle,
There she fought along with the rest;
But the wind being high, blew her waistcoat apparel,
And there they spied her lily white breast.

As soon as the captain he did see her,
Says he – 'What wind has blown you here?'
'I've come to seek my dearest William Taylor,
You've pressed the man that I loved so dear.'

'Is William Taylor your true lover?
If he is, he's a false young man,
For tomorrow morning he's going to be married,
To some lady of this land.

'If you rise early tomorrow morning,
Early by the break of day,
Then you will see your dearest William Taylor
Walking with some lady gay.'

Then she rose early the next morning,
Early by the break of day,
And there she saw her dearest William Taylor
Walking with his lady gay.

She boldly called for a brace of pistols,
Which were brought at her command,
And there she shot her dearest William Taylor
With his bride at his right hand.

Then the captain being a brave-hearted fellow,
Well pleased was he to see the fun;
Saying – 'If you'll be the captain I'll be commander,
And over the seas we will roll on.'

Soon as the captain he beheld her,
For the deed she had done,
Then he made her his chief commander,
Over a ship of five hundred men

She's married and is the captain's wife,
Was married in October,
They live a sweet and contented life,
There's none in the world above her.

Part 6, Number 7, 6 November 1915

The frequency with which this song was found by collectors confirms that it was a favourite among the old rural singers. The first recorded instance is in *The Female Sailor's Garland*, published by Sarah Bates in the early eighteenth century. It continued to appear in cheap print throughout the nineteenth century and a number of variants evolved from the original story. The rather worrying thought of this murderous young woman being rewarded for her crime did not prevent the song from travelling throughout the country and to the New World. Gale Huntington found it recorded in the journal of the sloop *Nellie* of Edgartown, Martha's Vineyard, dated 1769.[8]

16. Barbara Allen

Roud 54, Bathe-Clissold Gl.144
James Mills, South Cerney, Gloucestershire

Barbara Allen dates from at least the opening years of the seventeenth century. It is claimed as a Scotch song, and such, indeed, it may be, though I am of the opinion that more than one of the songs generally accepted as Scotch have had an English origin. The references to Reading Town and Newbury Town may be merely of local import, though in a 'Bundle of Ballads', published in 1891 by Henry Morley, LL.D., Professor of English language and literature at University College, London, the opening line has 'In Scarlet Town' which is obviously Reading Town disguised. The piece was very popular in the Thames Valley and occurs in several forms. As an illustration of the manner in which a piece may vary in one

[8] Gale Huntington, *The Gam; More Songs the Whalemen Sang* (Suffield, CT: Loomis House Press, 2014), pp. 155–56.

locality I am printing three versions [see also *FSUT*, pp. 204–05, 206–07] *procured within a space of twenty five miles. It is difficult to say which is the oldest and most nearly original form. Obtained of J. Mills, South Cerney and Latton.*

In Reading town, where I was born,
A fair maid there was dwelling,
I picked her out to be my wife,
And her name was Barbara Allen.

'Twas in the merry month of May,
When green leaves they were springing,
A young man on his deathbed lay,
For the love of Barbara Allen.

He sent to her a servant man,
To the place where she was dwelling,
Saying – 'Fair maid, to my master you must go,
If your name is Barbara Allen.'

So slowly, slowly she walked in,
So slowly she went to him,
And when she got to his bedside,
She said – 'Young man, you're dying.

'Nothing but Death's prints on thy cheeks,
All joys they are fled from thee,
I cannot save thee from the grave,
So farewell, my dearest Johnny!'

As she was walking in the fields,
She heard the bells a-ringing,
And as they rang they seemed to say –
Hard hearted Barbara Allen.

'Hard hearted creature, sure, I was,
To one that loved me so dearly;
I wish I had more kinder been,
In the time of life, when he was near me.'

'Twas he that died on one good day,
And she that died the morrow;
'Twas only he that died of love,
And she that died for sorrow.

Part 7, Number 1, 13 November 1915

Unquestionably the most frequently collected folk song in Britain and the English-speaking world, many readers of sufficient age will remember 'Barbara Allen' as one of the songs that they were required to learn at school. Its enduring success is hard to explain, given that neither of the two principal characters has much to recommend them. Yet Barbara's dreadful behaviour and subsequent remorse have some romantic appeal. I commented above on the large number of recordings still being made of 'Pretty Polly'. A similar exploration for 'Barbara Allen' reveals an even greater number of recordings and treatments, the earliest of which is that of Joseph Taylor made by Percy Grainger in 1907.

The song dates from the seventeenth century and Samuel Pepys wrote in his diary entry for 2 January 1666 about a meeting with friends and 'my dear Mrs. Knipp, with whom I sang; and in perfect pleasure I was to hear her sing, and especially her little Scotch song of *Barbary Allen*'. The description of it as a 'Scotch song' probably refers to the style in which it is written. Scottish origin cannot be assumed, particularly since, as Williams points out, 'Scarlet Town' could be taken to mean Reading.

The earliest broadside version, from *c.*1690, carries the lengthy title *Barbara Allen's Cruelty; or, the Young-Man's Tragedy, with Barbara Allen's Lamentation for her Unkindness to her Lover, and her Self*, 'To the tune of Barbara Allen'. The texts heard by some of the early song collectors contain intriguing details that are missing from broadside versions, such as a bowl of blood at the foot of the bed and the young man's gold watch at its head, which Barbara Allen refuses to accept.

17. John Barleycorn

Roud 164, Bathe-Clissold Wt.404
Elijah Iles, Inglesham, Wiltshire

John Barleycorn is another ballad that exists in a variety of forms. It is undoubtedly of English origin. The poet Burns gave it a Scotch cast and is said to have improved it, but it will not require a very astute critic to perceive that the English versions, with all their rudeness are much better than the one penned by Burns: they are more pointed, simpler, stronger and truer than his. This ballad was extremely popular in the South, especially at harvest homes. I have given two versions, both current around Highworth and Lechlade. Obtained of Elijah Iles, Inglesham.

There came three men out of the West,
Their scheming for to try,
And they have sworn a solemn oath,
John Barleycorn should die.

They ploughed him in the earth so deep,
Put clots upon his head,
Then these three men they did conclude,
That Barleycorn was dead.

They let him stay a whole fortnight,
Till rain from heaven did fall,
John Barleycorn sprang a green blade,
Which quite amazed them all.

They let him stay till Midsummer,
Till he grew pale and wan,
And Barleycorn had a long beard,
Much like unto a man.

They hired men with scythes so sharp,
To cut him off at knee,
See how they served poor Barleycorn!
They served him bitterly.

They hired men with forks and rakes,
To stab him through the heart,
But the carter served him worse than that,
For he bound him to a cart.

They drove him round and round again,
Until they came to a barn,
And there they made a barley-mow –
A mow of John Barleycorn.

They hired men with crabtree sticks,
To beat him, skin from bone;
And the miller served him worse than that,
For he ground him between two stones.

They flung him in a cistern deep,
And drowned him in water clear,
The brewer served him worse than that,
For he brewed him into beer.

Put white wine in a bottle
And cider in a can,
John Barleycorn, in a brown bowl,
Will prove the stronger man

Part 7, Number 4, 13 November 1915

Williams had two versions of 'John Barleycorn', the second of which was published in *FSUT* (pp. 246–47). A ballad called 'Sir John Barleycorne' was entered with the Stationers' Company in December 1624. *A Pleasant New Ballad to Sing both Euen and Morne, of the Bloody Murther of Sir John Barley-corne* in Samuel Pepys's collection of broadside ballads was printed in London in the first half of the century.

The song has sometimes been assigned mystical origins, for which there is no evidence. What it does do is to use the personification of John Barleycorn to explain the agricultural and technological processes that go into making beer. As a poet himself, Williams could not refrain from commenting on Robert Burns's reworking of the song, and he found little to commend it.

18. Auld Robin Gray

Roud 2652, Bathe-Clissold Wt.420
The Keylock Family, Latton, Wiltshire

Auld Robin Grey was written in 1771 by Lady Ann Barnard whose husband was librarian to George III. It was printed on the ballad sheet and sung by the more intelligent of the rustics. The following version is not identical with that in some collections, the chief difference being in the last line of each stanza, which is shorter. I copied it from an old broadside which I found at Latton, where the piece was sung by the Keylock family.

When the sheep are in the fauld and the kye at hame,
And a' the world to sleep are gane,
The waes o' my heart fa' in showers frae my e'e,
When my gude man lies sound by me.

Young Jamie lo'ed me weel and socht me for his bride,
But, saving a croun, he had nothing else beside;
To mak' that croun a pund young Jamie gaed to sea,
And the croun and the pund were baith for me.

He hadna been awa a week, but only twa,
When my mother she fell sick and the cow was stolen awa;
My father brak his arm, and young Jamie at the sea,
And auld Robin Grey cam' a-courtin' me.

My father couldna work, and my mother couldna spin,
I toiled day and nicht, for their bread I couldna win;
Auld Rob maintained them baith, and, wi' tears in his e'e
Said – 'Jennie, for their sakes, oh, marry me.'

My heart it said Nay – for I looked for Jamie back;
But the wind it blew high, and the ship it was a wrack,
His ship it was a wrack – Why didna Jamie dee?
Or why do I live to say – 'Wae's me.'

My father argued sair, my mother didna speak,
But she lookit in my face till my heart was like to break;
So they gied him my hand – my heart was in the sea,
And auld Robin Grey was gudeman to me.

I hadna been a wife a week, but only four,
When mournfu' as I sat on a stane at the door,
I saw my Jamie's wraith, but I couldna think it he,
Till he said – 'I'm come hame to marry thee.'

Ah! sair, sair did we greet, and mickle did we say,
We took but ae kiss and we tore ourselves awa';
I wish I was dead, but I'm na likely to dee,
And why was I born to say – 'Wae's me?'

I gang like a ghaist, and I care na to spin,
I daurna think on Jamie for that wad be a sin,
But I'll do my best a gude wife to be,
For auld Robin Grey is kind to me.

Part 7, Number 6, 13 November 1915

This famous and widespread song first appeared anonymously in 1771, but several years later Lady Barnard revealed to Sir Walter Scott that she was its author. Although no other song collector has said that they heard it, that is probably because it did not meet their ideas of what a folk song was, rather than because its operatic plot appealed more to the drawing room than the cowshed. Henry Burstow, the old shoemaker and bell-ringer of Horsham, Sussex, included it in the list of songs that he sang.

19. The Banks of Green Willow

Roud 172, Bathe-Clissold Gl.85
George Grubb, Ewen, Gloucestershire

A very old song, possibly of Scotch origin. Obtained of George Grubb, the old shepherd of Ewen, near Cirencester, and formerly of South Marston, Wiltshire.

It's of a sea captain,
Lived near the seaside O,
He courted a farmer's daughter,
All for to make her his bride O.

'Fetch some of your father's gold,
Likewise your mother's money,
Then I will gang overseas,
Along with my Annie.'

She fetched some of her father's gold,
Likewise her mother's money,
And I gangéd overseas,
Along with my Annie.

We had not been on the sea,
Scarce six weeks or so many,
Before she wanted women's help,
But she could not get any.

'Can I do you women's help?
Can I do you my Annie?'

'You cannot do me women's help,
For love nor for money.'

'Tie a napkin around my head,
Tie it round easy,
Then throw me overboard,
Both me and my baby.'

He tied a napkin round her head,
He tied it so round easy,
And then threw her overboard,
Both she and her baby.

'Then see how she swims, my boys!
See how she quivers!
She will sink or she will swim, my boys,
To the banks of green willow.

'My love shall have a coffin made,
With the bright gold so yellow,
And she shall be buried,
On the banks of green willow.

'My mind it is tormented,
I cannot be easy;
The drowning of this pretty girl,
And her innocent baby.'

Part 7, Number 9, 13 November 1915

Francis James Child described this ballad, which he knew as 'Fair Annie' (Child 24), as 'pretty and touching, but much disordered'. He included two versions taken from books, Motherwell's *Minstrelsy: Ancient and Modern*, and Kinloch's *Ancient Scottish Ballads*, both published in 1827. The first to record it being sung in England was Sabine Baring-Gould, who heard it from five different singers. He never put it into print himself, but sent some versions to Child, including a fifteen-stanza collation from two singers to which he gave the title 'The Undutiful Daughter'. In his manuscript notes Baring-Gould drew a parallel with an eighteenth-century broadside, *The Faithless Sea Captain.* Although the plot is rather different, Baring-Gould mused that it might have been a rationalization of an earlier ballad.

Subsequently, the song was collected many times in England, but the 'disorder' continued and none of the versions make a lot of sense. In Kinloch's Scottish version the superstition about the ship being unable to move is invoked (cf. no. 8 above, 'Johnny, the Ship's Carpenter') and a ballot is drawn to see who must die to release the vessel. The English collected versions offer no satisfactory explanation for the woman being thrown overboard. When preparing the songs for the first series of Cecil Sharp's *Folk Songs From Somerset*, Charles Marson found it necessary to invent a stanza that included the supernatural event.

George Grubb's version has an unusual final stanza in which the sea captain expresses remorse for his actions, though he does not go as far as his counterpart in *The Faithless Sea Captain* and throw himself overboard. The song is frequently performed by revival singers and its familiarity is aided by the wonderful 'idyll' composed by George Butterworth, based on two tunes he collected for 'The Banks of Green Willow' in Sussex.

20. Sweet Molly O'Mog

Roud 21204, Bathe-Clissold Gl.143
Thomas Baughn, South Cerney, Gloucestershire

Obtained of Thomas Baughan, South Cerney. The song was a favourite of his father's and of his grandfather's, who bought it on a broadside at Cirencester Mop, where it was sung at least as early as 1793. I know nothing more concerning it, having heard it nowhere else.[9]

Zaays my uncle – 'I pray you discover,
What hath been the cause o' your woes,
That ye hakker and pine like a lover?'
'I have zeen Molly Mog o' the rose.'

'O nephew your zuit is all volly,
In town ye may vind better prog,
O go there and vind you a Molly,
A Molly much richer than Mog.'

'I know that by wits 'tis rezited,
That women at best are a clog;
But I'm not so easily vrighted,
From loving zweet Molly O'Mog.

I veels I'm in love to distraction,
My zenses all lost in a vog,
And nothing can give zatisfaction,
But thinking o' sweet Molly O'Mog.

Part 7, Number 10, 13 November 1915

This was the song that caused the angry termination of the correspondence between Alfred Williams and Frank Kidson (*Appendix A*). Thomas Baughn has given, in dialect, stanzas 1, 2, 3, and 9 of the

[9] The correct spelling of the name, from official documents, is 'Baughn'.

'The Ballad of Molly Mogg; or, the Fair Maid of the Inn', a fifteen-stanza poem written jointly by three giants of literature, John Gay, Alexander Pope, and Dean Swift, about the daughter of the landlord of the Rose Inn in Wokingham, Berkshire, where they were forced to shelter from the weather. No copy of the broadside that Williams mentions has been discovered and the song has not been recorded by any other collector. A tune, 'Molly Mogg', was published in *The New Country Dancing Master* (third book) by J. Walsh and J. Hare in 1728.

21. The Female Robber

Roud 289, Bathe-Clissold Ox.293
Thomas Smart, Blunsdon, Wiltshire
Henry Potter, Standlake, Oxfordshire

Formerly a very special favourite in the Vale. I have been offered the piece at least twelve times, though I have heard it but once quite accurately – assuming that the following version is accurate: it is the best I have obtained. Communicated by Thomas Smart, Blunsdon, and corrected by Henry Potter, Standlake, Oxfordshire.

It's of a pretty fair maid in London did dwell,
For wit and for beauty none could her excel;
To her master and mistress she servéd seven years,
And what follows after you quickly shall hear.

She put the box upon her head and gangéd along,
The first that she met was a stout and able man;
He said – 'My pretty fair maid, where are you going this way?
I'll show you a nearer road across the countree.'

He took her by the hand and led her to a lane,
Said he – 'My pretty fair maid, I mean to tell you plain,
Deliver up your money, without fear or strife,
Or else, this very moment, I'll take away your life.'

The tears from her eyes like two fountains did flow –
'Oh, where shall I wander? Oh, where shall I go?'
But while this young fellow was feeling for his knife,
This beautiful young damsel took away his life.

She put the box upon her head and gangéd along,
The next that she met was a noble gentleman;
He said – 'My pretty fair maid, where are you going so late?
And what was the noise that I heard at yonder gate?'

'The box on your head to yourself does not belong,
To your master or your mistress you have done something wrong;
To your master or your mistress you have done something ill,
For one moment from trembling you cannot keep still.'

'The box upon my head to myself it does belong,
To my master or my mistress I have done nothing wrong;
To my master or my mistress I have done nothing ill,
But I fear in my heart it's some man I have killed.

'He demanded my money and I soon let him know,
And when he took his knife I proved his overthrow.'
She took him by the hand and led him to the place,
Where this stout and able fellow lay bleeding on his face.

They searched him all over to see what he had got,
He had three loaded pistols, some powder and some shot;
He had three loaded pistols, some powder and some ball,
A knife and a whistle, more robbers for to call.

He put the whistle to his lips and blew both loud and shrill,
And four stout, able fellows, came tripping down the hill;
The gentleman shot one of them, and that most speedily,
And this beautiful young damsel she shot the other three.

He says – 'My pretty for maid, for what you have done,
I'll make you my lawful bride, before it is long,
I'll make you my lawful bride, love, before it is long,
For the taking of your own part, and the firing of your gun.'

Part 8, Number 1, 20 November 1915

It seems perverse of Williams to have called this song 'The Female Robber' when she was the one who would have been robbed had she not defended herself. This song, usually called 'The Box upon her Head', was first published as *The Staffordshire Maid* on an eighteenth-century broadside printed by Dicey. Nineteenth-century broadsides are much shorter, as the printer had to fit the story on to a smaller sheet. Most opted for an eleven-stanza version, and there are very few differences between editions.

Williams's version is nearly identical to the broadsides. Looking at the manuscript fair copy, it is possible to see his editing of Thomas Smart's version. He omitted the first two lines of stanza eight, which meant that stanza nine had six lines. Presumably this was the correction made on Henry Potter's advice. The song has been widely collected; after all, who could resist such a redoubtable young woman?

22. The Mantle of Green

Roud 714, Bathe-Clissold Wt.457
David Sawyer, Stratton St Margaret, Wiltshire
Alice Rowles, Witney, Oxfordshire

One of the many folk songs proceeding from incidents connected with the Battle of Waterloo. Obtained of David Sawyer and Mrs Rowles, Witney. This piece was popular in Marston Meysey.

As I was walking one morning in June,
To view the gay fields and the meadows in bloom,
I spied a young female, she appeared like a queen,
With costly fine robes and a mantle of green.

I stood in amaze and looked on her with surprise,
I thought her an angel had fallen from the skies,
Her eyes shone like diamonds, her cheeks like a rose,
She's one of the finest that Nature composed.

I said – 'Lovely fair one, if you can agree,
We will join in wedlock and married we'll be;
I'll dress you in riches, you'll appear like a queen,
With costly fine robes and a mantle of green.'

She quickly made answer – 'You must be refused,
For I'll wed with no man, and I must be excused;
To the green woods I'll wander and shun all men too,
For the boy that I love is in famed Waterloo.'

'Then if you will not marry me, tell me your love's name,
For I've been a soldier and might know the same.'
'Draw near to my mantle and there it shall be seen,
His name is embroidered in my mantle of green.'

Then, raising her mantle, it was there I did behold,
His name and his surname in letters of bright gold;
Young William O'Riley appeared to my view;
He was my companion at famed Waterloo.

'We fought there so valiant, the bullets did fly,
In the field of battle your true love he did die;
We fought for three days till the third afternoon,
He received his death wound on the eighteenth of June.

'When he was dying I hear his last sigh –
'Where are you my Nancy? Contented I die.
Now peace is proclaimed, the truth I declare,
Here is your love's token, this gold ring I wear.'

The longer she viewed it the paler she grew,
And fell in my arms with her heart full of woe –
'To the green woods I'll wander for the boy that I love.'
'Oh, stop here, lovely Nancy, for your grief I'll remove.

'Oh, Nancy, lovely Nancy, since I've won your heart,
In your father's garden no more we will part;
I will clothe you in rich attire, and you'll look like a queen,
With a cluster of roses round your mantle of green.'

Part 8, Number 2, 20 November 1915

The theme of the returning lover who, rather cruelly, tests his sweetheart by pretending to be someone else who saw him die is very common in traditional song, but rarely as beautifully expressed as in this ballad, which probably of Irish origin. The evidence for when it was actually written is very limited since the earliest broadside version currently known is set in the Crimean War, so not earlier than 1854. It seems likely that there was an earlier printing yet to be discovered. The song travelled to the USA and was recorded in the journal of the bark *Ocean Rover* of New Bedford in 1869.

23. As I Walked Out One May Morning

Roud 419, Bathe-Clissold Wt.342
Robert King, Castle Eaton, Wiltshire

A quaint old song, composed by one who, whatever other qualifications he might have possessed, was never a naturalist, or he would not have wished to climb up to the highest tree top to rob the cuckoo's nest. Obtained of Robert King, *Castle Eaton. Heard also at Bishopstone, Wilts.*

As I walked out one May morning,
One May morn in the spring,
I leaned my back on a low-land gate,
For to hear my true love sing.

To hear my true love sing a song,
And to hear what he had to say,
For I wished to know more of his mind,
Before he went away.

I never will believe what an old man does say,
For his days they cannot be long,
And I never will believe what the young men say,
For they promise but marry none.

There's T stand for Thomas, as I have heard them say,
And I'm certain that J stands for John;
And W stands for sweet William,
But Johnny is the handsomest man.

Now I'll climb up to the highest tree top,
To rob the cuckoo of her nest,
I will not tarry long, but soon will return,
And be married to the lad I love the best.

Part 8, Number 7, 20 November 1915

In his manuscripts, Williams gave the title of this song as 'T Stands for Thomas'. Many variants of have been found in Britain, Ireland, and North America. Williams's concern about ornithological accuracy is met in many versions by referring simply to a 'wild bird's nest'. The earliest known copy in print is on a broadside published by W. Armstrong of Liverpool in the 1820s. This has a number of passages in common with Williams's text. It has been suggested that the song is of Irish origin, and one of the best-known versions is the beautiful song 'The Verdant Braes of Skreen'. The song was collected a number of times in southern England.

24. Old Dorrington

Roud 281, Bathe-Clissold Gl.101
Elizabeth Mackie, Lechlade, Gloucestershire

Obtained of Mrs Mackie, Lechlade, who learned it while a school-girl on the banks of the Thames, about 1860. I have also met with it at Hinton Parva, Wiltshire where it was sung by the Clargo family a hundred years ago. I think the version is incorrect, though it is the best I could get. I have an idea there should be another stanza or two.

Old Dorrington was a most terrible Turk,
As I've often heard people say;
He swore he'd do more work in an hour
Than his wife would do in a day.

'Upon my word,' said the good old dame,
'I'm willing, any hour;
If thou all day in the house wilt stay,
I'll go and drive the plough.

'But thou must feed the brindle sow,
And the little pigs in the sty,
And thou must milk old Tiny the cow,
Or Tiny will go dry.

And thou must watch the speckled hen,
Or she will lay astray,
And don't forget the hank of yarn,
That I spun yesterday.'

So the good old dame, with whip in hand,
Went out to drive the plough,
And the old man took the milking-pail,
And went to milk to cow.

Tiny winced and bounced about,
'Woa, Tiny,' and 'Wutt, Tiny,' and 'Drat the cow, be still!
And if ever I milk such a maggoty cow again,
'Twill be much against my will.'

He went to serve the brindle sow,
And the little pigs in the sty,
When he knocked his head against the post,
And nearly knocked out his eye.

He left the cream to stand in the churn,
While he went to fetch a clout,
And, e'er Massy knew, in came the old sow,
And slushed in her snout.

He turned to find a whirling stick,
Surprising so to see –
'More harm thy snout will do in an hour,
Than I can mend in three.'

And he forgot the speckled hen,
And she went and laid astray,
And he never once thought of the hank of yarn,
The old woman had spun yesterday.

Just at that moment in came the old woman,
And thus in haste she spoke –
'John, John, the old horse is on his back in the pond,
And the plough and the tackle are broke.'

So old Dorrington swore by the sun and the moon,
And all of the green leaves on the tree,
If his wife would but take to the indoors again,
He never would grumble at she.

Part 8, Number 9, 20 November 1915

This salvo in the battle of the sexes dates from the beginning of the nineteenth century and is usually called 'The Old Man and his Wife', though in North America it is known as 'Father Grumble'. Widely anthologized, it is rare on broadsides. Some versions were heard by early collectors and it seems to have had a resurgence in the later part of the twentieth century, as several collectors have made sound recordings of it. The wife is not as incompetent in all the versions, and in some the old farmer runs out to the field and finds her enjoying herself with a farmhand. This did not happen in the version in Sabine Baring-Gould's manuscripts, which was entered into a notebook kept by his maiden aunt, Emily Baring-Gould, about 1838.

25. Rodney So Bold

Roud 8167, Ox.302
Leah Sirman, Stanton Harcourt, Oxfordshire

Rodney was Admiral of the British fleet in the naval battle off Cape St. Vincent, 1780, in which he won a gallant victory. He also defeated the French fleet off St. Lucia in 1782. The song has little to do with Rodney; it merely relates the homecoming of one of his Jack Tars. Obtained of Miss Leah Serman, Stanton Harcourt, Oxfordshire. It was her father's favourite piece.

Last night at ten o'clock,
As I a-reading sat
Letters of love I received from my dear,
Somebody at the door

Just like a Jack Tar did roar,
It drove my poor senses I can't tell you where.
I rose up at the shock,
And did the door unlock,

Such a fine sight my eyes did behold!
Trousers as white as snow,
Buckles down to the toe,
With his flashy cockade and his hat laced with gold.

As I stood gazing at the view,
Into my arms he flew,
Giving me kisses more sweet than rue;
Seeing Jack half so smart,

It quite revived my heart,
And nothing was want but my mind to bring to.
As I stood gazing at the view,
Into my apron he threw,

Into my apron he threw handfuls of gold,
Saying – 'I will you deck
With a gold chain about your neck,
For I have been sailing with Rodney so bold.'

Here's a health to each lad and lass!
Drink of a flowing glass,
Drink a good health to the lads on the sea,
That they may safe return
Into their own native home:
Oh, what a comfort and joy that will be!

Part 8, Number 11, 20 November 1915

One of only five collected versions, this is a comparatively rare song. Cecil Sharp heard a version at Clewer, near Windsor, from the Anglican nun Sister Emma. Sabine Baring-Gould recorded two versions in his manuscripts, the first from his most prolific singer, Samuel Fone, which he collected in 1892. The second was sent to him by the entertainer, poet, and quack nutritionist Reddie Mallett, who had taken it down from an unnamed singer at Harlyn Bay in Cornwall. The song appears in print as *Jack Tar's Return*, the earliest known instance being a late eighteenth-century slip in the British Library's Roxburghe Collection. Williams's version is very close to the broadsides.

26. The Admiral's Return

Roud 12876, Bathe-Clissold Wt.480
William King, Purton, Wiltshire

The Admiral's Return is a superior folk song. The subject is a good one, and it is developed with skill and considerable imagination. I do not know the age of the piece – it probably dates from the seventeenth century. Obtained of William King, Purton, Wiltshire.

How gallantly, how merrily, we ride along the sea!
The morning is all sunshine, the wind is blowing free;
The billows are all sparkling, and bounding in the light,
Like creatures in whose sunny veins the blood is running bright.

All nature knows our triumph, strange birds about us sweep,
Strange things come up to look at us – the masters of the deep;
In our wake, like any servant, follows even the bold shark,
Oh! Proud must be the Admiral of such a bonny barque.

Oh! Proud must be our Admiral, though he is pale today,
Of twice five hundred iron men who all his nod obey;

Who've fought for him and conquered, who've won with sweat and gore,
Nobility, which he shall have whene'er he touch the shore.

Oh! Would I were an Admiral, to order with a word!
To lose a dozen drops of blood and straight rise up a lord!
I'd shout to yonder shark there, which follows in our lee –
'Some day I'll make thee carry me like lightning through the sea.'

Our Admiral grew paler and paler as we flew,
Still talked he to the officers, and smiled upon the crew;
He looked up at the heavens, and he looked down on the sea,
And at last he saw this creature that was following in our lee.

He shook – 'twas but an instant, for speedily the pride,
Ran crimson to his heart, till all chances he defied;
It threw boldness on his forehead, gave firmness to his breath,
And he looked like some warrior now risen up from death.

That night a horrid whisper fell on us where we lay,
And we knew our fine old Admiral was changing to clay;
And we heard the dash of waters, though nothing we could see,
But a whistle and a plunge among the billows on our lee.

Till morn we watched the body in its dead and ghastly sleep,
And next evening at sunset, it was flung into the deep;
And never from that moment, save one shudder on the sea,
Saw we, or heard the creature, that had followed in our lee.

Part 9, Number 1, 27 November 1915

Here Williams has certainly not got it right. 'The Return of the Admiral', of which this is a good replica, is a poem by Bryan Proctor (1787–1874), who wrote under the *nom de plume* of 'Barry Cornwall' in the mid-nineteenth century. It appeared frequently on broadsides, on some of which the author was acknowledged. William King's is the only collected version.

27. Pat Maguire

Roud 16887, Bathe-Clissold Wt.483
William King, Purton, Wiltshire

Of Irish origin, and not one of the best and most popular songs, though it was current around Wootton Basset sixty years ago. Obtained of William King, Purton.

You muses nine with me combine, assist my tender quill,
And grant me your kind endeavours to every line I fill;
My name is Pat Maguire and how can I conceal?
By the cruelty of Mary Kayes I lie in Lifford Jail.

When I came from the colleges, my parents for to see,
She did her whole endeavours to prove my destiny;
She said – 'Young Pat Maguire, come join in wedlock's band,
You will consent to go with me and leave your native land.'

The answer that I gave her – 'My parents would me blame,
If I should wed with anyone and not be ordained;
For in this holy order, I mean to spend my life,
So, Mary dear, don't persevere, I'll never wed a wife.'

'Twas on a Sunday morning, before the sun did rise,
The cavalry surrounded me, and, to my great surprise;
They said to young Maguire – 'Come, rise and do not fail,
You know our duty we must do: You're bound for Lifford Jail.'

When I got my committal a letter I did send,
Unto brave Captain Hamilton, thinking he'd stand my friend;
As soon as he read my letter, an answer he sent down -
'I'll bail young Pat Maguire, if it costs ten thousand pounds.'

And when my aged father he came for to hear,
He said – 'My dear and only child, be not the least to fear!
For I have money plenty and God will stand your friend,
On Shield, that noble counsellor, your life you may depend.'

My parents reared me tenderly and very well it's known,
They gave me education for the Church of Rome;
They ought to have comfort with me in future days,
But now I lie in irons by Cruel Mary Kayes.

But when my trial it came on, to let the world to see,
In spite of all her interest the jury set me free;
And now I'm out of Lifford Jail, with honour I got home,
In hope to be a member of the holy Church of Rome.

Part 9, Number 4, 27 November 1915

There can be no mistaking the Irish setting and origin of this song. It was printed on several broadsides, from the late 1830s onwards, which are consistently silent as to what Maguire's crime actually was. Frank Purslow suggested that Mary Kayes had denounced Maguire to the authorities in a fit of pique, accusing him of rape, and made the comparison with 'Father Tom O'Neil' (Roud 1013).[10] Williams is the only collector to have found it in Britain. More recently, though, it has been collected by John Meredith from Sally Sloane in Australia, and by Helen Hartness Flanders from Jack McNally in Maine. William King's text is very close to the broadsides, his stanza seven corresponding to stanza two of the printed versions.

28. To Hear the Nightingale Sing

Roud 140, Bathe-Clissold Wt.495
Edward Kemble, South Marston, Wiltshire

This also was very popular in and around South Marston. I have not met with it elsewhere. The tune is very sweet, which accounted for its success. It is, of course, rarely sung now, and there is less chance of it being revived in the future. We must march forward. There is nothing either good or bad but is so comparatively, in the folk song, as elsewhere, and if we lose in one direction we gain in another. Obtained of Edward Kemble, South Marston.

It was early one morning in the month of May,
When I saw a young couple together at play;
One was a pretty fair maid, whose beauty shone clear,
And the other was a soldier, a bold Grenadier.

There were kisses and sweet compliments they gave to each other,
They went hand in hand, like sister and brother,
They went hand in hand, till they came to a spring,
Where they both sat together to hear the nightingale sing.

He undid his knapsack and drew out a long fiddle,
He put one arm round her, yes, right round her middle;
He played her a merry tune, which made the valleys ring -
'Oh hark!' said the fair maid, 'How the nightingales sing!'

'Oh now,' said the soldier, 'It is time to give o'er.'
'Oh no,' said the fair maid, Play me one tune more,
For the listening of your music and the touching of your string,
I'd rather much more have it than to hear the nightingale sing.'

[10] Frank Purslow, 'The Williams Manuscripts', *Folk Music Journal*, 1.5 (1969), 301–15 (pp. 312–13).

'Oh now,' said the fair maid, 'Will you marry me?'
'Oh no,' said the soldier, 'That never can be,
I've a wife and three children in my own country,
Such a nice little woman as ever you did see.

'I am bound for old India for seven long years,
To drink wine and whisky instead of strong beers;
But if ever I return again, may it be in the spring!
Then we'll both sit down together to hear the nightingale sing.'

Part 9, Number 6, 27 November 1915

Williams's headnote alludes to the metaphorical eroticism of this song in a roundabout way, echoing some of the comments that he made about risqué pieces in other places. Far from its time being past, it has survived into the present time in most parts of the English-speaking world. It is, though, from the seventeenth century and is to be found in Samuel Pepys's broadside collection with the title *The Nightingales Song; or, The Souldiers Rare Musick, and Maids Recreation* – 'The Song adviseth Maids to have a care, / And of a Souldiers Knap-sack to beware'. This tells the same story in sixteen delightful stanzas, offering plentiful opportunity to enjoy the gentle seduction of his willing partner. The opening stanzas give an idea of the different style:

As I went forth one Sun-shining Day,
A dainty young Couple were gathering May;
The one a fair Damosel, of beauty most clear,
The other a Souldier, as it doth appear.

With kisses and compliments, to her he said,
Good morrow sweet honey thou well favour'd maid,
I think myself happy, I met with you here
As you are a Virgin, and I a Souldier.

It takes eight stanzas before the soldier 'gave her a green Gown' (i.e. laid her down in the grass) and 'pull'd a rare Fiddle' from out of his knapsack. Surprisingly, the song did not feature on many later broadsides. It is perhaps because the song is naughty, rather than explicit, that it has been enjoyed by singers for so long and is still being recorded today.

29. John Returned from Sea

Roud 276, Bathe-Clissold Ox.271
Richard Gardner, Hardwick, Oxfordshire

Obtained of Richard Gardner of Hardwick, near Witney, Oxfordshire. Gardner is an old carter, and a most cheerful and vivacious man. Though of the advanced age of eighty three he goes daily to work on the land and is capable of rendering at least a dozen lengthy songs.

A story, a story well-known,
It's of a young man whose name it is John;
Long time he went to sea and now he's come on shore,
In ragged apparel, like one that is poor.

He went to an alehouse and knock'd at the door,
He went to an alehouse where he spent all his store –
'You're welcome home from sea, dear John,' Mrs. Molly did say,
'Last night my daughter Molly was dreaming of thee.'

'Where is your daughter Molly? Go, fetch her unto me.
We'll laugh, and we'll sing, and I'll set her on my knee.'
'My daughter Molly's busy, John,' Mrs. Molly did say,
'My daughter Molly's busy and cannot come to thee.'

After supper was over John hung down his head,
And called for a candle to light him to bed –
'The beds are all full, John, and have been for this week,
And now for fresh lodging I'd have you go and seek.'

'O landlord, O landlord, O landlord,' cried he,
'Come tell me my reckoning that I may pay thee.'
'My reckoning is forty shillings, John, Now you have been told.'
Then out of his pocket he pulled handfuls of gold.

To see the gold glittering it made the people stare,
Down ran Miss Molly with her curly hair;
She huddled him, she cuddled him, and called him her dear,
Saying – 'The green bed is empty, John, and you can lie there.'

'Since it being so late, no lodgings I could get,
Before I would lie there now, I'd lie out in the street;
If I had not got any money out of doors I had been turned,
So thou and thy old mother can go and get burned.'

Part 9, Number 7, 27 November 1915

Tales like this about sailors getting the better of ladies of negotiable affection are common in folk songs. This song is usually known as 'The Green Bed'. A version appeared in *Philander's Garland* in the late eighteenth century.

30. No Money and Plenty

Roud 393, Bathe-Clissold Gl.148
James Mills, South Cerney, Gloucestershire

Obtained of James Mills, South Cerney. I have also heard it spoken of at Bradon. The style discovers its age; it is of eighteenth century date, or earlier.

I often travelled the North Countree,
Seeking for good company;
Good company I could always find,
But never one girl to my mind.
Whack fol i dee,
Whack fol i dee,
And in my pocket not one penny.

I saddled my pony and away I did ride,
Till I came to an alehouse close by the roadside;
I boldly got off and I sat myself down,
And called for a jug of good ale that was brown.
Whack fol i dee, *etc.*

As I sat drinking in front of my eyes,
There were two gentlemen playing at dice;
As they were at play, and I looking on,
They took me to be a respectable man.
Whack fol i dee, *etc.*

As I sat there, they asked me to play,
I asked them the wager, what would they lay;
One said a guinea, the other five pound,
The wager was laid, but the money not down.
Whack fol i dee, *etc.*

I picked up the dice, I threw them all in,
It happened to be my good fortune to win;
If they had won, and I should have lost,
Then I must have sold my little black horse.
Whack fol i dee, *etc.*

I stopped there all night, until the next day,
I asked the landlady what I had to pay;
She said, 'Kiss me and love me, and then go your way,
If you stop any longer you'll have money to pay.'
Whack fol i dee, *etc.*

Part 9, Number 8, 27 November 1915

This song, often called 'The Penny Wager', represents another popular theme, the likeable rogue. It appeared on broadsides early in the nineteenth century.

31. I Had an Old Father

Roud 5487, Bathe-Clissold Wt.428
Unknown singer, Minety, Wiltshire

The subjects of drinking and squandering the inherited – or not yet inherited – estate were productive of many pieces. The majority were however, not of a very high quality. We shall have several other songs, dealing with the drunkard presently. Obtained at Minety.

I had an old father and a noble estate,
Besides a rich uncle, whose fortune was great,
Till I took to drinking and spent all my store –
Now I'll be a food fellow and do so no more.

I sat in the ale house with Kit, Moll and Sue,
And five or six drunkards we had in our crew
We'd stay up till midnight and make the town roar –
Now I'll be a good fellow and do so no more.

A little time after to prison I was sent,
With a cold, empty belly it was time to repent;
I could eat any hard crust that lay on the floor –
Now I'll be a good fellow and do so, no more.

The doors being open, the bolts being unfast,
'Twas a long time to look for, but 'tis come now at last;
I've paid for all my folly which I did before –
Now I'll be a good fellow and do so, no more.

I'll go home to my own trade, I'll go home to my wife,
And work for my Betsy all the days of my life;
I'll instruct every young man his drinking to give o'er,
To be a good fellow and do so, no more.

Part 9, Number 10, 27 November 1915

This appeared on broadsides as *I'll Be a Good Fellow and Do So No More* from the early eighteenth century. Apart from Williams's version, only a fragment found by George Gardiner in Dorset has survived in England. However, a few versions have been collected in North America.

32. My Bonny Boy

Roud 293, Bathe-Clissold Wt.488
Amelia Phillips, Purton, Wiltshire

Obtained of Mrs Philips, Purton. It is an old song, and, as may be seen, was well fitted to be sung by the ladies. Elsewhere I have not heard of it.

Once I was courted by a bonny boy,
And for him I could never take any rest,
I loved him so well, ah! so very well,
I could build him a nest in my breast;
I could build him a nest in my breast.

'Twas up the green alley, and down the green valley,
Like one that is troubled in mind.
I whooped and I called, and I played on my lute,
But no bonny boy could I find;
But no bonny boy could I find.

But now he is gone o'er the waters so far,
And I'm afraid he will never return;
But, if he loves another girl better than I,
He may have her; and why should I mourn?
He may have her, and why should I mourn?

Part 9, Number 12, 27 November 1915

This is another song that was published several times on broadsides in the seventeenth century, under the title *Cupid's Trappan; or, Up the Green Forrest*, subtitled 'The Scorner Scorned; or, Willow Turned into Carnation, Described in the Ranting Resolution of a Forsaken Maid'. There the object of the protagonist's anger is her 'bonny bonny Bird', and the first five stanzas provide the core of the song as it has survived in numerous collected versions. In the remaining fourteen stanzas she curses him roundly.

When he comes disfigur'd and crippl'd from war,
I'll jeer him, and laugh him to scorn;
His Wife too will scoff, when he comes lamely off,
And give him a night-cap of horn, brave Boys,
And give, *etc.*

The song was noted by the major collectors of Victorian and Edwardian times, but was not often found outside England. Despite Williams's comment, other collectors found it sung roughly equally by men and women. A few weeks after this version, Williams published 'My Bonny Girl' from William Wise of Alvescot, Oxfordshire, in Part 15 (22 January 1916) and later printed it in *FSUT* (p. 209). Mrs Philips's version has only three stanzas of the usual five, yet it stands on its feet.

33. The Bugle Played for Me

Roud 469, Bathe-Clissold Wt.374
Ann Sparrow, Crudwell, Wiltshire

Communicated by Mrs Sparrow, Crudwell, Wiltshire. The piece is extremely old, and a specimen of the pure folk song.

My grandmother died and left me fifty pound,
I bought me a house and a little bit of ground;
I sold my house and bought me a cow,
For how to get on, I could not tell how.
I sold my cow and I bought me a calf,
Now I believe in my heart I lost half.
    Jack stock sliddle uck, fatty fiddle uck,
    Ban to the broom,
    Pick and hack, Jimmy Prack, ti mi diddle,
    Ti mi diddle tum tay,
    Hang the day that the bugle played for me.

So I sold my calf and bought me a mouse,
On purpose to have a pretty thing to run about my house,
In came a neighbour's cat and stole away my mouse,
I flung a fire stick at his tail, which burned down my house,
So played I till I played it all away.
    Jack stock sliddle uck, *etc.*

Part 9, Number 13, 27 November 1915

Often called 'My Father Died', different versions of this song were popular both in Britain and in North America, where it was often known as 'The Swapping Song'. The earliest known mention of it occurs in a book of children's rhymes, *Gammer Gurton's Needle*, which was published in 1810. It did not appear on many broadsides, but was included in numerous books of nursery rhymes.

34. The Spider and the Fly

Roud 13006, Bathe-Clissold X.789
Alfred Howse, Latton, Wiltshire

Obtained of Alfred Howse, The Basin, Latton. The fable is well known, though, perhaps, not in the following form.

'Will you walk into my parlour?' said the spider to the fly,
'Tis the prettiest little parlour that ever you did spy,
You've only got to peep your head inside of the door,
You'll see so many curious things you never saw before,
Will you walk in, pretty fly?'

'My house is always open,' says the spider to the fly,
'I'm glad to have the company of all that do go by.'
'They all go in but don't go out, I've heard of you before.'
'Oh, yes they do! I always let them out at my back door.
Will you walk in, pretty fly?'

'Will you grant me one sweet kiss?' says the spider to the fly,
'To taste your charming lips I've a curiosity.'
Said the fly – 'If once our lips do meet a wager I would lay,
Of ten to one you would not after let them come away.'

'If you won't kiss, will you shake hands?' says the spider to the fly,
'Before you leave me to myself to sorrow and to sigh.'
Says the fly – 'There's nothing handsome that unto you belongs.
I declare you should not touch me with a pair of tongs.'

'What handsome wings you've got!' says the spider to the fly,
'If I had such a pair I in the air would fly.
'Tis useless all my wishing for I can only talk,
You can fly up in the air, whilst I'm obliged to walk.'

'For the last time I will ask you, will you walk in Mister Fly?'
'No. If I do I will be shot. I'm off now, so goodbye!'
Then up he springs but both his wings were in the web caught fast,
The spider laughed – 'Ha! Ha! my boy, I have you safe at last.'

'And pray! how are you now?' cries the spider to the fly,
'You fools will never wiser grow unless you dearly buy.
The vanity that ever made you come in now too late,
And you who into cobwebs run dearly deserve your fate.'

Now all young men take warning by this foolish little fly,
Pleasure is the spider that to catch you fast will try,
For although you think that my advice is quite a bore,
You're lost if you stand parleying outside Pleasure's door.
Remember, O remember the spider and the fly.

Part 10, Number 7, 4 December 1915

This song, of which the first line has become a familiar tag, is a source of some confusion. It is not, as stated authoritatively by some commentators, the poem by Mary Howitt published in 1829, which shares only the first line with this version. Sabine Baring-Gould got closer when he published in his *English Minstrelsie* the version by the writer and performer Thomas Hudson, which is in most respects the same as that sung by Alfred Howse.[11] Baring-Gould refers to an edition ascribed to Hudson published in Paternoster Row in 1853. Since Hudson died in 1844 this is not likely to have been its first appearance, and Michael Kilgariff suggests that it was written *c.*1835.[12] It is Hudson's text (or variants of it) that can be found on the broadsides in the Bodleian collection and which was printed a number of times in songsters and chapbooks. This is the only instance of it having been collected from a singer in Britain, though it has been heard (one time each) in Nova Scotia and Virginia.

35. Down in Moorfields

Roud 578, Bathe-Clissold X.761
David Sawyer, Stratton St Margaret, Wiltshire

An old song, that was sung to a plaintive melody. I have heard of it but near the Downs of Wiltshire. Obtained of David Sawyer.

Down in Moorfields I walked one evening in the spring,
I heard a maid in Bedlam, how sweetly she did sing;
Her chains she rattled with her hands, and thus replied she –
'I love my love because I know my love he does love me.'

'My love was forced from me, his parents proved unkind,
They sent him far across the sea all to torment my mind;
But though I suffer for his sake as he rolls upon the sea,
I love my love because I know my love he does love me.

'I'll make my love a garland, and it shall be very fine,
I'll stick it up with roses red, and lilies mixed with thyme,
I will preserve it for his sake while he rolls upon the sea –
I love my love because I know my love he does love me.

[11] Sabine Baring-Gould (ed.), *English Minstrelsie: A National Monument of English Song*, 8 vols (Edinburgh: T. C. & E. C. Jack, 1895–[97]), I, xxxii, 108–10.
[12] Michael Kilgariff, *Sing Us One of the Old Songs* (Oxford: Oxford University Press, 1998), p. 86.

Just as she was lamenting here true love came on land,
Hearing she was in Bedlam and straightway out of hand,
Just as he entered in the gates he heard her sigh and say –
I love my love because I know my love he does love me.

'Oh, stand away, don't frighten me! Are you my love or no?'
'Oh, yes my dearest Nancy. What makes you lament so?
I'm come to make you full amends for all your injury'
I love my love because I know my love he does love me.

He brought her to her senses and married her with speed,
And now they love together in love and unity,
Pretty maidens, wait with patience, all you that love so true,
And love your love; in time you'll find your love he does love you.

Part 10, Number 8, 4 December 1915

In search of this song I have visited several 'Maids in Bedlam' and discovered that the theme of the young woman incarcerated in Bedlam after her lover has been pressed to sea goes back at least as far as an eighteenth-century broadside called *The Distracted Maiden's Love to the Farmer's Son*. There are several more versions, but they are so different that they are distinct songs.

The song Williams heard from David Sawyer is a version of 'A Maid in Bedlam' which Lucy Broadwood found in a garland in the British Museum and attached to a tune collected near Helston, Cornwall, with the title 'I'll Love my Love, Because I Know my Love Loves Me'.[13] This was later arranged very successfully by Gustav Holst.

36. Fanny Blair

Roud 1393, Bathe-Clissold X.763
Alfred Howse, Latton, Wiltshire

Obtained of Alfred Howse, The Basin, Latton. It was formerly popular around Cricklade.

Come all you young females, wherever you may be,
Beware of false swearing and all sad perjury,
For by a young female I'm wounded full soon,
For you see I am cut down in the height of my bloom.

[13] *Journal of the Folk-Song Society*, 2.2 (no. 7) (1905), 93–94.

Last Monday morning, as I lay on my bed,
A young man came up to me and these he said –
'Rise up, Thomas Hegan, and fly you elsewhere,
For vengeance is sworn you by young Fanny Blair.'

Young Fanny Blair she's eleven years old,
And as I must die the truth I'll unfold;
I never had dealings with her in my time,
It's a hard thing to die for another man's crime.

The day of my trial Squire Vernon was there,
And on the green table they handed Miss Blair;
False oaths she a-swearing, I'm ashamed for to tell,
Till at length the Judge cries – 'Your mother tutored you well!'

The day that Hegan was doomed to die,
The people rose up with a murmuring cry –
'If we catch her we'll crop her. She falsely has swore;
Young Hegan dies innocent, of that we are sure.'

There is one thing more which I beg of my friends,
To take me in Bloomfield one night by themselves,
And bury my body in Mary-le-Mould,
And I hope that the great God will pardon my soul.

Part 10, Number 9, 4 December 1915

None of the broadside versions give a clear idea of what Thomas Hegan's crime was, but when A. L. Lloyd introduced the song into the modern repertoire he was sure that it was about the rape of a child. He used broadsides to construct his version around a wonderful tune collected by Cecil Sharp.[14]

John Moulden, in his article 'Ballads and Ballad Singers: Samuel Lover's Tour of Dublin in 1830', provides good evidence that the song is of Irish origin and points towards a real-life court case in Ireland in the late eighteenth century.[15] The subject matter makes it virtually impossible to sing this song today. The old singers may have been more focused on the probable innocence of Hegan, and Sabine Baring-Gould's version, for example, carries the subtitle 'The Perjurer'.[16]

---

[14] Sharp's informant was George Say of Axbridge, Somerset, and though his words were garbled they were redeemed a little by the wonderful phrase 'he was handcuffed and shackledised'.

[15] John Moulden, 'Ballads and Ballad Singers: Samuel Lover's Tour of Dublin in 1830', in *Street Ballads in Nineteenth-Century Britain, Ireland, and North America: The Interface between Print and Oral Tradition*, ed. David Atkinson and Steve Roud (Farnham and Burlington, VT: Ashgate, 2014), pp. 127–46 (pp. 141–45).

[16] Baring-Gould heard the song from William Aggett in Chagford on 30 September 1890, but although Frederick Bussell noted the tune in the Rough Copy manuscript the song was not carried forward into any of Baring-Gould's fair copies.

37. The Maid and the Sailor

Roud 264, Bathe-Clissold Ox.307
Alice Rowles, Witney, Oxfordshire,
Amelia Phillips, Purton, Wiltshire

An old and fairly well known song. The wives of villagers especially were fond of it. Obtained of Mrs Rowles, Witney, Oxfordshire, and Mrs Phillips, Purton.

As a pretty maid in the garden was walking,
A brisk young sailor she chanced to see,
He stepped up to her to ask her favour,
Saying, 'Pretty maid, can you fancy me?'

'I think you are some man of honour,
Some man of honour, you seem to be;
How can you impose on a poor young woman,
That is not fit your servant to be?'

'If you are not fit to be my servant,
A real regard I have for thee;
I mean to marry and make you my lady,
And I'll have servants to wait on thee.'

'I have a sweetheart of my own, sir,
And seven years he's been at sea;
And seven more I will wait for him,
If he's alive he'll return to me.'

'If it is seven years since your true love has left you,
I'm sure he's either dead or drowned.'
'If he's alive I will love him dearly,
And if he's dead, he's in glory crowned.'

Then when he found her love was loyal –
'It's a pity that true love be crossed,
I am thy poor and single sailor,
Many a time on the wide ocean tossed.'

'Then if you are my poor and single sailor,
Show me the token I gave to thee;
For seven years makes an alteration,
Since my true love has been gone from me.'

He took his hand out of his bosom,
His fingers being both long and small,
He showed her the ring that was broke betwixt them,
Soon as she saw it she down did fall.

He took her up all in his arms,
And gave her kisses by two and three,

Saying, 'I am thy poor and single sailor,
I've just returned to marry thee.'

So now this couple they are married,
In wedlock's bounds they are bound with joy;
Now these two lovers they live contented,
So here's an end to my sailor boy.

Part 10, Number 10, 4 December 1915

Usually known as 'The Young and Single Sailor', this is one of the best examples of the genre of 'broken-token' songs, though the returnee does not push the test of his sweetheart so far as to tell her that her lover has died, as happens in other songs of this ilk. The earliest known version is 'The Sailor's Return' in a chapbook, *The Shepherd's Lament for the Loss of his Sweetheart*, published in Glasgow in 1802. It appeared on further broadsides in the nineteenth century. The song was very popular among the old singers in Britain and North America, and was been found by many collectors. Alice Rowles's version is a good representative of this well-loved song, retaining key features like his fingers 'long and small' from the 1802 publication.

38. The Sailor and the Farmer's Daughter

Roud 993, Bathe-Clissold Gl.110
John Pillinger, Down Ampney, Gloucestershire

A very old and simple piece. Obtained of John Pillinger, formerly of Lechlade.

A sailor courted a farmer's daughter,
Who lived convenient in the Isle of Man;
And mark, good people, what follows after;
Long time this courtship was carried on.

Long time been courting, and still discoursing
All things concerning the ocean wide –
'I've one more voyage to cross the ocean.
You know, my darling, I cannot 'bide.'

As soon as his mother heard the story,
Before he stepped one foot on board,
That he'd been courting a farmer's daughter,
Whom her parents could not afford.

When he pushed down into the ocean,
Like one distracted his old mother ran,
Crying in a passion – 'If you don't forsake her
I will disown you to be my son.'

'Oh, mother, mother, I'm very sorry,
I'm sorry you have spoke too late,
Don't you remember the first beginning,
When my father married you, a servant maid?

'Oh, don't despise her, I mean to rise her,
As my own father by you has done;
I mean to take her, and my bride I'll make her,
If you will disown me to be your son.'

Part 10, Number 13, 4 December 1915

Usually titled 'The Constant Lovers', this is a much shortened version of 'The Sailor's Courtship' in a chapbook, *Captain Barber's Gallant Behaviour,* published in 1773. The story was simplified on nineteenth-century broadsides but the theme is still that of money versus love. Although it is slightly incoherent in places, the essence of the story is captured in John Pillinger's version.

39. Old Daddy Reynolds

Roud 131, Bathe-Clissold Ox.241
John Chambers, Broadwell, Oxfordshire

Obtained of John Chambers, Broadwell, Oxon. The song was better known at the Oxford end of the Thames Vale.

Old Daddy Reynolds jumped out of the wood,
Upon his hind legs he boldly stood,
Saying – 'A little fresh meat for to do me good,'
And away he went to the town O.
    The town O, the town O
    And away he went to the town O.

Old Daddy Reynolds got to the park gate,
Where he'd often been both early and late;
It made his poor bones for to shiver and to shake,
When he heard the cry of the hounds O,

The hounds O, the hounds O,
When he heard the cry of the hounds O.

Old Mother Prittle-Prattle jumped out of bed,
And out of the window she tucked her old grey head –
'Oh husband! O husband! the grey goose is dead,
And the fox is gone through the town O,'
The town O, *etc.*

Then up jumped the old man with heart and goodwill,
Blowing his horn both loud and shrill;
Says old Daddy Reynolds – 'Catch me if you will,
For I'm glad I'm safe through the town O,'
The town O, *etc.*

Then old Daddy Reynolds got back to his den
Where there were young ones, eight, nine, or ten;
Saying – 'Daddy, oh Daddy, I wish you'd go again,
For I think it's a lucky little town O,'
The town O, *etc.*

Old Daddy Reynolds and his old wife,
Never eat a bit of mustard all the days of their life;
They picked the goose's bones without fork or knife,
And the meat it went merrily down, O.
Down O, down O, *etc.*

Part 11, Number 4, 25 December 1915

This is one of very few English folk songs the roots of which can be traced to the fifteenth century. Even so, scholars believe that when it was first copied into manuscript as 'The Fox and the Goose' *c.*1500 it was a well-known piece.[17] There is subsequently no appearance of it in print until the nineteenth century, when a single stanza about 'Old Mother Widdle Waddle' was printed by Joseph Ritson in his *Gammer Gurton's Garland* in 1861. After this, the song reappeared in full in a number of nursery rhyme collections, but it is very rare in cheap print. Despite this, it made its way around Britain and to North America and the late nineteenth- and early twentieth-century collectors came across it frequently, in a form that retained the basic pattern from more than four hundred years before. This is a remarkable survival.

17 George Perkins, 'A Medieval Carol Survival: "The Fox and the Goose"', *Journal of American Folklore*, 74 (1961), 235–44.

40. Gilderoy

Roud 1486, Bathe-Clissold Wt.482
William King, Purton, Wiltshire

Of Scotch origin, and formerly common on broadsides. It should be borne in mind that many of the finest folk songs, the older ones especially, are not to be found on ballad sheets. The choicest songs seem often to have escaped the notice of the ballad printer. Obtained of William King, Purton, Wiltshire.

Gilderoy was a bonny boy, had roses on his shoon,
His stockings made of the finest silk, his garter hanging down;
It was a comely sight to see, he was so trim a boy,
He was my joy and heart's delight - my handsome Gilderoy.

O such a charming eye he had, his breath sweet as a rose,
He never wore a Highland plaid, but costly silken clothes;
He gained the love of ladies gay, and none to him were coy,
Ah, woe is me! I mourn the day for my dear Gilderoy.

My Gilderoy, that love of thine, good faith! I'd freely bought,
A wedding gown of Holland fine with silken flowers wrought;
And he gave me a wedding ring, which I received with joy,
No lads and lasses e'er could sing like me and Gilderoy.

While we together both did play, he kissed me o'er and o'er,
Good day it was, as blithe a day as e'er I saw before;
He filled my heart in every vein with love and mickle joy –
But when shall I behold again my handsome Gilderoy.

'Tis pity a man should e'er be hanged for taking women's gear,
Or for pilfering a sheep or calf, or stealing cow or mare;
Had not our laws been made so strict I ne'er had lost my joy,
Who was my dearest heart's delight – my handsome Gilderoy.

At Leith they took my Gilderoy, and there God wot, they tried him;
They carried him to fair Edinburgh, and there God wot, they hanged him;
They hanged him up above the rest, he was so trim a boy,
My only love and heart's delight – my handsome Gilderoy.

Thus, having yielded up his breath, in a cypress he was laid,
Then, for my dearest after death, a funeral I made;
Above his grave a marble stone I fixed for my joy,
Now I am left to weep alone for my handsome Gilderoy.

Part 11, Number 6, 25 Dec 1915

This story of a lovable Scottish rogue, told from the point of view of his lover, was also found by some of the other early song collectors. According to William Aytoun, Gilderoy was a cattle robber and highwayman, whose real name was Patrick MacGregor, and was brought to trial on 7 June 1636.[18] His legend grew after his death and he was credited with a life of crime across Europe which included robbing both Cardinal Richelieu and Oliver Cromwell.

There is a song about Gilderoy in the *Westminster Drollery* (1671) which begins, 'Was ever a grief so great as mine'. Eighteenth-century broadsides are similarly structured, but, like William King's version, they begin, 'Gilderoy was a bonny boy, had roses to his shoon'. The song was later shortened to fit the nineteenth-century broadside format.

41. Old Age

Roud 13247, Bathe-Clissold Gl.74
Arthur Halliday, Culkerton, Gloucestershire

A naive and admirable little song, well worth the printing, and of which the sentiment might profitably be committed to memory by many young and middle aged people. Obtained of Arthur Halliday, Culkerton.

The subject of my little song,
I do not think you will say it's wrong;
Though youth and beauty are all the rage,
I never will despise old age.
    Never will I despise old age,
    Though youth and beauty are all the rage;
    But drink to the health of those who clung,
    And cared for us when we were young.

I have a father eighty three,
And a mother soon that age will be;
To me their duty they have done;
May Heaven protect them for their son!
    Never will I despise old age, *etc.*

When I was quite a little babe,
No troubles I knew, but troubles gave,
Kicking, squalling and shouting out,
And knocking all the crocks about.
    Never will I despise old age, *etc.*

[18] William Edmondstoune Aytoun (ed.), *The Ballads of Scotland*, 2 vols (Edinburgh: William Blackwood and Sons, 1858), II, 147–50.

Sometimes mother would get cross,
Then on her knees she would me toss,
Saying this to Mr Brown –
'He's the finest boy in all the town.'
    Never will I despise old age, *etc.*

Some say- 'Let the old wear first!'
But in my mind it should be reversed.
For many years for us they toiled,
It's time for them our hands were soiled.
    Never will I despise old age, *etc.*

May Heaven bless them for their grey hairs,
And keep them from all grief and cares;
Let us do to them as they have done!
It's the duty of every mother's son.
    Never will I despise old age, *etc.*

Part 11, Number 7, 25 December 1915

This was printed on broadsides as *Never Despise Old Age*. A newspaper search reveals that it was being performed on stage by several amateur and professional singers from 1873 until 1905. I have not discovered any sheet music for the song, but it appeared in the *Albion Songster* in 1840 and there is a broadside from an unidentified printer in Frank Kidson's broadside collection. No song collector other than Williams heard it.

42. In the City of Limerick

Roud 21203, Bathe Clissold Gl.105
John Pillinger, Down Ampney, Gloucestershire

Offences against the law, their consequent punishment and the repentance of the culprit afford the ballad writer abundant materials. The songs themselves seldom exhibit any particular brilliance, but they are interesting, if only as being illustrative of the weaker side of human nature. Obtained of John Pillinger, Lechlade.

In the City of Limerick, where I was first born,
All young men, my companions, looked on me with scorn;
In the City of Limerick, they bound me a slave,
For in my own country I could not behave.

My foot's on the ocean, my heart's on dry land,
When I think of my Polly dear it puts me to stand;

If I was on board ship and my Polly dear with me,
Bound down in strong irons, I would think myself free.

I can't tell the reason why women love men,
I can't tell the reason why men do love them;
For a woman's my ruin, my sudden downfall,
She's caused me to lie betwixt lime and stone wall.

Here's a health to my father, who's living today,
Likewise to my mother, she's cold in her grave;
Then you may wear the red rose, and I'll wear the thyme,
You drink to your true love and I'll drink to mine.

The time is approaching when I shall get free,
Straight home to old Ireland my Polly dear to see;
If I was on board ship and my Polly drear with me,
Bound down in strong irons, I should think myself free.

Part 11, Number 8, 25 December 1915

This song was printed on several broadsides in the middle of the nineteenth century as *The Irish Transport*. John Pillinger's is the only collected version. It is very similar to the printed texts.

43. The Farmer's Daughter and her Servant Man

Roud 18, Bathe-Clissold Ox.270
Richard Gardner, Hardwick, Oxfordshire

The subject of the following piece is a well laboured one: it has provided the ballad singers with much capital material. The frequent appearance of the type of story may be tedious, but the rustics do not tire of hearing the pieces. Obtained of Richard Gardner, Hardwick, Oxfordshire.

It's of a brisk and gay old farmer,
He had two sons and a daughter dear;
The servant man being much admired,
Not one in the world she loved so dear.

They asked him to go to a field of hunting,
He went without any fear or strife,
And those two brothers they proved so cruel,
They took away this young man's life.

When they returned from the field of hunting,
The sister inquired for the servant man –
'Now, brothers, tell me, because you whisper,
Now, brothers, tell me, if you can.'

'Sister, sister, I much divine you,
To see you look so pale and wan;
We've left him in the field of hunting,
No more to be your servant man.'

Then she rose early the next morning,
Early by the break of day;
She searched all round where there was no water,
And there she found his body lay.

And on his lips there was blood drying,
Tears more salt than any brine,
Three times she kissed him, loudly crying –
'Here lies the bosomest friend of mine.'

Three nights and days she stood lamenting,
'Till her poor heart was filled with woe;
Until sharp hunger came creeping on her,
And then off to home she was forced to go.

And those two brothers both were tried,
And were bound up in irons strong;
All for this murder they both were guilty,
All for this murder they both were hung.

Part 11, Number 12, 25 December 1915

Francis James Child did not include this fine ballad in his *English and Scottish Popular Ballads.* Also known as 'The Field of Hunting' and 'Bruton Town', among other titles, it is frequently compared to Boccaccio's story of 'Lisabetta' in the *Decameron* (Day 5, Story 5), whose brothers murdered her lover. The story was retold by John Keats in 'Isabella, or the Pot of Basil' in 1818, and then captured in a by William Holman Hunt's painting *Isabella and the Pot of Basil* (1868), where the wronged woman moons over the pot in which she keeps her lover's head as a grisly memento.

The earliest written version of the song is in a manuscript discovered by Harry Douglass of Arcade, New York state, among the manuscript songs compiled by his ancestors, the Stevens family, during the years 1841–56.[19] The manuscript carried the name of one of his great-aunts who died in the early 1850s. The surprise here is not so much that the earliest confirmed version of the song is American, as that the date is so late for what feels like an older song. There are no surviving broadsides, though a ballad with a similar plot, 'The Constant Farmer's Son' (Roud 675), was printed on

[19] Harold W. Thompson, *A Pioneer Songster: Texts from the Stevens-Douglass Manuscripts of Western New York, 1841–1856* (Ithaca, NY: Cornell University Press, 1958), pp. 63–66.

broadsides in the nineteenth century. Steve Gardham speculates that an early ballad lurks unseen somewhere.[20]

The song has been widely collected in southern England but even more frequently in the USA. The American versions often end with the brothers escaping on board a ship, and justice is served by the ship's sinking in a storm. The English versions, of which Richard Gardner's is a good example, end with the sister's threat that her brothers will be hanged. No versions have the dead lover's head removed and used to feed a plant.

44. The Bold Fisherman

Roud 291, Bathe-Clissold Ox.282
Henry Harvey, Cricklade, Gloucestershire
Sarah Calcott, Northmoor, Oxfordshire

I have heard of this piece in several quarters of the Thames Valley. I obtained my first copy of 'Wassail' Harvey, Cricklade, and a slightly better version, given below, of Mrs Sarah Calcott, Northmoor, Oxon. Northmoor is a lonely little village on the banks of the Thames between Standlake and Oxford. The road is broken by the river which must be crossed by ferry to Babcock, Hythe and Appleton. The old woman, who lives alone, sang me several songs including Lord Bateman, while her pet jackdaw sat upon the arm of her chair in the fire light. At the same time, though extremely poor, she insisted upon my taking tea with her, and filled my pockets with choicest apples to eat on my way home.

As I walked out one May morning,
Down by the riverside,
'Twas there I saw a bold fisherman
Come rowing down the tide.

'Good morning to you, bold fisherman!
How came you fishing here?'
'I came a fishing for you, my love,
All down this river clear.'

Then he rowed his boat unto the shore,
And to the maid he went;
He took her by the lily white hand
Which was his full intent.

[20] Steve Gardham, 'The Bridgewater Merchant', Musical Traditions https://www.mustrad.org.uk/articles/dungheap.htm.

Then he pulled off his morning gown,
And laid it on the ground;
And there she saw three chains of gold
All hanging round and round.

Then she on her bended knees did fall,
Saying – 'Lord, have mercy on me,
For calling you a bold fisherman,
All on those briny seas.'

'Rise up, rise up, my pretty fair maid,
And go along with me,
There's not one word that you have spoke
That's least offended me.'

'Stop till I get to my father's gate,
And married we will be;
Married, I say, without delay,
And married we shall be.'

Then he took her to his father's hall,
And married her the next day;
And now she has her bold fisherman,
To row her down the sea.

Part 12, Number 5, 1 January 1916

A very popular song frequently found from singers and in print. It has been suggested that it is a religious allegory, but the words of the broadside versions offer a more earthy interpretation. By folk song standards it is not too shocking, but in a letter to Lucy Broadwood in 1893 Sabine Baring-Gould wrote: 'The song of which you send me the first stanza is, I fancy, a variant of "The Bold Fisherman" a disgusting broadside ballad.'[21] He was not normally shocked by the shenanigans in folk songs, so it may be that he had seen something more than we know of. There are broadsides of the song in his collection, but they conform with the majority in being quite similar to the text that Williams obtained from Sarah Calcott.

The version about which Broadwood wrote to Baring-Gould may well have been the one she had heard from Thomas Gray of Weston, Hertfordshire, which was published in her *English County Songs*.[22] Gray told her it was 'ancients of years old', but the earliest record in print is a broadside by Catnach of London from the early nineteenth century.

[21] VWML, Lucy Broadwood Manuscript Collection, LEB/4/6, Sabine Baring-Gould to Lucy Broadwood, 29 January 1893.

[22] Lucy Broadwood and J. A. Fuller Maitland (eds), *English County Songs* (London: Leadenhall Press, 1893), p. 110.

45. Captain Brooks and his Gallant Crew

Roud 963, Bathe-Clissold Gl.138
Edwin Roberts, Siddington, Gloucestershire

An old sea song, descriptive of a fight between the British frigate 'Shannon' and the American frigate 'Chesapeake' at the time of the American War of Independence. The incident also gave rise to another song, one verse and the chorus of which I give below.

The Chesapeake so bold out of Boston, I am told,
Came to take a British frigate neat and handy O!
The people of the port came out to see the sport,
With their music playing Yankee doodle dandy O!
Yankee doodle, Yankee doodle dandy O!
The people of the port came out to see the sport,
With their music playing Yankee doodle dandy O!

It will be seen that our version is more nearly in line with the folk ballad. I obtained the piece of Edward Roberts, Siddington, Gloucestershire, and he learnt it of an old sailor, who took part in the bombardment of Alexandria.

On the twenty-ninth of May, my boys, off Boston Light we lay,
Watching the bold American while at anchor she lay,
The *Chesapeake* lay in harbour, a frigate stout and fine,
Four hundred and fifty was our crew, and our guns were forty-nine.

Now Captain Brooks commanded us, a challenge he did write,
To ask the bold Americans if they would come out to fight,
Our captain says – 'Brave Lawrence, it is not for enmity,
But it is to prove to all the world that Britain rules the sea.'

Now the challenge was accepted, the Americans they came down,
But never a finer frigate belonged to the British Crown;
We brought her into action, and the true old British plan,
Not fire a gun till all was well, and then the fight began.

It was broadside for broadside, which caused a tremendous roar,
Like thunder it did rattle along that sacred shore;
Oh, the dreadful fire it lasted for three quarters of an hour,
The enemy's ship bore down on us, and their yards were locked with ours.

Then our Captain went to the ship's side to see how she did lie,
And he perceived the enemy's men all from their guns did fly,
'All hands to board her now, he cried, 'the victory is sure,
Come bear a hand, my gallant boys, and the prize we'll soon secure.'

Then like lions we rushed on board and fought them hand to hand,
And though they did outnumber us they could not us withstand;
They fought in desperation, disorder and dismay,
And then, a few minutes after, they were forced to give way.

Our Captain and five lieutenants and fifty of our crew,
Were killed in that short action, one hundred wounded, too;
The news we told to Halifax, our Captain buried there,
And the remainder of his ship's company his honourship did wear.

So come all you true born Englishmen that wear the jackets blue,
Come, drink a health to Captain Brooks and all his gallant crew,
That fought those bold Americans, boys, and laid their courage low,
That fought those bold Americans, boys, and laid their courage low.

Part 12, Number 6, 1 January 1916

Williams was wrong in assigning this song to the American War of Independence because it actually describes a naval action that took place in on 1 June 1813 during the so-called War of 1812. The two frigates involved were the USS *Chesapeake* and HMS *Shannon*. The *Chesapeake* was theoretically superior to the *Shannon* but her captain, James Lawrence, had only just taken her over after a refit. By contrast, Philip Broke, commander of the Shannon, had been at sea for a long time and had drilled his crew to a high level of skill with their guns. Though Broke did, as the song describes, send a challenge to Lawrence, the latter never received it and left Boston of his own accord to meet the *Shannon*. The battle was short and both captains were wounded, Lawrence mortally and Broke so seriously that he never commanded a ship again.

The titles of the various songs about the battle are very similar, but the short extract in the headnote is from 'Chesapeake and Shannon' (Roud 1583) and was sung to Williams by Henry 'Wassail' Harvey of Cricklade, Wiltshire. The manuscript copy of that version has not survived. Edward Roberts's song is more usually titled 'The Battle of the Chesapeake and the Shannon' and corresponds with the broadside text, although two details are incorrect. The 'dreadful fire' lasted only twelve minutes, and in the penultimate stanza it should have been '*their* captain' who was buried. Both of these songs were printed on broadsides and were noted by collectors, though not in great numbers.[23]

[23] Martin Graebe, 'The *Chesapeake* and the *Shannon*: A Battle and its Broadsides', in *Printers, Pedlars, Sailors, Nuns: Aspects of Street Literature*, ed. David Atkinson and Steve Roud (London: Ballad Partners, 2020), pp. 1–22.

46. The Spendthrift

Roud 969, Bathe-Clissold Ox.272
Richard Gardner, Hardwick, Oxfordshire

An old piece, of irregular composition, one of many dealing with a common subject. Obtained of Richard Gardner, Hardwick, near Witney, Oxfordshire.

Once I was big and little I grew,
Once fat, now ready to starve O,
They buried me alive in a cluster of stones,
And they said, 'twas all I deserved O.

Here's now and then one that will tell the truth,
Being a wild and extravagant youth,
Many hundreds I spent on Rachel and Ruth,
And now they have got me in limbo.

Fine fox hunting hounds and rambling nags,
I hunted about till I'd emptied my bags;
My fine fronted shirts all are torn to rags,
And now they have got me in limbo.

Once I did hunt, till I thought I could fly,
I'd strut like a crow in the gutter,
The people did say, as they saw me pass by –
'There goes Mr Flob in a flutter.'

I had an old uncle lived down in the West,
He heard of my sad disaster,
His poor heart it was ready to break,
And his sorrows came thicker and faster.

As soon as I saw him, I well knew his face,
And stood gazing on him like one in amaze;
He looked me all over and pitied my case,
And I hoped for to get out of limbo.

Then he gave me a purse of five hundred pounds,
And the most of it ran into guineas;
As soon as this glorious money I'd got,
I went to see Peggy and Jenny.

I in my rags – not knowing my gold –
How they did box me for being so bold!
You would have laughed to see how they did scold,
To think I was got out of limbo.

As soon as they saw I had so much gold,
They to my pockets were picking;
And I to reward them for being so bold,
Straightway fell to cuffing and kicking.

I, to reward them for being so bold,
To pick my pockets and rob me of my gold;
Banged both of their bodies for the good of their soul,
And teach them to leave me in limbo.

Part 12, Number 9, 1 January 1916

Sabine Baring-Gould heard 'In Limbo' sung by Mary Knapman of Kingswear, Devon, in 1893, and later found it as 'The Fantastick Prodigal' in *The Merry Musician; or, A Cure for the Spleen* (1716), though he suggested it was probably written a few decades earlier.[24] On nineteenth-century broadsides it was often called *The Rake's Complain in Limbo.* The only others to have collected the song were George Gardiner in Hampshire and Cecil Sharp in Gloucestershire. 'Limbo' is a slang term for debtor's prison.

47. In the Lowlands of Holland

Roud 484, Bathe-Clissold Wt.456
David Sawyer, Stratton St Margaret, Wiltshire

One of the many songs composed at the time of Marlborough's campaign in the Netherlands, 1702. Obtained of David Sawyer. I have heard it but once. I do not think it is very well known.

Oh, Holland is a pretty place, and there my love does lie,
And there shall be a resting place for my true love and I;
Since the liquors are as plentiful as the leaves upon the trees,
May the heavens above protect my love as he sails upon the seas.

There came five hundred seamen bold, and it was their full intent,
To fight for King and Country, so boldly then they went;
But four score of them were wounded and the rest of them were slain,
And my true love was one of them that died upon the main.

Said the mother to the daughter, 'What makes you to lament,
Is there never a lad in all the world can give your heart content?'
'There are lads enough in our own town, but never a one for me,
Since the Lowlands of Holland parted my true love and me.

There shall never a cap go on my head, or a comb all in my hair,
Neither fire nor candle bright shall show the clothes I wear;

[24] Sabine Baring-Gould (ed.), *English Minstrelsie: A National Monument of English Song*, 8 vols (Edinburgh: T. C. & E. C. Jack, 1895–[97]), II, iv.

And neither will I married be until the day I die,
Since in the Lowlands of Holland, my true love does lie.'

Part 12, Number 10, 1 January 1916

The earliest printed versions of this song discovered to date are from the second half of the eighteenth century, such as *The Drowned Mariner; or, The Lowlands of Holland Hath Twin'd my Love and Me.* There are two distinct forms of the song in England and Scotland. John Ord's *Bothy Songs and Ballads* gives version of both.[25] His Scottish version has the opening line 'The lad that I had chosen' and is about a young man who builds a ship and is lost at sea. It includes a stanza in which the woman's mother consoles her with the thought that there are plenty of other men in Galloway. William Stenhouse offered this as evidence for the Scottish origin of the song. Ord's English version begins 'The first night I was married and laid in marriage-bed', about a young man who is called away (not necessarily pressed) to fight for his country and is presumed dead. This is the usual form recorded by a number of English collectors. Although Williams's version does not have this first stanza, it clearly follows this pattern.

48. Wait for the Waggon

Roud 2080, Bathe-Clissold Wt.514
John Goddard, Stratton St Margaret, Wiltshire

'Wait for the wagon' was very popular in most villages of the Thames valley when I was a boy, and I often sang it on the way to the hayfield at the time I worked for the farmer. An old man named Jonathon Keene, of Wanborough, told me he remembered when the song came out: that would have been about the year 1824. I obtained the full copy of John Goddard, Stratton St. Margaret, Wiltshire.

Will you come with me Phyllis, dear, to yon blue mountains free?
Where the blossoms smell the sweetest, come, rove along with me,
And every Sunday morning, when I am by your side,
We'll jump into the waggon and all take a ride.
    Wait for the waggon; wait for the waggon;
    Wait for the waggon, and we'll all take a ride.

[25] John Ord, *Bothy Songs and Ballads of Aberdeen, Banff, and Moray, Angus, and the Mearns* (Paisley: Alexander Gardner, 1930), pp. 328–31.

Where the river runs like silver, and the thrushes sing so sweet,
I have a cabin, Phyllis, and something good to eat;
Come listen to my story, it will relieve my heart,
So jump into the waggon and off we will start.
Wait for the waggon, *etc.*

Do you believe, my Phyllis dear, old Mike, with all his worth,
Can make you half so happy, as I with youth and health?
We'll have a little cottage dear, a horse, a pig, a cow,
And you shall mind the dairy, while I will guide the plough.
Wait for the waggon, *etc.*

Your lips are red like poppies, your hair is thick and neat,
All braided up with dahlias and hollyhocks so sweet;
And every Sunday morning, when I am by your side,
We'll jump into the waggon and all to take a ride.
Wait for the waggon, *etc.*

Together on life's journey, we'll travel till we stop,
And if we have us trouble, we'll reach the happy top;
Then come with me, sweet Phyllis, my dear, my lovely bride,
We'll jump into the waggon and all will take a ride.
Wait for the waggon, *etc.*

Part 13, Number 2, 8 January 1916

A version of this American song is on a sheet in the Library of Congress dated 1851 and published by F. D. Benteen of Rhode Island. It is described as an 'Ethiopian Song' (that is, a blackface minstrel song) composed by George P. Knauff, though Knauff may just have been the arranger. An 1850 version is reported to have been written 'by a lady' with music by Wiesenthal. Other authorities, including Michael Kilgariff, attribute the song to R. Bishop Buckley, and there is some evidence that Buckley's Minstrels were performing the song as early as 1843. It was printed on a number of British broadsides. Jonathon Keene's memory, as recorded by Williams, places the song earlier still.

49. The Transport

Roud 3913, Bathe-Clissold Ox.222
Charles Tanner, Bampton, Oxfordshire

Obviously of late eighteenth century date. Obtained at Bampton of Charles Tanner, the aged Morris dancer. I have not heard it elsewhere.

There was an old miser in London did dwell,
He had but one daughter, a most beautiful girl,
And when this old miser was out of the way,
She was always a-courting, by night and by day.

And when this old miser he heard of the news,
Straightway to the captain he immediately goes –
'O honoured bold captain! good news I've to tell,
I've got a jolly transport unto you I'm to sell.'

'What do you want for him?' the captain said he,
'I want nothing for him but to send him to sea.
I'll send him a-sailing right over the main,
Where he shall never come to England to courting again.'

Soon as this fair lady she heard of this news,
Straightway to the Captain she immediately goes -
'O honoured bold captain! Bad news I'm to tell,
You've got my jolly sailor as a transport to sell.'

Then out of her pocket she pulled handfuls of gold,
Down on the main deck she immediately them told –
'O honoured bold captain! All this I'll give to you,
For my jolly young sailor, my right and my due.'

'O it's honoured fair lady! That never can be,
He was sold as a transport the other day to me;
I will send him a-sailing right over the main,
Where he'll never come to England to court you again.'

'O bad luck to my father, wherever he may be,
For I think in my own heart he has quite ruined me,
I'll away to my cottage and lay myself down,
And all this night long for my true love I'll mourn.'

Part 13, Number 6, 8 January 1916

More frequently called 'The Old Miser', this is an unusual ballad in that the young woman is unsuccessful in her attempt to save her lover from the machinations of her father. Although it has not been collected frequently, it has travelled widely and has twice been found on Tristan da Cunha.

50. The Sailor Boy Just Come from Sea

Roud 531, Bathe-Clissold X.806
Edwin Warren, South Marston, Wiltshire

This seems to have enjoyed considerable popularity. It is old and the words appealed to the villagers. I obtained the copy of Edward Warren, South Marston, though I have heard of it in several neighbouring localities.

'Come my own one; come my dear one,
Come my loved one unto me,
Will you wed a poor sailor boy,
That has just come from sea?'

'You are ragged love; you are dirty,
And your clothes smell much of tar.
So begone, you saucy sailor boy!
So begone, you Jack Tar!'

'If I am ragged, love, if I'm dirty,
If my clothes smell much of tar,
I've got silver in each pocket, love,
And gold in great store.

'I am frolicsome, I am easy,
I am good tempered love, and free,
And I don't care a single pin, boys,
What the world may say of me.'

As soon as she heard these words,
Down on her bended knees she fell,
Saying – 'To be sure I'll wed you, Henry,
For I love the sailors well.'

'Do you think I am crazy, love?
Do you think I'm going mad,
To wed a poor country wench,
With no fortune to be had?

'I will cross the briny ocean,
Where the wild birds sweetly sing;
Since you have refused my offer, love,
Some other girl shall wear the ring.'

Part 13, Number 7, 8 January 1916

Usually called 'The Saucy Sailor Boy', this song was very popular in England. Only a few examples made their way into the repertoire of North American singers. It appeared widely in print from the middle of the nineteenth century.

51. The Lakes of Cold Finn

Roud 189, Bathe-Clissold Ox.295
Henry Potter, Standlake, Oxfordshire

I am unable to locate the Lakes of Finn, or to suggest the locality referred to in the song. The piece is old, and not very well known. I have heard of it at Latton. The copy I obtained of Henry Potter, Standlake, Oxfordshire.

It was early one morning young William arose,
Straightway to his comrades' bed chamber he goes,
Saying – 'Comrades, loyal comrades, let nobody know,
It is a fine morning, and a-bathing we'll go.'

So they walked right along till they came to a lane,
And the first that they met was a keeper of game;
He advised them in sorrow to turn back again,
For their doom was to die on the watery main.

Young William stepped in and he swam the lake round,
He swam round the island but not the right ground,
Saying – 'Comrades, loyal comrades, don't you venture in,
There's depths of false waters in the lakes of Cold Finn.'

Next morning, next morning, when his uncle went there,
He rode round the island like one in despair,
Saying – 'Where was he drownéd? Or did he fall in?
For there's depths of false waters in the lakes of Cold Finn.

The day of his funeral there will be a grand sight,
There will be four-and-twenty young men all dressed in white;
They will carry him along and will lay him on clay,
Saying – 'Adieu to young William!' and they'll all march away.

Part 13, Number 8, 8 January 1916

Often the young swimmer is called Willie Leonard and there are persistent stories that it commemorates a real event. As a result, there are a number of contenders for the 'real' location and the name of the lake varies between versions of the song. It is most likely an Irish song and it appeared in print early in the nineteenth century. Although Williams thought that it was not well known, it has been collected a number of times in Britain, Ireland, and North America, but surprisingly few times in Ireland itself.

52. Sarah Gale

Roud 22074, Bathe-Clissold Ox.219
Charles Tanner, Bampton, Oxfordshire

Obtained of Charles Tanner, Bampton.

As I walked round by the walls of Newgate,
I thought I heard a female say –
'I am condemned my days to linger
In the land called Botany Bay.

'For now from him I'm separated,
Scorned by everyone all round,
Tried before a British Jury,
All for the murder of Anna Brown.

'With Greenacre I did cohabit,
When I knew he had a wife;
With Greenacre I did cohabit –
A most abundant, wicked life.

'It was one very Tuesday morning,
About the hour of eight o clock,
The dreadful groans, and shrieks, and rushes
Did my very bosom shock.

'When Greenacre on the scaffold died,
Pray! Do tell me a dismal tale;
Can anyone describe the feelings
Of the wretched Sarah Gale?

'Now all you females, by me take warning –
Rich and poor, and high and low –
What troubles you might yet encounter,
It is very hard for you to know.

'Strive to walk in the paths of virtue,
Take a lesson from my mournful tale;
Can anyone describe the feelings
Of this wretched Sarah Gale?'

Part 13, Number 10, 8 January 1916

In 1836, Hannah Brown, shortly to be the fourth wife of James Greenacre, a grocer from Camberwell, was murdered for her money. He cut her body up and distributed the parts around London. When her head was found in the Regent's Canal, Greenacre was arrested, along with his mistress, Sarah Gale. Both were tried and found guilty. Greenacre was hanged but Sarah Gale was transported to Australia, where she died in 1888. The case became notorious as 'The Edgware Murder' and a play was written about it. This is a very rare song of which only a handful of printed versions exist, and Alfred Williams is the only collector to have heard it.

53. The Disconsolate Lover

Roud 602, Bathe-Clissold Wt.440
David Sawyer, Stratton St Margaret, Wiltshire

A sweet old song. Written at the time of one of Britain's wars overseas. Obtained of David Sawyer, Ogbourne

The captain cries – 'All hands, and away tomorrow,'
Dry up your heavy tears, I must go from you.
Dry up your heavy tears, and leave your weeping,
How happy we shall be at our next meeting."

'How can you go abroad to fight a stranger?
You had better stay at home here, out of danger;
I'll roll you in my arms, my dearest jewel,
So stay at home with me, and don't be cruel.'

Down on the ground she fell, like one a-dying,
Spreading her arms abroad, sifing and crying. [*sighing*]
'There's no believing man – not my own brother!
So girls, if you can love, love one another.'

'Oh mother, don't weep for me, for I am going,
The lad I loved so dear has been my ruin.
He has courted me awhile, just to deceive me,
Now my poor heart is won, he's going to leave me.'

Part 13, Number 13, 8 January 1916

This appeared first on a broadside by Catnach with the title of *The Distressed Maid* early in the nineteenth century. The song was recorded in the journal of the whaling ship *Polly* of Gloucester, Massachusetts, in 1794 as 'A Song concerning Love', predating the broadsides. Most of the collected versions have been found in southern England and are usually called 'Our Captain Cried/Calls All Hands'. 'Monk's Gate', the tune to which it is usually heard sung in modern performances, is familiar from its use by Ralph Vaughan Williams for the hymn 'He Who Would Valiant Be'.

54. On Compton Downs

Roud 2407, Bathe-Clissold Ox.197
Shadrach Haydon, Bampton, Oxfordshire

An old shepherd song, local to the Berkshire Downs between Wantage and Streatley, and one of the very few that were obviously written by rustics. Obtained of Shadrach Haydon, Bampton, late of Hatford and Lyford, Berkshire.

Once I was a shepherd boy, kept sheep on Compton Downs
About two miles from Ilsley, 'twas called a market town;
When we rise all in the morn, when daylight does appear,
Our breakfast we do get, to our fold we all do steer.

When we come to our sheepfold we merrily pitch them round,
And all the rest part of the day we sail the downs all round;
When we get upon the downs, gazing ourselves all round,
We see the storm is rising and coming on all around.

There we stand in our wet clothes, shivering with the cold,
We dare not change our garments till we've drove our sheep to fold;
Now the storm is over, and that you may plainly see,
I'll never keep sheep on the downs any more, for there's neither bush nor tree.

Part 13, Number 14, 8 January 1916

Only one other singer, Richard Read from Hampshire, has been found to have known this song and he only recalled the two stanzas that he sang to George Gardiner. Williams had little better luck with Shadrach Haydon and only recorded the three stanzas given here. A few years earlier, however, Haydon (or Hayden, the spelling varied) sang a slightly longer version for Cecil Sharp.[26] Sharp's version divides the four-line stanzas and has a 'fol-de-rol' refrain. Both Read's and Haydon's versions are located on the North Wessex Downs, the chalk uplands where sheep thrived in former times. The song has not been found in print and it is conceivable that it was a local production.

---

[26] Sharp's version, 'Once I Was a Shepherd's Boy', is in Maud Karpeles (ed.), *Cecil Sharp's Collection of English Folk Songs*, 2 vols (Oxford: Oxford University Press, 1974), II, 196–97. Karpeles gives no indication of where the text can be found, as it does not appear to be among Sharp's manuscripts.

55. Hist! The Mighty Winds Do Blow

Roud 22830, Bathe-Clissold Ox.182
David Ball, Aston, Oxfordshire

A very sweet and superior song. The first line of the chorus is probably incorrect. As it stands it is deficient in sense though in spite of the most careful inquiries, I could not discover another reading. The song was popular at Aston, near Bampton, Oxfordshire. I have not met with it elsewhere. As practically every song I have was obtained by the oral method there must necessarily be some defects; at the same time, I have been astonished at the accuracy of memory of most of the old men. They are often more trustworthy than the printed sheet. Communicated by David Ball, Aston.

Hist! The mighty winds do blow,
Hist! The mourning streams do flow,
Hist to every sounding noise,
I think I hear my true love's voice.
    Here's to the rock that breaks the tree!
    Hark! Hark! A voice. Don't you think it is he?
    No! It is not he, and the night is coming on,
    Where is my lovely wanderer gone?

Loud she calls to make him hear,
'Tis she that calls – 'My love! My dear!
Oh where does he wander? Oh where does he stay?
I am afraid my true love has lost his way.'
    Here's to the rock, *etc.*

The moon behind the clouds was lost,
And every crag appeared his ghost;
The lightning glanced, to cease no more,
Hark! How the awful thunders roar.
    Here's to the rock, *etc.*

Part 14, Number 3, 15 January 1916

Williams collected a version of this song from Mrs Anne Moss of Driffield, which was printed in *FSUT* (p. 234), but not in the *Wilts and Gloucestershire Standard.* This he called 'Cease, Ye Stormy Winds':

Cease ye stormy winds to blow,
Cease ye murmuring streams to flow,
Hushed be every sounding noise
I think I hear my true love's voice.
    Here is the rock, the brook, the tree,
    Hark, hark a voice! Don't you think it is he?
    No, it is not he, and the night is coming on,
    Where is my lovely wanderer gone? [. . .]

The song was published on a number of broadsides from the late eighteenth century onwards as *The Wanderer*. Williams's description of it as a 'very sweet and superior song' betrays its derivation from a composition by Johann Christian Bach, 'Cease a While ye Winds to Blow', from 1771. The piece was performed at Vauxhall Gardens and from there it made its way, eventually, to two singers in Wiltshire in the early twentieth century.

56. The Clowdy Banks

Roud 266, Bathe-Clissold Gl.61
Charles Messenger, Cerney Wick, Gloucestershire

An old ballad, which I have met with but once in the Vale, i.e. in the neighbourhood of Latton. Obtained of Charles Messenger, Cerney Wick.

As I walked out one evening, 'twas in the month of May,
Down by some flowery gardens with pleasure I did stray;
'Twas there I heard a damsel in sorrow to complain,
'Twas for her absent lover, who ploughed the raging main.

I boldly steppéd up to her, I put her in surprise,
I knew she didn't know me, for I was in disguise;
I said – 'My charming creature, you're my joy and heart's delight,
How far on this road do you travel this dark and rainy night?'

'I am bound for the Clowdy Banks, if you will please to show,
O pity a poor girl distressed, for there this night I must go,
In search all of some false young man, and Johnny is his name;
And on the banks of Clowdy I'm told he does remain.'

'Being six long months and better since your true love left shore,
For to cross that wide ocean where thundering cannons roar;
For to cross that wide ocean for honour and for gain,
Their ship's been wrecked, as I've been told, all on the coast of Spain.'

By hearing of this dreadful news she fell into despair,
By wringing her hands, and crying, and tearing of her hair –
'My vows unto no other man I never more will make;
In some lonesome woods and valleys I'll wander for his sake,'

By hearing of this joy, after he could no longer stand,
He flew into her open arms, crying – 'Betsy, I'm the man,
I am that faithful young man whom you did think was slain,
And since we've met on Clowdy banks we'll never part again.'

Part 14, Number 4, 15 January 1916

As Steve Roud and Julia Bishop point out in their notes to 'Claudy Banks' in *The New Penguin Book of English Folk Songs*, there is more to this song than meets the eye. It is not a 'broken-token' song, as there is no sign of a ring. And the 'false young man' has only been away six months ('six long weeks' in some versions), rather than the customary seven years. Not much time to engage with thundering cannons, either by land or sea. But we, and the old rural singers, would all like to believe that he is as faithful as he claims to be and that they really will 'never part again'. The earliest known version of the song in print is *A New Song Called the Banks of Claudy* published in Belfast in 1816. It was very widely collected in England, Ireland, and North America.

57. Sally M'Roe

Roud 526, Bathe-Clissold Wt.326
Daniel Morgan, Braydon, Wiltshire

An old Irish ballad, of uncertain date. Obtained of Daniel Morgan, Braydon, Wiltshire.

My name is Tom Dixon, I'm a blacksmith by my trade,
When, from the town called Newry where I was born and bred;
I packed up my tools, and to Belfast I did go,
And 'twas for the sake of young Sally M'roe.

Now it was some two years ago and more since from her I heard,
Not one word from that bonny girl I once loved so dear;
But abroad as I was walking, down by some shady grove,
Who should I meet there but young Sally M'roe.

'Now,' said I, 'my bonny girl, if you'll go along with me,
I'll take you straight to Newry and married we will be;
Then we'll cross the heaving ocean, and none shall ever know
That I've been and married young Sally M'roe.'

We went floating down that river with a sweet wind and tide,
Leaving our friends behind us to sorrow and complain,
Whilst many briny tears all down their cheeks did flow,
And whilst I was quite happy with young Sally M'roe

'Twas on one Sunday morning about six o clock,
Our ship she sprang a leak and went dash against a rock;
No one could be saved who lay down below,
And amongst that great number was young Sally M'roe.

It was from her parents I stole that girl away,
Which has caused me to lament unto my dying day;
Never to ill use her, but, since I have done so,
All my long life now I'll mourn for young Sally M'roe.

Part 14, Number 5, 15 January 1916

This first appeared in the early nineteenth century on broadsides printed in northern Britain. These have more stanzas than the above and provide greater detail, saying, for example, that the ship was called the *Newry*. It was this that led Roy Palmer to the discovery that a ship of that name left Warren Point, near Newry, in April 1830 carrying Irish emigrants bound for Quebec. The vessel was wrecked on Bardsey Island off the north Welsh coast. *The Times* reported that three hundred of about four hundred Irish emigrants aboard were saved. Apparently, the passenger list included the names of Sally Munro and John Dickson. Although the song has been collected several times, the majority of instances are sound recordings made in the 1930s and after the Second World War. The only other version heard by the early song collectors in England was that found by George Gardiner in Hampshire.[27]

58. The Lass with the Jet Braided Hair

Roud 12885, Bathe-Clissold Wt.333
Allan Cutts, Brinkworth, Wiltshire

The following I obtained of Mr Allan Cutts, Brinkworth, Wiltshire. I have not heard it elsewhere.

As I was a-walking one morn, a-viewing the meadows in spring,
The birds were sweetly in tune, I heard a poor damsel did sing;
I gazed on the spotless, poor creature, like Venus she then did appear,
For she was the grandest of nature, 'twas the lass with the jet braided hair.

Her neck was as fair as the lily, her teeth were as white as the pearl,
Like the roses that grow in the garden were the cheeks of this charming young girl;
A dress of bright crimson velvet this beautiful damsel did wear,
And a chain of pure gold with a diamond was wove in her jet braided hair.

[27] For a detailed study of the song, see Roly Brown, 'Glimpses into the 19th Century Broadside Ballad Trade, No. 36: Sally Munro', Musical Traditions https://www.mustrad.org.uk/articles/bbals_36.htm.

Long time did I court this fair damsel, and fixed our nuptial day,
Till her mind to some other did ramble, and scornful these words she did say –
'I have one more bolder and clever, my hand and my heart I will share.'
So I bid adieu now and for ever, to the lass with the jet braided hair.

So farewell all my friends and relations, I never may see you no more!
I'll travel through all foreign nations and seek for my dear native shore;
Since I am doomed for to wander, I'll try my fond heart for to cheer,
So I bid adieu now and for ever, to the lass with the jet braided hair.

Part 14, Number 6, 15 January 1916

This song appeared on broadsides in the middle of the nineteenth century. In the fourth stanza of the broadsides the hapless narrator sails down the river for Spain, and as he is departing he sees the lass with the jet braided hair walking out with another man. The only other instance of this song collected in England was found by Clive Carey in Sussex. It has, however, been collected more frequently in Ireland, sometimes with the title 'The Maid with the Bonny Brown Hair'.

59. Banks of the Nile

Roud 950, Bathe-Clissold Ox.175
William Wise, Alvescot, Oxfordshire

This suggests the French expedition to Egypt planned by Napoleon in 1798, and frustrated by Nelson at the Battle of the Nile. I obtained the piece of William Wise, Alvescot, Oxfordshire.

Hark! I hear the drums a-beating,
Here no longer I can stay,
I hear the trumpet sounding,
Love, now we must away;
I'm ordered off to Portsmouth,
It's many a long mile,
For to join the British Army,
On the Banks of the Nile.

O Willie, dearest Willie,
Don't leave me here to mourn,
'Twill make me curse and rue the day,
That ever I was born;
With the parting of my own true love,
And the parting of his life,

If you'll stay at home dear William,
Then I will be your wife.

If not, I'll cut off my curly locks,
And I'll go along with you,
I'll dress myself in velveteen,
I'll go and see Egypt, too;
I'll fight beneath your banner,
While Fortune seems to smile,
On the cold, sandy desert,
On the Banks of the Nile.

O Nancy, dearest Nancy,
You must not go with me,
Our Colonel gave us orders
That no women there must be;
We must forsake our sweethearts,
Likewise our native soil,
And we'll comfort one another,
On the Banks of the Nile.

It made me curse and rue the day,
When the war it first began,
For old Ireland has been robbéd,
Of many a clever young man;
But now the war is over,
We're all a-going home,
Unto our wives and sweethearts,
We left behind to mourn.

Part 14, Number 7, 15 January 1916

The earliest version of this in print is in a chapbook, *The Banks of the Nile, a Love Song; to which is annexed, Prince Charles Answer to the King of France; and Rouse Britons, Rouse*, and it appeared on many other broadsides in later years. It was collected in Britain, Ireland, and North America, but did not come to the notice of the early collectors other than Gardiner, Williams, and Vaughan Williams. Alfred Williams is slightly out with his history as, rather than Nelson's Battle of the Nile in 1798, the song refers to the campaign of the British expeditionary force under Sir Ralph Abercromby that drove Napoleon's army out of Egypt in 1801.

60. The Three Jolly Huntsmen

Roud 796, Bathe-Clissold Ox.274
George Keen, High Cogges, Witney, Oxfordshire

This version I obtained of Mr George Keen, roadman, High Coggs, near Witney, Oxfordshire. It is shorter than the preceding and differs from it in several other respects. It appears to have been rather more local. I have not heard of its chorus anywhere else.

There was three jolly huntsmen,
To hunting they did go,
To chase poor bold Reynolds,
It was the hue and cry.
    Yoicks, my boys! The huntsman cried,
    And so did every one,
    Wivvy, wivvy wink, chivvy, chivvy, chink,
    And over the hills they ran,
    And over the hills they ran.

The first they met was a ploughboy,
A-ploughing of his land,
He swore he saw bold Reynolds,
Run up the fallow land
    Yoicks, *etc.*
    And up the fallow they ran,
    And up the fallow they ran.

The next they met was a blind man,
As blind as he could be,
He swore he saw bold Reynolds,
Run up a hollow tree,
    Yoicks, *etc.*
    And up the tree they ran,
    And up the tree they ran.

The next they met it was an old woman,
A-curling of her locks,
She swore she saw bold Reynolds,
Among the hens and cocks.
    Yoicks, *etc.*
    And through the farm yard they ran,
    And through the farm yard they ran.

The next they met was a soldier,
And he was dressed in red.
He swore he saw Bold Reynolds,
Lie on the ground for dead.
    Yoicks, *etc.*

And now poor Reynolds is dead.
And now poor Reynolds is dead.

Part 14, Number 9, 15 January 1916

This first appeared as 'The Pursuit of Reynard' in a collection of songs from the theatres and pleasure gardens called *The Woody Choristers.* It has much in common with 'Three Men Went A-Hunting' or 'Three Jovial Welshmen' (Roud 283), which has antecedents in the early seventeenth century. Williams included two versions of 'The Three Jolly Huntsmen' in the newspaper series and published one of them in *FSUT* (pp. 67–68). This version does not have the shepherd, the carter, and the miller, who appear in *FSUT*, but it gains a ploughboy and a soldier. It also has a chorus that varies each time, while in *FSUT* the chorus is repeated.

61. The Copy Boy

Roud 1030, Bathe-Clissold Ox.207
Charles Tanner, Bampton, Oxfordshire
Shadrach Haydon, Bampton, Oxfordshire

This dates from about 1798, and refers to the rebellion in Ireland, which was effectively suppressed by the Lord Lieutenant, Lord Cornwallis, the Lord Cornwall in the second verse of the song. I obtained the copy in parts, of Charles Tanner, Bampton, and Shadrach Haydon, also now being at Bampton. Neither knew of the others' acquaintance with the song.

It was early, early in the spring,
The birds did whistle and sweetly sing,
Changing their notes from tree to tree,
And the song they sang was, 'Old Ireland Free'.

It was early, early in the night,
The Yeoman Cavalry gave me a fright;
The Yeoman Cavalry was my downfall,
And taken was I by Lord Cornwall.

When I was standing at my father's door,
My brother William stood on the floor,
My sister Mary did grieve full sore,
My tender mother her grey locks tore.

'Twas in the guardhouse where I was laid,
And in the parlour where I was tried;

My sentence passed, and my courage low,
And to Dungara I was forced to go.

My sister Mary she heard the express,
And ran downstairs in her morning dress:
'Five hundred guineas I would pay down,
To see my brother march through Wexford town.'

As I was going up Wexford Hill,
Which did induce me to cry my fill;
I looked behind and I looked before,
But my tender mother I could see no more.

As I was walking down Wexford Street,
My own first cousin I chanced to meet;
My own first cousin did me annoy,
And for one burgala swore my life away.

When I was on the gallows high,
My aged father was standing by;
My aged father did me deny,
And the name he gave me was the Copy Boy.

All you good Christians that do pass by,
Pray drop one tear for the Copy Boy.

Part 14, Number 10, 15 January 1916

This song is correctly 'The Croppy Boy', which appeared on a number of broadsides in the early nineteenth century and has been collected widely in Britain, Ireland, and North America. The rebellion of 1798 was an important landmark in Irish history and the song has regularly appeared in collections of Irish national songs. The town mentioned in stanza four should be Dungannon. The puzzling 'burgala' in stanza seven is rendered in the broadsides as 'bare guinea'.

62. Yonder Sits a Pretty Little Creature

Roud 542, Bathe-Clissold Ox.225
Charles Tanner, Bampton, Oxfordshire

The following version of the above ['March Away', *FSUT*, pp. 196–97] *I obtained of Charles Tanner, Bampton, Oxfordshire. The chorus is worthy of note. Its composition and balance are perfect: one is surprised to find such in the bare enumeration of a score of figures.*

Yonder sits a pretty little creature,
Who she is I do not know,
I'll go court her for her sweet favour,
Let her answer me 'Yes' or 'No.'
With my twenty, eighteen, sixteen, fourteen,
Twelve, ten, eight, six, four, two, none;
Nineteen, seventeen, fifteen, thirteen,
Eleven, nine, seven, five, three, one.

'O madam, mind, I'm come a-courting,
If your favour I can gain;
If you make me kindly welcome,
Perhaps then I may come again.'
With my twenty, *etc.*

'Sit you down, you're kindly welcome,
If your face I never see no more,
I must and I will have a handsome fellow,
Let him keep me, rich or poor.'
With my twenty, *etc.*

'Madam! don't think much of beauty,
Beauty's a flower that soon will fade,
The fairest flower that grows in the summer,
Soon it'll die and fade away.'
With my twenty, *etc.*

Part 15, Number 3, 22 January 1916

The earliest version so far discovered in print is 'The Lovely Creature' in a mid-eighteenth century chapbook, *The Tom-Tit*, published by Dicey of London. Both of Williams's texts are close to that early version. Although it was not reprinted on nineteenth-century broadsides the song has been collected in a number of variants, many of them incoherent. The problem is often caused by the introduction of floating verses. These obscure the simple message of the song, which is that even though she has rejected him because he is not handsome enough, her own beauty will fade like the flowers. Williams comments on the numerical chorus; to be able to sing it was sometimes treated as a demonstration of a singer's sobriety.

63. I Courted a Bonny Lass

Roud 154, Bathe-Clissold Wt.400
Elijah Iles, Inglesham, Wiltshire
Sarah Calcott, Northmoor, Oxfordshire

An old favourite, formerly widely known. Words obtained of Elijah Iles, Inglesham and Sarah Calcott, Northmoor, Oxfordshire

A week before Easter, the day is long and clear,
So beautiful shone the sun and so cold blowed the air,
I went to the forest some flowers to get there,
But the forest would yield me no posies.

I courted a bonny lass many a long day,
I hated all people that against her did say,
But now she's rewarding me well for my pains,
For she's going to be wed to another.

So, when I heard my true love asked in the church,
I rose from my seat and sat in the porch,
Thought I to myself – 'I am left in the lurch,
So adieu to my false love for ever!'

When I saw my love unto the church go,
Bride's men and bride's maidens they made a fine show,
And I followed after with my heart full of woe,
To see how my false love was guarded.

When I saw my love within the church stand,
Gold ring on her finger, and love in her hand, [*glove*]
Thought I to myself – 'If I could by her stand,
Although she is tied to another!'

When that I saw my love dressed in her white,
The tears in my eyes quite dazzled my sight;
I picked up my hat and I wished them Goodnight,
And adieu to my false love for ever!

The parson that named them so loudly did cry –
'All you that forbid it, I'd have you draw nigh.'
Thought I to myself – 'A good reason have I.'
But I had not the heart to forbid it.

And when that I saw my love sat down to meat,
I sat myself by her, but nothing could eat;
For I loved her sweet company better than meat,
Although she was wed to another.

Now dig me a grave, long large, wide and deep,
And strew it all over with flowers so sweet,
That I may lie down, and take a long sleep,
For that's the right way to forget her.

Part 15, Number 6, 22 January 1916

Known as 'The False Bride' or 'The Week before Easter', this is derived from *The Forlorn Lover*, a sixteen-stanza ballad entered in the Stationers' Register in 1675. The Bodleian Library holds a copy printed in London assigned to the period 1663–74.The song was shortened in later broadside versions, and there is a lot of variation in the collected versions, of which there are many. Williams's nine-stanza song is more complete than most and constitutes a very satisfying narrative.

64. In Sheffield Park

Roud 860, Bathe-Clissold Wt.339
Miss E. King, Castle Eaton, Wiltshire

This song I have heard but once, i.e. at Castle Eaton, where I obtained it of Miss E. King. It is a very old piece, rather plain and simple, but with an admirable ending.

In Sheffield Park there once did dwell,
A brisk, young lad – I loved him well.
He courted me, my heart to gain,
He's gone and left me full of pain.

I went upstairs to make my bed,
I laid me down, but nothing said;
My mistress came to me and said –
'What is the matter with you, my maid?'

My mistress then from me did go –
'Some help, some help, some help for you!'
'No help, no help, no help I crave,
Sweet William has brought me to my grave.

You take this letter to him with speed,
And give it to him, if he can read;
Bring me an answer without delay,
For he has stolen my heart away.'

He took the letter immediately,
And read it over while I stood by;

And soon he did this letter burn,
Leaving the maid to weep and mourn.

'Oh, foolish girl, to weep for me!
Think I could fancy none but thee?
The world was not made for one alone;
I take delight to hear thee moan.'

We gathered the green leaves for her bed,
And a flowery pillow for her head;
And the leaves that grow from tree to tree,
Shall be a covering over thee.

'Oh, mistress, mistress, you little know,
What pain and sorrow I undergo;
Oh, put your hand on my left breast,
My aching heart can take no rest.'

Part 15, Number 7, 22 January 1916

The earliest version of this that I have discovered is 'The Unfortunate Maid' in an Aldermary Churchyard chapbook of the second half of the eighteenth century, *The Choice Spirits Delight, Part II, being a Choice Collection of New Songs, Sung this and the Last Season, at Renelagh, Vauxhall, Sadler's Wells, the Theatres, and in the Politest Companies.* Other chapbooks of similar date also have the song. It reappeared on broadsides in the early nineteenth century and was collected several times, mainly in southern England. Williams's version runs along the same lines as the broadsides, but with the usual third stanza placed at the end of the song.

65. Catch Me If You Can

Roud 1028, Bathe-Clissold Wt.329
Jonathan Cole, Brinkworth, Wiltshire

For the following old song I am indebted to Mr Jonathon Cole of Brinkworth, Wiltshire. The subject is that eternal and well laboured one of love in spring time. I have not heard the piece elsewhere.

Early, early in the spring,
The cuckoo and the nightingale so sweetly they did sing,
Down by the riverside a pretty girl I chanced to spy,
  She was taking of fresh air,
  She was taking of fresh air.

I said – 'Pretty maid will you go along with me?
I will show you a nearer way across the countree.'
'Sir Tittle-tattle,' she did say,
'I have a mind to go that way.'
    And he soon gained her favour,
    And he soon gained her favour.

'Now you have the will of me,
Pray, tell me what your name may be.'
'My name is Catch-me-if-you-can,
And marry me when I return.
    I'm going for recreation,
    I'm going for aggravation.

Then her parents set out, both horse and foot,
To catch this young man if they could;
They catched the rogue and bound him fast,
They took the young man in at last.
    They robbed him of his leisure.
    They robbed him of his pleasure.

Part 15, Number 9, 22 January 1916

The story of a young man seducing a maid and leaving her to face the consequences is as old as time. A search for the origins of this version of the story has yielded only one broadside edition, printed by Pitts of London in the early nineteenth century under the title *The Recreation.*

The song was first collected by Sabine Baring-Gould in the early 1890s. The words, as he heard them originally, are not recorded in his manuscripts. In his Personal Copy manuscript he has a rewritten version (never published) which he describes as 'A softened version of a not very savoury song sung by a man at South Zeal'. His collection of broadsides includes the Pitts version of *The Recreation.* Later, several other collectors heard the song, notably in the South-West, where it was recovered from Travellers near the end of the twentieth century.

Unusually, in Jonathan Cole's version the parents go after the young man and bring him back to face the consequences, which are hinted at in the menacing final two lines.

66. O Then, O Then

Roud 437, Bathe-Clissold Gl.150
James Mills, South Cerney

Here again I am required to give two versions [the other is 'Once I Was Single', *FSUT*, p. 111] *of a song which has for its subject the sarcastic relation of the taking of a wife and the ill natured rejoicing of the husband over her death and burial. Obtained of James Mills, South Cerney.*

Once I was a young man, O then, O then,
Once I was a young man, O then;
A-courting I went, and my money I spent,
And the world went merry with me just now, then.

I married me a wife, O then, O then,
I married me a wife, O then;
My wife she fell sick and the fever took her quick,
And the world went merry with me just now, then.

I went for the doctor, O then, O then,
I went for the doctor, O then;
He couldn't do her good, nor I didn't wish he would,
For the world went merry with me just now, then.

My wife she did die, O then, O then
My wife she did die, O then;
My wife she did die, be hanged if I could cry,
For the world went merry with me just now, then.

I went for the coffin, O then, O then
I went for the coffin, O then;
I went for the coffin, and I couldn't speak for laughing,
For the world went merry with me just now, then.

I put her in the coffin, O then O then,
I put her in the coffin, O then,
I put her in the coffin and I saw the bitch a-laughing,
And the world went merry with me just now, then.

I took her to the grave, O then, O then,
I took her to the grave, O then;
I heard the bands play and I danced all the way,
And the world went merry with me just now, then.

And now she's in, O then, O then,
And now she's in, O then,
And now she's in, we'll have a glass of gin,
For the world went merry with me just now, then.

Part 15, Part 10, 22 January 1916

Another salvo in the battle of the sexes. The earliest version known is 'When I Was a Young Man' in a Scottish songbook, *The Entertaining Songster*, of 1791. A broadside was printed around the same time by Jennings of London with the title *The First Wife the Best.* For some reason the song seems to have been collected and published more often in the USA than in Britain.

67. The Country Blade and his Scolding Wife

Roud 434, Bathe-Clissold Ox.194
Shadrach Haydon, Bampton, Oxfordshire

This, like the two preceding ['O, Then, O Then' (no. 66) and 'Once I Was Single', *FSUT*, pp. 111–12] *relates of the marriage experience and is not very complimentary to the better half. The 'oil of hazel' means the hazel rod and suggests beating her as the only effective cure. Our sympathies are with the 'weaker vessel.' Obtained of Shadrach Hayden, Bampton.*

It's of a country blade,
And he loved a country maid,
And in vain he conducted her home, home, home,
She could sew and she could make,
She could brew and she could bake,
And she could sweep up the house with the broom, broom, broom.

She could card and she could spin,
And do many another thing,
And at last she cried she was dumb, dumb, dumb,
Then to the doctor John did go,
For to see whether or no,
He could cure any woman that was dumb, dumb, dumb.

Then the doctor John did bring,
And he cut her chattering string,
And her clapper it began for to run, run, run,
In the morning she did rise,
She filled the house with noise,
And it rattled in my ears like a drum, drum, drum.

Then to the doctor John did go,
For to see whether or no,
He could make a scolding woman hold her tongue, tongue, tongue,
'For my wife has took to scold,
And her tongue will never hold,
And I'd give all the world if she was dumb, dumb, dumb.

Then the best advice I could give –
Let her die or let her live –
Is to get the oil of hazel that is strong, strong, strong,
And every time she frowns,
Give her a good dressing down,
That will make a scolding woman hold her d—n long tongue.

Part 15, Number 12, 22 January 1916

Distasteful as it is, this is a song of some antiquity. Sabine Baring-Gould reported hearing it from a number of Devonshire men and referred to a version in the Roxburghe Ballads, *The Dumb Maid; or, The Young Gallant Trappan'd*, from *c.*1678.[28] It was more usually called *The Dumb Wife* on nineteenth-century broadsides. It has been heard from singers on both sides of the Atlantic.

68. The Silvery Tide

Roud 561, Bathe-Clissold Gl.142
Thomas Baughn, South Cerney, Gloucestershire

I have heard a few lines of this song in several villages far removed from each other, but I have only met with once in its complete form. This was at South Cerney, where I obtained the copy of Mr Thomas Baughan.[29]

It's of a fair young creature who dwelt by the sea side,
Her lovely form and feature, she was called the Village Pride;
She was admired by lords and squires, but still it was all in vain,
For true she was to Henry whilst on the watery main.

As a nobleman was walking one morning to take the air,
Down by the foaming ocean he met this lady fair;
'Now,' says this artful villain, 'consent to be my bride
Or you'll sink or swim, far, far from him who is on the silvery tide.'

With trembling lips says Mary – 'My vows I ne'er can break,
For Henry I love dearly, I will die for his sweet sake.'
With his handkerchief he tied her hands and plunged her o'er the side,
And quickly she went floating down on the silvery tide.

[28] Sabine Baring-Gould (ed.), *English Minstrelsie: A National Monument of English Song*, 8 vols (Edinburgh: T. C. & E. C. Jack, 1895–[97]), II, vi.
[29] The correct spelling of the name, from official documents, is 'Baughn'.

Now it happened, a few days after, young Henry came from the sea,
And, thinking to live happy, he thought on the wedding day;
'We believe your love is murdered,' her aged parents cried,
'She has caused her own destruction down in the silvery tide.'

As young Henry on his pillow lay he could not take his rest,
For the thought of pretty Mary disturbed his wounded breast;
So he arose at midnight gloom, and at midnight gloom goes he,
To wander the sandbanks over, down by the raging sea.

It was daybreak in the morning when young Mary's corpse he spied,
As to and fro it went floating down on the silvery tide;
He knew it was young Mary, by his own ring on her hand,
And when he saw this silk handkerchief it put him to a stand.

As he undid this silk handkerchief, therein full soon he spied,
Who had cruelly murdered Mary down on the silvery tide:
This nobleman was taken and the gallows was his doom,
For ending pretty Mary, who'd scarcely attained her bloom.

Part 16, Number 3, 29 January 1916

Though worthy of a Victorian melodrama, this song appeared on broadsides by printers such as Catnach early in the nineteenth century. It was also collected frequently because this was exactly the sort of story that the old singers loved. The identification of the squire from his monogrammed handkerchief is a deduction worthy of Hercule Poirot. There are some elements missing from Thomas Baughn's version, such as a stanza in which the squire's jealous rage develops into intent to murder, and the dream that reveals Mary's fate to Henry. And, of course, the song should properly end with:

Young Henry so dejected, he wandered till he died,
His last words were for Mary, who died in the silvery tide.

69. Phoebe and her Dark-Eyed Sailor

Roud 265, Bathe-Clissold Wt.409
Elijah Iles, Inglesham, Wiltshire

A special favourite, both of men and maidens and also loved of the old folks. Words obtained of Elijah Iles, Inglesham, Wiltshire.

It's of a comely young lady fair,
Who was walking out to take the air;

She met a sailor all on her way,
So she paid attention,
So she paid attention, to all he had to say.

Said William – 'Lady, why roam'st alone?
The night is coming, the day's near gone.'
She said, while tears from her eyes did fall –
'Tis my darkeyed sailor,
'Tis my darkeyed sailor, that has proved my downfall.'

Says William, 'Drive him from off your mind,
Some other sailor as good you'll find.
Love turns aside and soon cold doth grow,
Like a winter's morning,
Like a winter's morning when the land is covered with snow.'

These words did Phoebe's fond heart inflame,
She said – 'On me you shall play no game.'
She drew a dagger and then did cry –
'For my darkeyed sailor,
For my darkeyed sailor, a maid I'll live and die.

'It's two long years since he left the land,
He took the gold ring from off my hand;
He broke the token, here's a part with me,
And the other's rolling,
And the other's rolling at the bottom of the sea.

'But still,' said Phoebe, 'I'll not disdain,
A tarry sailor, but treat the same.
So drink his health – here's a piece of coin,
But my darkeyed sailor,
But my darkeyed sailor still claims this heart of mine.'

Then half the ring did young William show;
She seemed distracted midst joy and woe –
'Oh, welcome, William, I've lands and gold,
For my darkeyed sailor,
For my darkeyed sailor, so true and bold.'

Then in a village, down by the sea,
They joined in wedlock and well agree;
So maids, be true when your love's away,
For a cloudy morning,
For a cloudy morning brings forth a sunshiny day.

Part 16, Number 5, 29 January 1916

That this, another 'broken-token' song, was a favourite with the old singers is confirmed by the number of times it has been collected. It does not, though, appear to be any older than the first part of the nineteenth century, when it appeared on a Catnach broadside with the title *Fair Phoebe and her Dark-Eyed Sailor.*

70. The Tinker's Courtship

Roud 863, Bathe-Clissold Ox.179
William Wise, Alvescot, Oxfordshire

The tinker is celebrated in many songs and ballads though he is never treated with any degree of seriousness. As a rule, he was always looked upon as a meddler and a 'gay spark', and he consequently comes in for much satirical criticism and caricature. Obtained of W. Wise, Alvescot, Oxfordshire.

In Dublin there once did dwell,
A pretty fine girl and I knew her well;
Her age it was just twenty-two,
And for a man she had to do.
 Sing fol the rol lara li gee o,
 Fol the rol lara li gee o.

The gentleman being come home one day,
The tinker with her did skip and play;
He courted her behind the door,
And there he kissed her o'er and o'er.
 Sing fol the rol lara, *etc.*

Now when this courtship was at an end,
She tipped him twenty guineas in hand;
Saying – 'Call again as soon as you can,
I'll find you another old kettle to mend.'
 Sing fol the rol lara, *etc.*

Now, if all be true as I've been told,
The tinker he spent all the gold;
Then he must do as he'd done before,
And kiss the girl behind the door.
 Sing fol the rol lara, *etc.*

Part 16, Number 8, 29 January 1916

Among the Roxburgh Ballads is one from the 1660s called *Room for a Joviall Tinker, Old Brass to Mend*, with an elaborate subtitle:

Here is a Tinker full of mettle
The which can mend pot pan or Kettle,
For stopping of holes is his delight
His work goes forward day and night
If there be any women brave,
whose Coldrons need of mending have
Send for this Tinker nere deny him
He'l do your work well if you try him.
A proof of him Ile forthwith show
Cause you his workmanship may know.

Subsequent editions of the song became steadily earthier until it reached a point in the later twentieth century when it was to be found mainly in collections of bawdy songs. Alfred Williams is the only early collector to admit to having heard it. William Wise's version navigates safely through these murky waters, while retaining the metaphor of the mended kettle.

71. The Shepherd on the Mountain

Roud 1433, Bathe-Clissold Ox.220
Charles Tanner, Bampton, Oxfordshire
Richard Gardner, Hardwick, Oxfordshire

This is a very old country song, rude and unpolished, but not without a certain charm of language and sentiment. Obtained of Charles Tanner, Bampton, and Richard Gardner, Hardwick, Oxon.

Young William the shepherd kept sheep on the mountain,
And his echoing voice made the valleys to ring;
With his bagpipes so neatly, he played them so sweetly,
And his echoing voice made pretty Sally to sing.

Says William to Sally – 'My dear, let us go walking
Down in yonder gay meadows to take the fresh air,'
Where the lambkins were playing Sally and I went a-straying,
So sweetly the nightingale sang to my dear.

Says Sally to William – 'My dear, I must leave you,
For the night is approaching, and I must go home;
All my friends will chastise me and unto me will prove cruel,
If I and my William should tarry too long.'

Says William to Sally – 'Let's join and be married,'
We'll live in a cottage, contented with home,
'Let's join and be married,' replies the young shepherd,
'Let's join and be married, with our sheep all on.'

Now this couple are married and are united,
They live in a cottage down by the sea,
Where they're never dejected, but always respected,
And always a-striving each other to please.

Part 16, Number 11, 29 January 1916

Cecil Sharp had heard this from Charles Tanner in September 1909, when he sang four stanzas, with some garbling. Williams's manuscript is heavily edited and added to in red ink, as was his practice when preparing a song for publication. The original entry in blue-black ink is similar to Sharp's stanzas one, three, and four, along with the final verse in which the couple are married. His edited version adds stanza two (though it is not identical to that noted by Sharp) and makes some modifications to the other stanzas. There is no indication as to where he obtained this additional material.

The song does not appear to have been printed on broadsides, but the style suggests that it may have been written for the pleasure gardens or the theatre. George Gardiner found a version at Farnham, Surrey, and Henry Hammond noted a version from Thomas Henry at the workhouse at Yate, Gloucestershire, though the tune has been lost. Sharp also noted the song (words and tune) from Thomas Henry in April 1907.

72. At Seventeen Years I Was Young

Roud 1479, Bathe-Clissold Ox.204
Charles Tanner, Bampton, Oxfordshire

This also is of good age, is plain and simple, yet not unworthy of interest. Obtained of Charles Tanner, Bampton.

At seventeen years of age I was young,
I fixed my mind all on a pretty maid,
There's no one does know what I did undergo,
When my poor silly heart she betrayed.

Home to her father's house I did go,
Thinking to gain her as a prize;
Her hair it was like the velvet so soft,
She had a diamond in each of her eyes.

Her cheeks were like the roses so red,
That grew on yonder high tree;
Her lips were like unto cherries sweet –
What a charming creature was she!

Now I'll sit myself down and I'll cry,
To think of the sorrows I've done,
To think I was deluded and had a deluding tongue,
When I was but a boy so young.

Part 16, Number 12, 29 January 1916

This song of male teenage anguish appears to be unique to Charles Tanner. Cecil Sharp had heard it from him in September 1909, and the text he noted is essentially the same, apart from the sort of variations that a singer struggling to remember the song might introduce. Thus Sharp's version of stanza three is:

> Her cheeks were like the cherries,
> Growing on yonder tree,
> Her lips were like unto the violets so blue,
> What a charming sweet creature was she.

73. The Pretty Ploughing Boy

Roud 186, Bathe-Clissold Bk.5
Jonas Wheeler, Buscot, Berkshire
Robert Carpenter, Cerney Wick, Gloucestershire

Formerly an exceedingly popular song throughout the Thames villages. There are several versions of it with considerable variations. Of the three that I give the first was the best known as a matter of fact. I have not heard the second and third but at Highworth and Castle Eaton. Copy obtained of Jonas Wheeler, Buscot, Berkshire and Robert Carpenter of Cerney Field. Mr Carpenter gained the prize for singing this in a competition held at Kemble Flower Show in the year 1893.

> It's of a pretty ploughing boy stood gazing on his plough,
> While his horses stood underneath the shade;
> It was down in yonder grove he went whistling to his plough,
> And by chance O there he spied a pretty maid.
>
> And this was his song as he ploughed along,
> 'Pretty maid, you are of a high degree,
> And if I should fall in love, and your parents not approve,
> The next thing, they'll send me to the sea.'
>
> As soon as her aged parents came to know,
> That the ploughing boy was ploughing on the plain,
> The press gang it was sent for and they pressed him away,
> And sent him to the wars to be slain.
>
> Then herself she dressed all in her very best,
> And her pockets were well lined with gold,
> She trudged the street with tears in her eyes,
> A-searching for her jolly sailor bold.

The very first she met with was a jolly sailor –
'Have you seen my pretty ploughing boy?' she cried;
'He's just crossing the deep and sailing for the fleet,'
And he said, 'My pretty maid will you ride?'

Then she rode till she came to the ship her love was in,
And unto the captain did complain,
Said she – 'I'm come to seek the pretty ploughing boy,
That was sent unto the wars to be slain.'

A hundred bright guineas then she freely pulled out,
And so gaily she told them on the floor,
And when she had her ploughing boy in her arms again,
She hugged him till she'd got him safe ashore.

When she'd got her ploughing boy in her arms again,
Where he oft times had been before,
She set the bells to ring, and so sweetly she did sing,
When she met with the lad she did adore.

Part 17, Number 1, 5 February 1916

This was, as Williams says, a very popular song, whose simple story of the rich girl who buys her true-love back from the navy against her parents' wishes, had great appeal to ordinary country folk. The song first appeared on a slip printed by Evans of London *c.*1790, *The Pretty Plow-Boy, a New Song.* Even though impressment ended with the defeat of Napoleon in 1814, the powerful threat of the press-gang ensured that it remained a staple of British broadsides and folk songs throughout the nineteenth century.

Although Williams saw this group as being three versions of the same song, I believe that he is incorrect. 'Once I Courted a Beauty Bride' (no. 75) is a different song, and 'Pressed Off to War' (no. 74) seems to be a mixture of the two. He did not choose any of these three songs for inclusion in *FSUT.*

74. Pressed Off to War

Roud 405, Bathe-Clissold X.805
Thomas King, Castle Eaton, Wiltshire

A very old version of the 'Pretty Ploughing Boy'. Obtained of the late Thomas King, Castle Eaton. He was ninety eight years of age when he sang me the song.

As this young fellow was ploughing along,

His furrow was wide, and deep, and long,
Breaking his clats to pieces some barley for to sow,
And this was his song as he ploughed along –
'If I should fall in love, and her parents not approve,
They shall send me to the wars to be slain.'

As soon as the parents came for to know,
That he courted their daughter, and darling also,
The press-gang it was sent for and pressed him away,
And he's gone to the wars to be slain.

And when in the wars he had servéd seven years,
'Twas then he returned to find his dearest dear,
He asked her father for her, and thus he replied –
'She broke her heart in love, and for her love she died.'

'Oh, don't tell me more than I'm able to bear,
For in a silent grave I wish I was but there;
Then should I be free from all sorrow, grief and woe,
For I know not where to wander, nor where for to go.

And so in Bedlam this young man was confined,
All for the sake of a comely young maid;
With the rattling of his chains on a straw bed he was laid,
And he called for his Polly on the day that he died.

Part 17, Number 2, 5 February 1916

Although Williams presented this as a version of 'The Pretty Ploughboy' (no. 73), it does not have the happy ending that is an essential feature of that song. In this alternative unreality the young woman fails to buy him out of the navy and dies broken-hearted instead, which drives the sailor into Bedlam when he returns. In this respect it is more like the next song, 'Once I Courted a Fair Beauty Bride' (no. 75), which was sung by Thomas King's nephew, William King.

75. Once I Courted a Fair Beauty Bride

Roud 405, Bathe-Clissold Wt.346
William King, Highworth, Wiltshire

This version also originally came from Castle Eaton. I obtained it of William King, Highworth, nephew of the Thomas King mentioned above.

O once I courted a fair beauty bride,
And she was the joy and comfort of my life;
I courted her for love, it was for her love to gain,
And I'm sure she had no reason at all to complain.

As soon as her father came for to know,
That I courted his daughter, and darling also,
O then he ordered me that I should be sent to sea,
Away from my Polly and her sweet company.

O then for a soldier I was forcéd for to go,
To see whether I could forget my love or no;
But as I entered in with my sword, it shone so bright,
I could not forget her by day nor by night.

And when I returned unto my dearest dear,
O then to New Bedlam I was forced to draw near;
I asked her father for her, and he made this reply –
'She broke her heart in love, and for her love she died.'

'Don't tell me, don't tell me more than I can bear!
For if she's in a silent grave I wish I was there;
Then I should be free from all sorrow, grief, and woe,
For I know not where to wander, nor where for to go.'

O then in New Bedlam this young man was confined,
And the thoughts of his Polly ran hard in his mind;
With the rattling of his chains on a straw bed he did lie,
And he called for his Polly till the day that he died.

Part 17, Number 3, 5 February 1916

This is another song derived from a broadside produced in the seventeenth century, in this case *The Distracted Young-Man; or, The Overthrow of Two Loyal Lovers.* Pepys had a copy printed by J. Deacon of London, which has been assigned to the period 1685–88. There are only a few nineteenth-century broadsides, but one published in Liverpool in the 1820s has words similar to those sung by William King.

Although it has only been collected a few times in England, it seems to have been particularly well established in the USA. It is not, though, a variant of 'The Pretty Ploughing Boy' (no. 73), as Williams suggests.

76. The Bold Recruit

Roud 12878, Bathe-Clissold Wt.311
John Eggleton, Broad Blunsdon, Wiltshire

This song dates probably from the opening of the nineteenth century, i.e. the time of the wars on the Continent. I obtained the words of John Eggleton, Broad Blunsdon, Wilts. He is in his ninetieth year.

See these ribbons gaily streaming!
I'm a soldier now, Lizette,
And of battle I am dreaming,
And the honour I shall get;
With a bayonet by my side,
And a helmet on my brow,
And a proud steed to ride,
I shall rush through the foe.

We shall march away tomorrow,
By the breaking of the day,
When the trumpets will be sounding,
And the merry cymbals play;
But before I say goodbye,
And, alas! a parting take,
Take this ring as a proof,
And wear it for my sake.

Shame, Lizette! to still keep weeping,
While there's fame in store for me,
Think of home when I'm returning,
What a joyful day 'twill be;
When to church you're fondly led,
Like a lady, proudly drest
With a hero to be wed,
With a medal on his breast.

Cheer up, my own Lizette!
Let not grief your beauty stain!
Soon as the battle's ended,
Your recruit you'll see again;
There is not a maiden fair,
But will welcome the salute,
And will envy the gay bride,
Of a bold, young recruit.

Part 17, Number 7, 5 February 1916

This song was written by George Linley to music by Friedrich Kücken in about 1859. It seems to have been popular in Britain and North America and, as well as sheet music, appeared on a number of broadsides. Williams is the only collector to have noted it.

77. When We Are Homeward Bound

Roud 1104, Bathe-Clissold Gl.88
George Grubb, Ewen, Gloucestershire

I have seen a more lengthy version of this song in print, though the following is the whole I have obtained in the neighbourhood. The copy I noted down from Mr George Grubb, Ewen, near Cirencester.

To Blackwall Docks I will bid adieu,
To charming Kate and lovely Sue;
Our anchor's weighed, our sail's unfurled,
We're about to plough the watery world –
That's when we are homeward bound.

And when we arrive in London docks,
The pretty girls come down in flocks,
One to the other you hear them say –
'Here comes Jack with his three year's pay!'
That's when we are homeward bound.

When we get to the Dog and Bell,
They have very good liquors to sell;
In comes the landlord with a smile,
Saying – 'Drink my lads, for it's worth your while.'
That's when we are homeward bound.

But when our money's all gone and spent,
There's none to be borrowed, and none to be lent;
Then in comes the landlord with a frown,
Saying – 'Get up Jack, and let John sit down.'
That's when we are outward bound.

Part 17, Number 9, 5 February 1916

'Outward Bound' was printed in *The Apollo*, a songbook published by R. Paddock of Bath in 1794. This gives the first half of the song, though it lacks the continuation of the story told in later broadsides where Jack, having spent all his money, has to give up his place to John who has just come into port.

The location in which the song is set varies greatly, but the Dog and Bell in Deptford is also mentioned in several nineteenth-century broadsides (but not in the 1794 edition). Some versions mention the landlord as 'Old Arch' or 'Archer', and a David Archer was landlord of the Dog and Bell in the 1820s.

'Outward Bound' has been heard from singers on both sides of the Atlantic and appears in a number of collections of maritime songs.

78. I'm a Stranger in this Country

Roud 1081, Bathe-Clissold Ox.259
John Flux, Filkins, Oxfordshire

The following is in the true ballad singer's style; it dates from the early part of the nineteenth century. I obtained the words of Mr John Flux, Filkins, near Lechlade.

I'm a stranger in this country, from America I came,
There's no one who knows me, who can tell me by name;
I'm a stranger from America, I will tarry here for awhile,
And ramble for my darling for many a long mile.

Some say I am rakish, some say I am wild,
Some say I am rakish, my friends to beguile;
But to prove myself loyal you shall go along with me,
I'll take you to America my darling to see.

Give my love to Polly, she's the girl I adore,
Likewise to my Susan, although she's quite poor;
Give my love to Bessie, she's my joy and delight,
I'll often think of her on many a cold and frosty night.

Now the moon shall be in darkness, and the stars give no light,
If ever I prove false to my own heart's delight;
In the middle of the ocean there shall grow a myrtle tree,
If ever I prove false to the girl that loves me.

Now we're bound for America, the ship she has set sail,
Kind Heaven protect us with a prosperous gale!
And when we are landed we'll dance and we'll sing,
In a plentiful country, and sing God save the King.

Part 17, Number 10, 5 February 1916

This appeared on a number of broadsides at the beginning of the nineteenth century as 'American Stranger', and was heard by several other collectors. John Ord, who published an eight-stanza version, inferred that the reference to the king in the final stanza indicated that the ballad was written before the American Revolution.[30]

79. Harry the Tailor

Roud 1465, Bathe-Clissold Bk.8
Harry Bennett, Cumnor, Oxfordshire

This also is of some age. A version appears in Bell's 'Songs of the Peasantry' 1862. Our copy has two extra stanzas, and differs in a few other particulars. Obtained of Mr Harry Bennett, Cumnor, near Oxford.

When Harry the tailor was twenty years old,
He began to be gamesome with courage so bold;
He told his old mother he was not in jest,
But he must have a wife as well as the rest.
Sing fol the rol laddle dee

'Twas early one morning before it was day,
To the house of a farmer he straked away;
Where he met with Miss Dolly a-making her cheese,
And he gave her a kiss, and a very hard squeeze.
Sing fol the rol laddle dee

Now she up with a bowl and the buttermilk flew,
Which made poor Harry look wonderful blue;
Then Harry cried – 'Dolly, what hast thou done?
From the back of my britches the buttermilk does run!'
Sing fol the rol laddle dee

She gave him a push and he blundered and fell,
From the door of the dairy right into the well;
And Harry cried out, with a pitiful sound,
'Oh help me, dear Dolly, or I shall be drowned.'
Sing fol the rol laddle dee

Young Roger the ploughboy ran in amain,
And soon skipped him up in the bucket again;
Crying out – 'Roger, how cam'st thou here?'
'It was Dolly that pushed me in, I declare.'
Sing fol the rol laddle dee

[30] John Ord, *Bothy Songs and Ballads of Aberdeen, Banff, and Moray, Angus, and the Mearns* (Paisley: Alexander Gardner, 1930), pp. 127–28.

'Believe me, young Roger,' this fair maid did say,
'He came to my dairy before it was day,
And as I was making my cheese all alone,
He kissed me and hugged me, and would not be gone.'
Sing fol the rol laddle dee

Then Harry ran home like a poor drowned rat,
And told his old mother what he had been at;
'Between buttermilk bowl, and the terrible fall,
And love, and the labour, the Devil take all.'

Part 17, Number 11, 5 February 1916

Sabine Baring-Gould, who heard this in Devon, mentioned in his notes that he had seen it in Bell's *Ancient Poems, Ballads, and Songs of the Peasantry of England* and that it appeared as *The Taylor's Courtship* on a broadside by Pitts of London from *c.*1800. Cecil Sharp found it in Somerset on two occasions. Baring-Gould's informant was Harry Westaway of Belstone, Devon, and Peter Kennedy heard the song from Harry Westaway's son in the 1950s.

80. The Wild Rover

Roud 1173, Bathe-Clissold Wt.476
David Sawyer, Stratton St Margaret, Wiltshire

We have had 'Spencer the Rover' [*FSUT*, pp. 130–31]. *This song is of a different kind and lacks the poetry and human feeling of the above mentioned. There are one or two other pieces concerning rovers which we shall print in due time. Obtained of David Sawyer, formerly of Ogbourne, Marlborough, Wiltshire.*

I've been a wild rover these several years,
I've spent all my money on strong ale, wine, and beer;
But the time it will come, my boys, when we're all in good cheer,
Lest poverty happens to fall to our share.
So now I will lay up my money in store,
And never will play the wild rover no more.

I went to an ale house where I used to resort,
Said I to the landlord – 'My money runs short.'
I asked him to trust me, but his answer was, 'Nay!
Such custom as yours I can get every day.'
So now I will lay up, *etc.*

Then I pulled out my handfuls of silver straightway,
It was only to try them to hear what they'd say -
'You're welcome kind sir, in my house to the best,
What I told you before, it was only in jest.'
So now I will lay up, *etc.*

'Oh, no! my brave boys. That never can be.
I'll see them all hanged ere I'll spend a pennee.
For a man that's got money may sing and may roar,
But a man that's got none must be turned out of doors.'
So now I will lay up, *etc.*

Part 17, Number 12, 5 February 1916

The Dubliners made 'The Wild Rover' one of the most regularly performed songs of the post-war folk revival, but its ancestor is *The Goodfellow's Resolution* written by Thomas Lanfiere, printed on a broadside in the 1670s. By the beginning of the nineteenth century the song had evolved into two separate forms.[31] David Sawyer's is the less familiar form and is similar to that written into a notebook by Thomas Hardy's father in about 1820.

81. You Gentlemen that Take Delight

Roud 1868, Bathe-Clissold Wt.316
G. Giles, Blunsdon Hill, Wiltshire

This version of Bold Reynolds was sung on the neighbourhood of Cricklade: it will be seen that the allusions were made to fit in with the locality. This copy I obtained of Mr G. Giles, Blunsdon Hill, Wiltshire.

You gentlemen that take delight
In hunting bold Reynolds the fox!
All in this wild wood he makes his den,
And he lives upon fat geese and ducks.

'They've sent for the Cricklade Hounds,
The huntsman has sworn I shall die,
But I've left two young brothers behind,
That love young lambs better than I.

'I've ofttimes been hunted before,
By dogs that could run like a cow,

31 Brian Peters, 'The Well-Travelled Wild Rover', *Folk Music Journal*, 10.5 (2015), 609–36.

But in the whole course of my life,
I've never had a breathing till now.

'Through woods and through valleys I've run,
Where the blood thirsty hounds they did follow,
It made my hair stand on an end
For to hear how the huntsmen did holloa.

'I've run them for fifty long miles,
I've run it in three hours space,
My strength it begins for to fail,
But the hounds come after apace.

'I've run them beyond Simon's Shore,
Where the game keeper shot through my thigh,
Oh, pardon, dear huntsmen and hounds!
For in this wild wood I must die.

'Now all alone I am left,
But I'll crawl back home and I'll die –
They'll dip my forefeet in the glass,
And drink my lord's health in good wine.

Part 18, Number 2, 12 February 1916

The earliest known version of this song is 'The Fox', published in a chapbook called *The Court of Apollo*, *c.*1770, and on broadsides in the early part of the nineteenth century. George Giles has localized it to Cricklade, the town nearest his home. Several of the early collectors found it, though not frequently, and since a few later twentieth-century collectors also recorded it, it evidently had great staying power – like the fox it commemorates.

82. Remember, Love, Remember

Roud 2674, Bathe-Clissold Wt.464
David Sawyer, Stratton St Margaret, Wiltshire
Mary Moss, Driffield, Gloucestershire

Old, and very well known. Words obtained of David Sawyer and Mrs Moss of Driffield, near Cirencester.

'Twas ten o clock one moonlight night,
I ever shall remember,
When every twinkling star shone bright,
One frosty cold December;

'Twas at the window, rat, tat, tat,
I heard a certain well known rap,
And with it were these words so clear –
Remember ten o clock, my dear,
Remember, love, remember.'

My mother dozed before the fire,
My dad his pipe was smoking,
I dared not, for the world, retire,
Now was not that provoking?
At last the old folks fell asleep,
'Twas then my promise for to keep,
But he did my long absence note,
And on the window shutter wrote,
'Remember, love, remember.'

Oh, did I read it o'er so sweet?
Ah, yes! 'Twas marked the warning;
It said at church we were to meet,
At ten o clock next morning:
And there we met, no more to part,
To join together, hand and heart;
And since that day in wedlock joined,
The window shutter brings to mind –
'Remember, love, remember.'

Part 18, Number 3, 12 February 1916

The earliest printed copy of this song was published by Catnach in the 1820s, followed by versions from other printers. It was published in songsters such as *The Quaver* (1844), and in the same year as sheet music in the USA, set to a tune by Mozart, and arranged by W. C. Peters. Despite being printed many times on broadsides and in books, it has not been collected very often.

83. Caroline and her Young Sailor Bold

Roud 553, Bathe-Clissold Wt.392
Elijah Iles, Inglesham, Wiltshire

A very old piece. The subject is a well laboured one: a score or more songs have been written describing a similar incident. The copy I obtained of Mr Elijah Iles, Inglesham, Wiltshire.

It's of a rich nobleman's daughter,
So comely and handsome we hear,

Her father possessed a great fortune –
Full thirty five thousand a year;
He had but one only daughter,
Caroline was her name, I've been told,
One day, from her drawing room window,
She admiréd a young sailor bold.

His cheeks they appeared like two roses,
His hair was a black as the jet,
Young Caroline watched his departure,
Walked round, and young William she met;
She said, 'I'm a nobleman's daughter,
Possessed of ten thousand in gold,
I'll forsake both my father and mother,
To wed with a young sailor bold.'

Said William – 'Young lady remember,
Your parents you are bound to mind,
And on sailors there is no dependence,
When their lovers are left far behind;
I'll advise you to stay at home with your parents,
And do as by them you are told,
And never let anyone tempt you,
To wed with a young sailor bold.'

She said – 'There's no one shall persuade me,
One moment to alter my mind,
But I'll ship and proceed with my true love,
He never shall leave me behind';
Then she dressed like a gallant young sailor,
Forsook both her parents and gold;
Four years and a half on the salt seas,
She ploughed with her young sailor bold.

Three times with her love she was ship wrecked,
And always proved constant and true,
Her duty she did like a sailor,
Went aloft in her jacket so blue;
Her father he wept and lamented,
And the tears from his eyes often rolled,
When at length they arrived safe in England –
Caroline and her young sailor bold.

Then her father admitted young William,
And vowed that in sweet unity,
If his life it was spared till the morning,
Together they married should be;
They were married and Caroline's portion,
Was two hundred thousand in gold,
So now they live happy and cheerful –
Caroline and her young sailor bold.

Part 18, Number 5, February 1916

The story is a familiar one and the song was heard frequently by the Victorian and Edwardian song collectors. It was printed on many broadsides, the earliest of which was published by Catnach with the title *The Young Sailor Bold, Answer to the Gallant Hussar.* Iles's song is nearly identical to the Catnach broadside, differing only in a few words, except that the fifth stanza was not sung to Williams. For the sake of the story I will supply it here:

Caroline went straightway to her father,
In her jacket and trowsers so blue
He received her and momently fainted
When first she appeared in his view,
She cried my dear father forgive me,
Deprive me for ever of gold,
Grant me my request, I'm contented,
To wed with my young sailor bold.

A later broadside published by W. Taylor of Waterloo Road, London, gives the name of the author as John Morgan, one of the few ballad writers of whom we have some knowledge. Between 1820 and 1870 Morgan wrote numerous ballads for Catnach and others. There are some 160 surviving ballads that bear his name and he is believed to have written many more. Several of his ballads were political, attacking the Poor Law, for example, as well as royalty. He was a shadowy figure, living always on the edge of poverty, and we know that he was born in Plymouth in about 1799.[32]

84. The Sailor Boy

Roud 273, Bathe-Clissold Gl.115
John Puffet, Lechlade, Gloucestershire

This I have met with in several versions, though the variations were not great. It is old and the air is very pleasant. Obtained of John Puffet, Lechlade

Early, early all in the spring,
I went aboard to serve the King;
'Twas the Regency and the mountains high,
That parted me and my sailor boy.
'Twas the Regency, *etc.* (*repeat*)

[32] There is a good deal of information about John Morgan in James Hepburn, *A Book of Scattered Leaves: Poetry of Poverty in Broadside Ballads of Nineteenth-Century England*, 2 vols (Lewisburg: Bucknell University Press, 2000–01).

I hadn't long been sailing down on the deep,
Before five King's ships I chanced to meet:
'Come, jovial sailors, tell me true,
Does my sweet William sail among your crew?
Come, jovial sailors, *etc.*

'Ah, no! fair lady, he is not here,
He's dead and drowned, I do declare;
On yonder island that we passed by
'Twas there we lost sight of your sailor boy.
On yonder island, *etc.*

Then she wrung her hands and tore her hair,
Like some wild creature in despair:
'My little boat against the rocks does run;
How can I live now my sailor's gone?'
My little boat, *etc.*

A few weeks after this lady died,
And a letter was found by her bedside;
The reason why she lost her life,
Was because she was not the sailor's wife.
The reason why, *etc.*

'Then dig me a grave, long wide and deep,
And strew it over with lilies so sweet;
Put on my stone a turtle dove,
To show the world that I died of love.'
Put on my stone, *etc.*

Part 18, Number 6, 12 February 1916

The earliest version of this song is *The Sailing Trade*, which was published by various Glasgow and Edinburgh printers around 1800. It was frequently printed on broadsides and, later, in folk song collections, and has been collected from Victorian times up to the end of the twentieth century. The words vary widely between the different versions, whether in print or collected from singers.

The mention of 'the Regency' in John Puffet's version is unusual. Because the song was in print before the beginning of the Regency in 1810, I rather think that it is actually a corruption of 'raging sea'.

85. As I Was Taking my Evening Walk

Roud 1734, Bathe-Clissold Bk.24
Alfred Smith, Watchfield, Berkshire

A plain old piece, that was not without some popularity, however. I have heard the piece in villages far remote. Obtained of Mr Alf Smith, Watchfield, Berkshire.

As I was taking my evening walk,
I met with a pretty girl, and to her did talk;
I asked her the question – 'Are you going home?
Why, 'tis a great pity you should walk alone.'

I asked her to go to the alehouse close by,
But the answer she gave me – 'No thank you. Not I!'
'But if you will go with me we'll not there long stay,
We'll both drink together and then come away.'

Now, she being a neighbour and one that I knew,
I thought to myself – 'This never will do!'
But I gave my consent and along with her went,
And this was the occasion caused me to lament.

Now her sweetheart being coming that very same day,
All in a sad humour, as I've heard them say,
And when he came in saying – How do you do?'
She answers – 'I'm never the better for you.'

'As you found your way out you may find your way in!
And as for your coming, I don't give a pin;
I have got my freedom, you can go as you come,
I wish you Good evening, and a pleasant walk home.'

Part 18, Number 7, 12 February 1916

This song has been found only a handful of times by collectors in southern England and, it appears, nowhere else. Neither have I found it on broadsides. When Frederick Keel heard a version from George Stacey in Surrey in 1913, Anne Gilchrist said that she thought both song and air to be of Irish origin, though she offered no evidence to back her belief.[33]

[33] *Journal of the Folk-Song Society*, 6.1 (no. 21) (1918), 16.

86. The Gay Ploughboy

Roud 1639, Bathe-Clissold Wt.443
David Sawyer, Stratton St Margaret, Wiltshire
Thomas Webb, Broadwell, Oxfordshire

A popular old ploughing song that was sung both by the carters, and by the women and girls who toiled in the open fields during summer and harvest. Obtained of David Sawyer and Thomas Webb, Broadwell, Oxfordshire.

Come all you pretty ploughing boys, and listen to my song,
A story I will tell to you – it won't detain you long;
For he will rise so early O and tends his team with joy,
And gladly does his duty like a gay plough boy,
A gay plough boy.

There was a youthful damsel that lived in the grove,
Whose heart did seem contented with loyal peace and love;
Down in her father's garden O she sang sweet songs of joy,
And in her melody was praising of the gay plough boy,
The gay plough boy.

Said the mother to the daughter – 'You seem to love him well,
It seems as if your tender heart all in his bosom does dwell;
For these lads are so rakish O young maidens to decoy,
Soon you shall see upon your knee the gay plough boy,
The gay plough boy.'

Then thus replied Miss Patty – 'That is just the lad for me,
For with him I could be happy, for his heart is gay and free;
For he would rise so early O and tend his team with joy,
And boldly do his duty like the gay plough boy,
Like the gay plough boy.'

'Young William with his team was returning home from plough,
He showed me a ring of gold, my tongue could not say No.
He said – 'My pretty Patty O the parson we'll employ,
Then none will be so happy as the gay plough boy,
As the gay plough boy.'

And now they are united and William goes to plough,
And Patty rises early to milk her spotted cow;
All in a rural cottage O there's none can them annoy,
How happy is Miss Patty and her gay plough boy,
And her gay plough boy.

Part 18, Number 8, 12 Feb 1916

This was printed on broadsides as *Young Patty and her Gay Ploughboy*, but the only other collected version was heard by the Hammond brothers in Dorset.

87. The Gipsy Girl

Roud 229, Bathe-Clissold Ox.247
Henry Harvey, Cricklade, Wiltshire
Frank Cook, Burford, Oxfordshire

This song I first encountered at Longworth, Berkshire, some few years ago, where it was sung by an old man named Polebrook. After many enquiries I at length obtained the copy, part from the late Wassail Harvey of Cricklade and part from Mr Frank Cook, Burford, Oxfordshire.

O once I was a gipsy lass, but now a squire's bride,
I have servants to wait on me, and in my carriage ride;
I left my friends and parents, likewise my sisters three,
And ran and met the squire beneath the greenwood tree.

My father he was king of the gipsies, you must know,
My mother she learnt me some cant words also;
With my pack at my back, and they all wish me well,
I went up to London some fortunes there to tell.

As I was a-walking through fair London street,
This wealthy young squire I chanced all for to meet;
He viewed my brown face and he liked it so well,
He said – 'My pretty gipsy girl, my fortune you shall tell.'

'O yes, kind sir. Give me hold of your hand,
For you have got riches, both houses and land,
Beside your pretty fair maid, which I'll put all aside,
For it is this little gipsy lass that is to be your bride.'

He took me to a house, it was a palace, I am sure,
Where ladies were waiting to open the door;
They were ladies of honour and of every degree,
But none for to equal my pretty Betsee.

Now adieu to each meadow and to each shady grove!
No more shall my gipsy girl from her home rove;
But now my song is ended, I hope it will please you well,
And when I come this way again your fortune I will tell.

Part 18, Number 9, 12 February 1916

There are a number of versions of this song and broadside texts vary considerably. The earliest version is 'The Fortune Teller' published in *The New Winter's Amusement and Jolly Toper's Companion* in the 1790s. In some versions it becomes clear that the honour of the ladies in the house to which the heroine was taken is questionable. Nine months later she has a child, which is looked after by her father, while she gets £20 a year as a pension and, in some versions, actually gets to marry the squire.

88. The Rover

Roud 1112, Bathe-Clissold Wt.411
Elijah Iles, Inglesham, Wiltshire
James Shilton, Lechlade, Gloucestershire

An ancient and simple piece, that is only remembered by the most aged men. I obtained the copy of Elijah Iles, Inglesham and James Shilton, Lechlade, one of whom is ninety four, and the other ninety years of age.

I am a rover and that's well known,
I'm just a-going to leave my home,
To leave my home and my friends to mourn;
Farewell, my bonny girl, till I return.

She drew a chair, and bid me sit down,
And soon she told me her heart was won;
She drew a chair, whilst I took my leave;
Farewell my bonny girl, don't grieve.

Then I sat down and wrote a song,
I wrote it wide, and I wrote it long;
At every line I shed a tear,
And at every verse I cried – 'Polly, dear.'

'I am not married, but I am free,
And I am not bound to marry thee;
But a married life I soon will see,
For a contented mind bears no jealousy.'

As I crossed over yon dreary moor,
There I lost sight of my true love's door;
My heart did ache, my eyes were blind,
Thinking on the bonny girl I'd left behind.

'I wish, I wish, but it's all in vain,
I wish I was a maid again;
But a maid again I'll never be,
Till apples grow on an orange tree.'

Part 18, Number 10, 12 February 1916

The earliest known version of this song appeared as 'I'm a Rover' in *The Golden Songster* published in Newcastle in the period 1828–37. The order of stanzas varies in different printed editions, probably due to the fact that, though the song makes a kind of sense, they all have the character of floating verses and rearranging them makes little difference to the story, such as it is.

89. Single I'll Go to my Grave

Roud 22620, Bathe-Clissold Ox.178
William Wise, Alvescot, Oxfordshire

An old song. We have had occasion to remark of several pieces that the subject of them was well-laboured, and we may say the same of this. At the same time, it was popular and, that being the case, there is no need for us to pretend to any tediousness. For the words I am indebted to William Wise, Alvescot, Oxfordshire.

'Awake! Awake! you drowsy sleepers.
Awake! Awake! for it's almost day.
How can you sleep, love, here, any longer,
Since you have stole my heart away?'

'Begone! Begone! you'll wake my mother;
My father he will quickly hear.
Begone! Begone! and court some other,
And whisper softly in her ear.'

My father heard those lovers talking,
And quickly jumpéd out of bed;
He put his head out of the window,
And this young man he quickly fled.

'Come back! Come back! don't be called a rover,
Come back! Come back! and stay with me,
And stay until his passion's over,
Your lawful bride then I will be.'

'O daughter, dear, now I'll confine you,
Your Jimmy dear shall go to sea;
Then you can write your love a letter,
So that he can read it when far away.'

'O father dear, pay me down my fortune,
Which is five hundred pounds, you know;
Then I will cross the watery ocean,
To where the hills are covered in snow.'

'No daughter dear, I'll not pay your fortune,
Which is five hundred pounds I know;
Nor you'll not cross the watery ocean,
To where the hills are covered with snow.

'But daughter, dear, now I'll confine you,
All in your own private room.
And you shall have naught but bread and water,
But once a day – and that's at noon.'

'I want none of your bread and water,
Nor any other thing you have;

If I can't have my heart's desire,
Then single I'll go to my grave.

Part 19, Number 3, 19 February 1916

This song has had a long life and has passed through many stages of evolution. 'Song XCVII' in Allan Ramsay's *Tea-Table Miscellany* is similar to the first few stanzas of William Wise's song. It begins 'Awake, thou finest thing in nature', and the stanzas are presented as a dialogue.[34] This was reworked around 1790 as 'The Drowsy Maid', which appeared in a chapbook called *The Silk Mercer's Daughter's Garland.* Both of these versions lack the main part of the story, in which the young man is sent off to sea and the daughter demands a down payment on her inheritance so that she can go and look for him. She is not one of those heroines who throws everything up to find him, however, and when her father refuses to fund her search she resolves to live comfortably but single for the rest of her life.

Wise's text is very similar to some broadside ballads printed around 1800, usually with the title *Awake, Awake, You Drowsy Sleeper* or *The Cruel Father.* Several of the other early collectors heard the song in this form in southern England. In Scotland and the north of England there is a song 'I Drew my Ship into the Harbour' (Roud 402) that is thought to have been derived from the same source.

A version widespread in America and also called 'Drowsy Sleeper' is considered to be a separate song. It sometimes goes under the title 'The Silver Dagger', which gives a clue to the fact that the American versions usually involve the death of one or both of the lovers.

90. The Poor Old Soldier's Boy

Roud 258, Bathe-Clissold Ox.172
William Wise, Alvescot, Oxfordshire

This is a song I have heard but once. I am unable to determine its date, but it is probably as old as Waterloo. This I also obtained of William Wise, Alvescot.

The clouds were fast descending,
Aloud the wind did roar,
The poor old soldier's boy he came,
Up to a mansion door;

[34] Allan Ramsay, *The Tea-Table Miscellany; or, A Collection of Scots Sangs*, 9th edn (London: A. Millar, 1733), p. 346.

Where a lady stood at her window,
He raised his eyes with joy,
Saying – 'Lady, gay, take pity, I pray!
On a poor old soldier's boy.'
    On a poor old soldier's boy,
    On a poor old soldier's boy,
    Saying – 'Lady, gay, take pity, I pray!
    On a poor old soldier's boy.'

'My mother died when I was young,
My father went to the wars,
On the battlefield he violently fell,
All shattered with wounds and scars;
But many a mile on his knapsack,
He carried me with joy,
So, lady, gay, take pity, I pray!
On a poor old soldier's boy.
    On a poor old soldier's boy, *etc.*

'All through the streets I wandered,
I oft heave many a sigh,
To see children run to their parents,
But no home or parents have I;
When hunger grows upon my heart,
I sit me down and cry;
So, lady gay, take pity, I pray!
On a poor old soldier's boy.
    On a poor old soldier's boy, *etc.*

'For the clouds are fast descending,
And the night is coming on,
Without you are befriending,
I shall perish before the morn;
Then O, I know it would break your heart,
And grieve your peace of mind,
To find we laid on the doorstep dead – [*me*]
The poor old soldier's boy.
    The poor old soldier's boy, *etc.*

Now the lady rose from her window,
She opened her mansion door,
'Come in,' she said, 'Misfortune's child,
You shall never wander more;
My son fell on the battlefield,
He was my only joy,
Now, whilst I live, O shelter I'll give,
To the poor old soldier's boy.'
    To the poor old soldier's boy, *etc.*

Part 19, Number 4, 19 February 1916

This appallingly sentimental song tells of the plight of just one of the many indigent orphans who plagued the consciences of Victorian ladies. Others were 'The Fisherman's Boy,' 'The Fisherman's Girl', 'The Poor Smuggler's Boy,' and, most popular of all, 'The Farmer's Boy'. This group of songs appeared early in the century, before Queen Victoria took the throne. The earliest known version of this one is a broadside titled *The Soldier's Boy* printed by Catnach, before 1832. Sabine Baring-Gould, who collected it in Devon in 1885, had eight different editions in his broadside collection.

91. Bonny Old England O

Roud 12879, Bathe-Clissold Ox.232
James Faulkner, Brize Norton, Oxfordshire

This is not a recent song. I thought when I first heard it that it might have originated during the agricultural disturbances fomented by the well known agitator, Joseph Arch, in the middle of the last century. As a matter of fact the piece is much older than that. My informant, who is nearly eighty years of age, told me that his father sang it as long ago as he could remember. From the phraseology I think it must date, at least, from the opening of the nineteenth century. Obtained of James Falconer, Brize Norton, near Witney.

Down by a crystal fountain, as I alone one morn did stray,
The Shamrock, Thistle and Rose unto each other they did say –
'Alterations must take place, for Britain seems in grief and woe,
Such times were never seen before in the land called Bonny Old England O.'

In former times my father said the times were different far from now,
The taxes were not half so high, the poor man kept a pig and cow;
His family was neat and clean, and cheerfully along did go,
Distress by few was seldom felt in the land called Bonny Old England O.

When Queen Elizabeth ruled the land she passed a law to feed the poor,
The people no occasion had to beg their bread from door to door;
Employment everyone could find, and cheerful to his labour go,
Now they've passed a law to starve the poor in Bonny Old England O.

The farmer's wives to market go upon the horse and promenade,
Their dress is linsey woolsey fine their clothing is so fine displayed;
Silk gowns with parasols and veils, and scented too, with musk they go,
And a fine blood horse to ride upon; what change in Bonny Old England O.

Come Britons! cheer your courage up, and let us hope the time will mend,
We're well aware it's almost time oppression should be at an end;
If men were for their labour paid, and rates and taxes both were low,
That would be the time to live and sing in the land called Bonny Old England O.

Part 19, Number 6, 19 February 1916

This appears to be the only instance of this song to have been heard by a collector, though there are broadsides from a number of printers from the middle of the nineteenth century. This type of ballad, harking back to the days of 'Good Queen Bess', was common at that time and there are many similar songs that take the farmer to task for parading his wealth while starving his workers.[35]

92. Down in the North Country

Roud 582, Bathe-Clissold Ox.233
James Faulkner, Brize Norton, Wiltshire

This also was told me by James Falconer, of Brize Norton. It is undoubtedly of good age. The piece is uncommon: I have not heard it elsewhere. Brize Norton has been famous for its singing in times past: few villages in the Thames Valley could surpass it either in the number or the quality of its singers. I unfortunately arrived on the scene too late by at least ten years to save the best of the Brize Norton songs.

Down in the North Country there lived a young couple,
A man and a maid so gallant and gay,
They long time were courting, but nothing of marriage,
Till at length this young maid to her lover did say –
'Come tell me plain, what is it you mean?
For from courting I'm very resolved for to marry,
Or else from your company I will refrain.'

'I must needs confess I do love you dearly,
For you are the joy of my heart's delight,
But when a man's wed his joys are all fled,
Freed from all liberty, bound down to slavery,
I cannot wed you. I wish you goodnight.'
She languished and laid, there came a brisk blade,
He stepped up to her, thinking for to woo her,
And he was a carpenter's son by his trade.

She wrote her old true love a charming, sweet letter,
For him to come on the nineteenth of June,
For him to do, instead of a better,
To wait at the table all on the bridegroom;
When these lines he read, it made his heart bleed –

[35] For further examples, see James Hepburn, *A Book of Scattered Leaves: Poetry of Poverty in Broadside Ballads of Nineteenth-Century England*, 2 vols (Lewisburg: Bucknell University Press, 2000–01).

'For the thoughts of my Polly drive me melancholy,
But now I have foolishly lost her indeed.'

He saddled his grey mare, and made down to the station,
Thinking to meet with his own true love there,
Then she came down, in her proper motion,
And from his bright eyes shed many a tear –
'If I had so soon thought you'd be so soon lost,
I had no longer tarried, but with you had married;
And now I have foolishly lost you indeed.'

Part 19, Number 7, 19 February 1916

In 1969 John Baldwin toured the Upper Thames area looking for descendants of Williams's singers and traces of the songs he had heard. He met Freda Palmer at Witney, not far from Brize Norton, and recorded her singing a slightly fuller version of this song.[36] The only other instance of the song found in England was a version heard in Dorset by the Hammond brothers, but it was found more widely in Scotland and North America.

John Ord had a version that he called 'The Tardy Wooer', which he described as 'a real bothy song, and a matter of thirty years ago it was a great favourite in the North of Scotland, and as it has been frequently asked for recently in the weekly newspapers it must be a favourite among a section of the community'.[37]

93. Creeping Jane

Roud 1012, Bathe-Clissold Wt.439
Thomas King, Castle Eaton, Wiltshire
David Sawyer, Stratton St Margaret, Wiltshire

Though this piece was once fairly well known I could only obtain the copy in parts, and with great difficulty. I first heard it at Castle Eaton. Old Thomas King, who was nearly a hundred, told me several verses: in time I obtained the remainder of David Sawyer, the sheep shearer. Creeping Jane was evidently the unexpected winner of a popular race, as the song itself testifies. There are one or two other old songs in the locality which I hope to obtain by and by.

---

[36] John R. Baldwin 'Song in the Upper Thames Valley: 1966–1969', *Folk Music Journal*, 1.5 (1969), 315–49 (pp. 328–30).

[37] John Ord, *Bothy Songs and Ballads of Aberdeen, Banff, and Moray, Angus, and the Mearns* (Paisley: Alexander Gardner, 1930), pp. 83–84.

I once had a mare, and a very pretty one,
Her name it was Creeping Jane,
She never ran a race with a horse or a mare,
That she valued one single pin.
    Fol rol the day, fol rol the rido,
    That she valued one single pin.

When Creeping Jane to the starting post she came,
She looked as lean as a hound,
And the people did say within themselves –
'She'll never run over the ground.'
    Fol rol the day, *etc.*

When she came to the first mile post
Creeping Jane was a-lingering behind.
The jockey clapped his whip to her little light neck,
And he said – 'My little lady, never mind.'
    Fol rol the day, *etc.*

And when she came to the second mile post,
The jockey began to take heart.
He cracked his whip to her little right side,
And she passed by them all like a dart.
    Fol rol the day, *etc.*

Now Creeping Jane has won this race,
And she scarcely sweat one drop,
She's able to gallop the ground over now,
While the others can scarcely trot.
    Fol rol the day, *etc.*

Now Creeping Jane is dead and gone,
She's lying in the cold hard ground;
I'll go straightway to my father's cot,
And beg her little body from the hounds.
    Fol rol the day, *etc.*

Part 19, Number 8, 19 February 1916

Notably sung in a competition at Brigg, Lincolnshire, in April 1905 by the fine singer Joseph Taylor, to whom the judges, including Percy Grainger, awarded the first prize. The song was heard by several of the early collectors and was printed on a number of broadsides in the early nineteenth century. There has been a lot of speculation about its origins and one of the stronger claims is for a horse named Yorkshire Jenny which raced successfully between 1762 and 1766. Her history and a version of a song similar to this one appeared in the *Sporting Magazine* in November 1831. It may, though, have been an adaptation of an existing song.

94. Prop of the Land

Roud 1254, Bathe-Clissold Gl.155
Robert Godwin, Southrop, Gloucestershire

Again we hear the voice of the poor, complaining of hard times, poverty, and lack of sympathy on the part of their betters and employers. The 'prop of the land' is a very good expression and there is optimism and good nature at the end of the piece. The song is old. I obtained the copy of Robert Godwin, Southrop.

The prop of the land is the hard working man,
His health let us pledge in a glass!
And they who say No, it will very soon show,
They don't belong to the working class.

Why should the rich man despise us, the poor,
When we toil for them hard, night and day?
The time it will come when the rich man will go,
By the side of the poor man he must lay.

Death lays low, ay! low, great and small,
If life was a thing we could buy,
The rich man would live – what thousands he would give!
While a poor man he might die.

A poor man is happy while he has work to do,
If the rich man only to him give
A fair day's pay for a hard day's toil:
His motto to live and let live.

Those rich grinding knives will have us poor slaves,
And take from the poor man what he earns;
To hear them boast how they carry every course!
And the poor man they treat like a worm.

The prop of the land is the hard working man,
His health let us pledge in a glass!
And they who say No, it will very soon show,
They don't belong to the working class.

Toast:

Here's luck to the swan that crosses yonder brook!
Here's luck to the house of industry!
Here's luck to every poor man's wife
That drinks health to her country!
If life was a thing that money could buy,
The rich would live and the poor might die.
Here's oceans of wine, rivers of beer,
A nice little wife, and ten thousand a year!

Part 19, Number 11, 19 February 1916

Considering that it has the makings of a socialist anthem, this song is very rare. There is just one broadside edition, from the London printer Henry Such in the second half of the nineteenth century, with the title *Here's a Health to the Hard Working Man.* The only other collected version was heard in Canada by Edith Fowke, from LaRena Clark of Ottawa in 1964.

95. The Rich Gentleman's Daughter

Roud 1651, Bathe-Clissold Gl.156
Sarah Godwin, Southrop, Gloucestershire

This is one of the old sort, by which I mean it is really in the common ballad singer's style. I have heard of it twice, i.e. at South Marston and Southrop, where I obtained the words complete of Miss Sarah Godwin.

It's of a rich gentleman in London did dwell,
He had a young daughter a farmer loved so well;
His parents being so cruel, and to him severe,
They sent him to a foreign land for seven long years.

He had not been gone but a month and one day
When he wrote a letter and sent it away;
An answer came back with haste and great speed,
Saying – 'My love, I will come to you, wherever you may be.'

As one was going up and the other coming down,
The damsel being a-tired she sat herself down;
And with her deep sighing her tender heart did break,
So she died for her true love, her true lover's sake.

Now when that young man got to his journey's end,
He called for a bottle to drink with a friend;
They asked of that young man, that which was sent abroad,
And told him of the poor girl that died on the road.

As soon as he heard the news he desired the corpse for to see,
As soon as he saw her he said, 'It is for me;
For me and me only, the only love I have;
Let me and my true love lie both in one grave.'

So all that long night, and part of the next day,
He kissed her cold cheeks, much colder than clay;
And with a deep sighing his tender heart did break,
So he died for his true love, his true lover's sake.

Come all you cruel parents, wherever you may be,
You should never part lovers, as lovers parted were we;
For what we have suffered, this world shall never know,
What I and my true love we both have been through.

Part 19, Number 12, 19 February 1916

This song was heard by seven other collectors in southern England, sometimes under the title 'The Shopkeeper' or 'In Rochester City'. Although it may appear to be a Victorian melodrama, it is a descendant of a ballad of the mid-eighteenth century called *The Two Loyal Lovers of Exeter.* It has been substantially reduced in length while retaining the basic plot and some original phrases.

96. Joe the Marine

Roud 1681, Bathe-Clissold Ox.172
William Flux, Alvescot, Oxfordshire

A very old and a very good song. I first heard of it at Blunsdon, where an old man who sang it bore the nickname, 'Joe the Marine' till his death some twenty years ago. I finally obtained the song at Alvescot, Oxfordshire, of William Flux, platelayer.

Now Joe the Marine was in Portsmouth well known,
No lad in that corps dressed so smart;
The lasses never looked on the youth with a frown,
But his manliness won every heart.
Sweet Polly of Portsmouth he took for his bride,
And surely there never was seen;
A couple so gay march to church, side by side,
As Polly and Joe the Marine.

The bright torch of Hymen was cast in a blaze,
And thundering loud guns did rattle;
And Joe, in an instant, was forced to the seas,
For to give the proud enemy battle;
The action was dreadful, each ship a mere wreck;
Such slaughter few soldiers had seen;
Two hundred brave fellows lay strewn on the deck,
And amongst them was Joe the Marine.

Now Victory, faithful to Britain's sailors.
At length put an end to the fight,
Then homeward they steered, full of glory and scars,

And soon had fond Portsmouth in sight;
The rampart was crowded the heroes to greet,
And, furthermost Polly was seen;
The very first sailor she chanced for to meet,
Told the fate of poor Joe the Marine.

Now the shock was severe as lightning's bright dart,
Her poor breast with frenzy was fired;
She flew from the crowd, softly cries – My poor heart!'
Clasped her hands, fainted, sighed and expired;
Now her body was laid 'neath the wide spreading yew,
And on a smooth stone may be seen –
'One tear let drop, all you lovers so true,
For Polly and Joe the Marine.'

Part 20, Number 1, 26 February 1916

This sentimental piece was written and composed by John Ashley in 1812, and subsequently appeared several times on broadsides. George Gardiner was the only other one of the early collectors to have heard it. Much later, Mike Yates recorded Mabs Hall singing it in Sussex in 1985.

97. The Old Woman of Hyslop Town

Roud 183, Bathe-Clissold Wt.417
George Keen, Kingsdown, Stratton St Margaret, Wiltshire

I have no less than four versions of this song. Below are two [see also 'Johnny Sands' (no. 98)]*, which I expect will be sufficient for the average reader. They are 'satirical', and, though not the best of pieces, appear to have been popular. As a rule such songs were brought in for the want of something better; or the singer fitted his piece to the mood of his audience, and introduced a variety to create 'diversion'. Obtained of George Keen, Kingsdown, near Stratton St. Margaret.*

There was an old woman of Hyslop Town,
The truth to you I'll tell,
She loved her husband dearly,
But another twice as well.
With my iddi fol i dol,
Iddi fol I dee.

Then she went to the doctor's,
All for to ease her mind,

For him to put her in the way,
To make her husband blind.
With my iddi fol i dol, *etc.*

'You get a store of cake and wine,
And brandy that is good,
And give it to the old man,
To nourish up his blood.
With my iddi fol i dol, *etc.*

'You get a store of marrowbones,
And beat them very small,
And then he will go stark blind,
And will not see at all.'
With my iddi fol i dol, etc.

As they were walking hand in hand,
Down by the river's brim,
All the old woman's intention was,
To push the old man in.
With my iddi fol i dol, *etc.*

The old woman ran with vengeance,
To push her husband in,
The old man stepped his foot aside,
And she went tumbling in.
With my iddi fol i dol, *etc.*

She how she roused and toused about,
And aloud for help did call,
The old man says – 'I am stark blind,
And I cannot see at all.'
With my iddi fol i dol, *etc.*

Then he being tender hearted,
For fear that she would swim,
Went straight and got a long pole,
And pushed her further in.
With my iddi fol i dol, *etc.*

Then the old man he went grumping home,
So happy in his mind -
'Ha, Ha!' says he, 'I'm heartily glad,
I've left the old woman behind.'
With my iddi fol i dol, *etc.*

Part 20, Number 3, 26 February 1916

This song was widely sung on both sides of the Atlantic, though the place where the event is supposed to have occurred varies. It is found on broadsides from the early 1800s. In some versions the man pretends to have lost his sight and asks his murderous wife to assist his suicide. Williams's observations about the place of a song like this in a singing session provide a valuable insight.

98. Johnny Sands

Roud 184, Bathe-Clissold Gl.99
James Collins, Lechlade, Gloucestershire

Johnny Sands is the Gloucestershire version of the above. This I obtained of James Collins, Lechlade.

A man, whose name was Johnny Sands,
Had married Betty Haig;
Although she brought him gold and lands,
She proved a terrible plague.

For Oh, she was a scolding wife,
Full of caprice and whim;
He said that he was tired of life,
And she was tired of him.

Says he – 'Then I will drown myself,
The river runs below.'
Says she – 'Pray do, you silly elf,
I wished it long ago.'

Says he – 'Upon the brink I'll stand,
Do you run down the hill,
And push me in with all your might.'
Says she – 'My love, I will.'

'For fear that I should courage lack,
And try to save my life,
Pray, tie my hands behind my back.'
'I will.' replied his wife.

She tied them fast as you may think,
And when securely done,
'Now stand,' said she, 'upon the brink,
And I'll prepare to run.'

All down the hill his loving wife,
Then ran, with all her force,
To push him in, he steps aside,
And she slipped in of course.

Now splashing, dashing like a fish –
Oh, save me Johnny Sands.'
'I can't, my dear, how much I wish,
For you have tied my hands.'

Part 20, Number 4, 26 February 1916

'Johnny Sands' was written by the singer John Sinclair in the 1840s and took its plot from the previous song, 'The Old Woman of Hyslop Town' (no. 97), though the mechanics of the murder were changed. Sinclair's song appeared on broadsides and was widely collected, like its predecessor, on both sides of the Atlantic. Its popularity was such that he wrote a sequel, 'Betty Sands', in which the wife returns and the couple make up their quarrels. This, however, did not prove as popular.

99. Thomas and Nancy

Roud 3232, Bathe-Clissold Ox.199
Shadrach Haydon, Bampton, Oxfordshire

An old coast song, that was formerly popular around Faringdon and Stanford in the Vale, Berkshire. The copy I obtained of Shadrach Haydon, the aged shepherd of Lyford and Hatford, Berkshire.

The boatswain's shrill whistle had sounded,
When young Thomas and Nancy must part;
The heart in her bosom high bounded,
The tears from her blue eyes did start.

'O Nancy, my dear, I must leave you,
The signal for sailing is made;
Our parting dear, let it not grieve you,
Nor, that I should prove false, be afraid.'

The vessel floats swift o'er the billow,
Like a sea-bird she breasted the foam;
Young Thomas then lay on his pillow,
Thought of Nancy, his parents, and home.

He prest to his lips his love's token,
And vowed to be constant and true;
He thought of the words she had spoken –
'Be constant, dear Thomas, adieu!'

The storm rose and loud pealed the thunder,
And the lightning flashed over the wave;
Till a rock dashed the vessel asunder,
And the crew found a watery grave.

To the beach then poor Nancy she hurried,
And beheld a most pitiful scene;
The corpse of young Thomas was carried,
To the spot where so happy they'd been.

Then she kissed his cold lips in her sorrow,
And her tears showed the depths of her grief;
And, ere the sun set on the morrow,
Death gave to poor Nancy relief.

Near the shade of the willow that's weeping,
Beside an old church in the vale;
In one grave these fond lovers lie sleeping,
Where sorrow nor care can assail.

And maidens, now they are departed,
Bring flowers to deck the cold grave;
For Nancy was fond and true hearted,
And young Thomas, her lover, was brave.

Part 20, Number 5, 26 February 1916

Thomas and Nancy appeared as a broadside printed by Catnach in the early part of the nineteenth century, the first of several printers to issue it. Shadrach Haydon's version has compressed the story. Alfred Williams seems to have been the only one of the early collectors to have heard the song in Britain, though it has been found several times in Newfoundland. The broadsides give the tune as 'The Gallant Hussar'.

100. Roger

Roud 1592, Bathe-Clissold Gl.64
Charles Messenger, Cerney Wick, Gloucestershire

A plain old ditty that used to be sung at Latton and Down Ampney. Both these villages were once famed for music and Morris dancing, and were full of choice old songs which have disappeared now however. Obtained of Charles Messenger, Cerney Wick.

Down in our village lived a parson and his wife,
They lived a very happy and comfortable life;
They kept a servant man and a maid as close as close could be,
But she only wanted Roger, and Roger wanted she.

The parson was an old man and he had done amiss,
He took her in the corner and asked her for a kiss;
But she answered him quite plain, as plain as plain could be,
She only wanted Roger, and Roger wanted she.

With love and work together this maid was taken ill,
The doctor soon was sent for to try his very best skill,
But she would not take his physic, though bad as bad could be,
She only wanted Roger, and Roger wanted she.

The doctor soon found out 'twas love that made her bad,
He very quickly said to her – 'You'd better take the lad.'
The thoughts of him soon made her as well as well could be,
Then, married, she had young Roger, and Roger he had she.

Part 20, Number 6, 26 February 1916

This song was printed with six stanzas in *Comic Songs* by Thomas Hudson in 1824. It is assumed that Hudson wrote the song. In 1912 Dorothy Marshall heard Bessie Knight of Minsted, Sussex, sing it, the only other instance of it having been collected. It was printed in the third volume of *The Universal Songster* in 1826 and was included by W. H. Long in his 1886 book *A Dictionary of the Isle of Wight Dialect.*

101. The London 'Prentice Boy

Roud 1501, Bathe-Clissold Gl.87
George Grubb, Ewen, Gloucestershire

The apprentice boy figures in several songs in our collection. The pieces are all rather dull and formal. They belonged to the commoner type of folk ballad, and were profusely distributed on broadsides. Obtained of George Grubb of Ewen, near Cirencester.

Come, all you wild young chaps, who live both far and near,
And listen with attention to these few lines you'll hear;
I once at ease did ramble till one did me destroy,
And sent unto Van Diemen's Land was the London 'prentice boy.

'Twas on the fourteenth of July a girl to me did say –
'Keep up your heart, from me depart, your master for to slay,'
A knife she gave me in my hand my master to destroy,
Till I said – 'No, that I'll not do, I'm a London 'prentice boy.'

She scorned and said – 'Begone from me. You know what you have done,
If gold you do not bring me, your race will soon be run.
Go boldly on! I'll shelter thee, if him you will destroy,
So take this knife, and end his life, you London 'prentice boy."

It was the hour of twelve at night, I to my master went,
All for to rob and murder him it was my full intent;
I took one hundred sovereigns, and the knife I threw away,
He was a master good and kind to the London 'prentice boy.

Then I returned with utmost speed unto my flashy dame,
The money I could show to her, she soon received the same;
Then I was sent to prison which did my hopes destroy,
All battered in a lonesome cell was this London 'prentice boy.

And when my trial it came on my heart was filled with woe,
The girl that I had long maintained she proved my bitter foe;
She was dressed in silks and satins, and sore she did annoy,
She tried to swear away the life of the London 'prentice boy.

My sister came to speak to me, she's the only friend I have.
All my parents are dead and gone, and lying in the grave;
Sentence was passed on me, which caused the court to cry –
'Twas the scornful dame that caused the same to this London 'prentice boy.

Part 20, Number 7, 26 February 1916

Although it was printed on several broadsides from the early part of the nineteenth century, this song does not seem to have been a favourite of many singers and Williams was the only one of the early collectors to have heard it. In the early 1970s a much shortened and slightly garbled version was recorded by Keith Summers from two Suffolk singers, Bob Scarce and Dick Woolnough.

George Grubb's version is very close to the broadsides, except that he did not sing the last two stanzas which round off the story of the unfortunate apprentice:

Then I was sent across the sea, likewise 300 more,
Some did sing, and some did cry, their hearts were griev'd full sore,
Our governor he did notice me, and gave me slight employ,
But still I think on happy days when a London prentice boy.

Come all you wild young people and take advice from me,
And never while you live keep bad company
I have a situation, which few that's here enjoy,
But ne'er again can free remain like a London prentice boy.

102. He's as Good as Gold

Roud 17008, Bathe-Clissold Wt.338
Miss E. King, Castle Eaton, Wiltshire

Perhaps not of great age, I cannot determine its date. At the same time it possesses the ordinary qualities of the folk song and I am induced to believe it should be reckoned of that order. Communicated by Miss King, Castle Eaton.

My true love is a shepherd lad,
A shepherdess am I,
We watch our flocks from morn till eve
Beneath the bright blue sky;
There's nothing troubles me, although
My fortune soon is told;
My calling poor in worldly wealth –
He's just as good as gold.
  He's just as good as gold, he is,
  He's just as good as gold;
  For I can see he's fond of me,
  And that's as good as gold.

His coat is somewhat worse for wear,
And is not trimmed with lace,
His hat would scarcely do for some
More fashionable place;
But what care I although he wear
A ragged suit so old!

His heart is in its proper place,
And that's as good as gold.
He's just as good as gold, *etc.*

He's going to build a little house,
And make a garden gay,
Soon as creation's ship comes back –
They say it's on its way;
Although a little house would do
To keep out rain and cold,
To me 'twill be a palace grand –
He's just as good as gold.
He's just as good as gold, *etc.*

He's going to take me to the church,
One happy day in spring,
When hedges will be white with may,
And the village bells will ring;
The sound will linger in our ears,
When we are both grown old,
And oh how happy we shall be!
For he's just as good as gold.
He's just as good as gold, *etc.*

Part 20, Number 8, 26 February 1916

This pretty song is 'As Good as Gold' written by Frank Green and Alfred Lee about 1870. Although unnoticed by the other early collectors, Fred Hamer heard it in Bedford sometime between 1950 and 1969. It was published in the USA as sheet music in 1871 and John Quincy Wolf recorded it from Emma Medlin of Arkansas in 1960.

103. The Wiltshire Labourers

Roud 21218, Bathe-Clissold Wt.521
Alfred Howse, Latton, Wiltshire

Here we have a song written by a rustic, evidently by a local leader at the time of the agricultural disturbances of the middle of the last century. It is, in reality, little more than a catalogue of place names, connected with an exhortation to the workers to stand out for better wages and conditions. It is, at the same time, of some interest, and I think it abundantly supports me in what I have said concerning the folk songs, i.e. that they could not have emanated from the illiterate population of the countryside. Words obtained from an old ballad sheet given to me by Alfred Howse, Latton.

Come all you gallant labourers, and listen to my song,
It's concerning of the labouring class, 'twill not detain you long;
Who, nobly standing out, my boys, for wages that is fair,
In Fovant, and in Codford, and Barford, in Wiltshire.
So here's to every labouring man who nobly stood their ground,
And by their roguish masters never will be trampled down.

In Stratford, and in Woodford, and Newton, true and bold,
In Durnford, and in Lake, my boys, as I've been lately told,
In Amesbury, and Durrington, and Bulford, brave and true,
In Netheravon they're inclined to bring their Masters to.
So here's to every labouring man, *etc.*

In Bourton, and in Liddington, Lydiard and Minety too,
In Wanborough, and Hinton, like gallant soldiers true,
Stand up you lads of Chippenham, and Lacock, one and all!
Recollect the time is coming when your Masters they must fall.
So here's to every labouring man, *etc.*

How can a man maintain a wife and poor young children too,
In Barwick or in Bishopstone? It's more than he can do
On six or seven shillings a week; it's starving by degrees,
But the time will come when every son of Wiltshire shall be freed.
So here's to every labouring man, *etc.*

In peace and quietness, my boys, in Ramsbury they intend,
In Overton, and Clatford, the gallant labouring men;
In Fifield, and Marlboro', and Lockeridge of fame,
They'll stand out for their wages from Swindon up to Calne.
So here's to every labouring man, *etc.*

May God protect the Ogbourne lads, for they are true and bold!
At Highworth, and in Cricklade they are worth their weight in gold:
The sons of Wootton Basset, and of Sutton, as you see,
Are like the lads of Malmesbury, who're determined to be free.
So here's to every labouring man, *etc.*

Here's to Cherhill, and Long Compton, and Hilmarton not behind,
In Lyneham, and in Clack, my boys, as we shall quickly find,
In Purton, and in Stratton, and Wroughton, as we hear,
They'll stand true to each other from Warminster to Mere.
So here's to every labouring man, *etc.*

Now in Bishop's Cannings, and in Potterne, it is said,
They'll do a fair day's labour for a fair day's wages paid,
Each labouring man shall get his rights, and that's before it's long,
Fair play's a jewel any day. How can you say it's wrong?
So here's to every labouring man, *etc.*

Part 20, Number 9, 26 February 1916

This song is unique to Williams's collection and I have not found a trace of it elsewhere, even though he reports that he had it in print on a broadside. He is probably correct in his assertion that it is from the period of unrest in agriculture in the nineteenth century. Farm wages in Wiltshire were low, even by the appalling level paid generally in England at that time. Farm labourers in Wiltshire were some of the most active in the Swing Riots which, in November 1830, resulted in 339 men, the largest number in any English county, being tried by a Special Commission. Though fifty-two death sentences were handed down, only one man was executed. A total of 152 labourers were transported to Australia.[38] This is one of the very few 'political' songs in Williams's collection. It was probably sung to one of the tunes used for 'Come All You Worthy Christians'.

104. There Is a Tavern in the Town

Roud 60, Bathe Clissold Wt.497
Lucy Lee, South Marston, Wiltshire

There is another song with this title, and which still enjoys some popularity: it is to be met with in modern song books and collections of 'Camp Songs'. There is no doubt but that this is the original version. The air is sweet, and well suits the words of the song. I remember hearing it sung at the first harvest-home I attended at South Marston, when I was eight years of age. Words obtained of Mrs George Lee, South Marston, Wilts.

There is a tavern in yonder town,
Where my young man is sitting down;
He takes another girl on his knee,
And don't you think it's a grief to me?

A grief to me, I'll tell you for why,
Because she has got more gold than I;
Her gold will fade, her beauty will die,
And she'll become a poor girl like I.

Her father came home, one stormy night,
And asked him for his daughter bright;
He went upstairs and opened the door,
And saw her hanging from a cord.

[38] Eric Hobsbawm and George Rudé, *Captain Swing* (London: Readers Union, 1970), pp. 308–09.

He took a knife and cut her down,
And in her bosom a note he found;
And on this note these words were wrote –
'My sweetheart knows that my heart is broke.

Dig me a grave, so long and deep,
And bury me under the lilies so sweet;
Put on my grave a turtle dove,
To show the world that I died in love.'

Part 20, Number 10, 26 February 1916

'There is a Tavern in Yonder Town' is part of a family of songs that have been derived from eighteenth-century originals and share themes and stanzas. Their long and complicated ancestry has proved difficult to unravel. The songs are, for convenience, grouped together under the title 'Died for Love' (Roud 60). The common theme is that of the young woman betrayed by a rakish lover, though his betrayal comes in many forms. It is tempting to think of this group of songs as a collection of stanzas that can be pulled out of a hat and placed in order. The most constant feature is the final 'Dig me a grave' stanza.[39]

The 'There is a tavern in yonder town' stanza that opens Lucy Lee's song is another that is found in a majority of the versions in this family. Songs from the 'Died for Love' group can be found in the collections of all of the Victorian and Edwardian collectors and also those working later in the twentieth century. Another example, 'When I Wore my Apron Low' appears below as no. 200.

The other song that Williams refers to in his headnote shares the title 'There is a Tavern in the Town' (Roud 18834) but was written in the latter part of the nineteenth century by William H. Hill, with an inappropriately jaunty tune and a 'Fare thee well for I must leave thee' chorus. Hill's song used the first and last stanzas of 'There is a Tavern in the Town'.

---

[39] For a picture of the complexity of the evolution of this song, see the listing at Bluegrass Messengers http://bluegrassmessengers.com/7-died-for-love-brisk-young-sailorrambling-boy.aspx.

105. The Emigrant Ship

Roud 21201, Bathe-Clissold Gl.86
George Grubb, Ewen, Gloucestershire

This, as the words of the song itself imply was written upon the loss of an emigrant ship bound for New Zealand, in the earlier part of the last century. I have heard it but once, i.e. at Ewen near Cirencester, where it is remembered by George Grubb, shepherd.

Beneath the rude and restless wave
Many brave men have found their grave;
This gallant ship, when tempest tost,
At length went down, with all hands lost.

This emigrant ship – how sad to hear!
Five hundred souls were lost with fear;
They left behind them old England's ground,
To New Zealand they were bound.

This gallant ship, which fate deplored,
Had near five hundred souls on board;
That was a dreadful death to meet –
A burning ship beneath your feet.

When fire and water both combined,
The raging flames and roaring wind;
It seized upon the doomèd ship,
When fear stood on each trembling lip.

There men and women, of a hardy crew,
One hundred and sixty children too;
The ship was burnt upon the sea,
And launched them into eternity.

Many a mother you know was there,
Whose heart was broken with despair;
God only knows what it is to be,
In an open boat ten days at sea.

Part 20, Number 105, 26 February 1916

This harrowing song was inspired by the sinking of the *Cospatrick* in November 1874. She was a sailing ship bound from Gravesend to Auckland, under charter from the New Zealand government. She was carrying a crew of forty-five, plus 433 passengers, most of whom were emigrants. She caught fire off the Cape of Good Hope and all were lost apart from the second mate and two of the crew. The ship was carrying 30 tons of coal and 27,000 litres of spirits and the cause of the fire was either spontaneous combustion or the result of a member of the crew or a passenger trying to tap some of the spirits with a naked light. It is still regarded as New Zealand's worst maritime disaster. Several broadsides about the sinking were printed but this text is not derived from any of those I have seen. Williams is the only collector to have heard the song.

106. The Milking Pail

Roud 114, Bathe-Clissold Wt.324
Daniel Morgan, Braydon, Wiltshire

This version of the above ['The Old Farmer and his Young Wife', *FSUT*, pp. 188–90] *was the most widely disseminated. The words of this I first obtained of Daniel Morgan, Braydon, Wiltshire.*

My husband he came late one night, home late, home late to me,
He looked into the stable, and a strange horse there did see;
'Whose horse is this? Whose horse is this? Or whose horse can it be?'
'Surely that's a milking cow my mother sent to me.'
'It's many a mile I've travelled, then thousand miles or more,
But a saddle on a milking cow, I never saw before.'

My husband he came late one night, home late, home late to me,
He looked into the kitchen, and a strange hat there did see;
'Whose hat is this? Whose hat is this? Or whose hat can it be?'
'Surely that's a milking pail my mother sent to me.'
'It's many a mile I've travelled, ten thousand miles or more,
But brims upon a milking pail, I never saw before.'

My husband he came late one night, home late, home late to me,
He looked into the kitchen, and a strange coat there did see;
'Whose coat is this? Whose coat is this? Or whose coat can it be?'
'Surely that is a blanket my mother sent to me.'
'It's many a mile I've travelled, then thousand miles or more,
But a buttons on a blanket, I never saw before.'

My husband he came late one night, home late, home late to me,
He looked into the kitchen, and strange boots there did see;
'Whose boots are these? Whose boots are these? Or whose boots can they be?'
'Surely they are two flowers pots mother sent to me.'
'It's many a mile I've travelled, then thousand miles or more,
But spurs upon a flower pot, I never saw before.'

My husband he came late one night, home late, home late to me,
He looked into the kitchen, and a strange whip there did see;
'Whose whip is this? Whose whip is this? Or whose whip can it be?'
'Surely that is a poker my mother sent to me.'

'It's many a mile I've travelled, then thousand miles or more,
But a lash upon a poker, I never saw before.'

My husband he came late one night, home late, home late to me,
He looked into the chamber, and a strange face there did see;
'Whose face is this? Whose face is this? Or whose face can it be?'
'Surely it is a new born babe my mother sent to me.'
'It's many a mile I've travelled, then thousand miles or more,
But whiskers on a new born babe, I never saw before.'

Part 21, Number 2, 4 March 1916

Another extraordinarily popular song the humour of which has struck a chord with the folk since the eighteenth century when it appeared on several broadside ballads. The song is usually known as 'Our Goodman' and the earliest known publication is *The Merry Cuckold and his Kind Wife*, published as a broadside by Dicey of London in the mid-century. It was a very popular song throughout Britain and was heard by most collectors from Victorian times through to the end of the twentieth century. The durability of its appeal is demonstrated by its having spent seventeen weeks in the UK pop charts in 1967, with the help of The Dubliners, who called their version 'Seven Drunken Nights'.

107. The Buxom Blade

Roud 7, Bathe-Clissold Ox.305
Alice Rowles, Witney, Oxfordshire

This song was formerly popular in and around Marston Meysey, where it was sung by an old carter named W. Barrett, of whose daughter, Mrs Rowles, Bridge Street, Witney, I obtained the copy.

In London there lived a buxom blade,
A jolly butcher all by his trade;
He fell in love with some damsel bright,
And he loved her dearly,
He loved her dearly as he loved his life.

With her silvery finery on one day,
She dressed herself in man's array;
With a sword and pistol hung by her side,
To meet her true love,
To meet her true love, she did ride.

And when she met him all on the plain,
She boldly bid him for to stand;
'Stand and deliver, kind sir,' she said,
'Or else this moment,
Or else this moment, your life I'll have.'

Then he delivered his gold in store,
She cried aloud – 'Sir, there's one thing more!
There's a diamond ring which I saw you wear,
Deliver it,
Deliver it, and your life I'll spare.'

'This diamond ring was a token given,
And I'll keep it too, if my life I lose.'
She being tender hearted, like a dove,
She rode away,
She rode away from her true love.

The very next day they both were seen,
Walking together in the garden green;
Seeing his watch hanging by her side,
It made him blush,
It made him blush like any rose.

'What makes you blush, you foolish thing?
'Twas I that wanted your diamond ring.
'Twas I that robbed you all on the plain;
So take your watch love,
So take your watch, and your gold again.

'The reason of my doing so,
Was to see whether you were a man or no;
But now I have a contented mind;
My heart and all,
My heart and all and my love is thine.'

Part 21, Number 6, 4 March 1916

This song is very similar to a broadside printed by Henry Disley of London in the third quarter of the nineteenth century. He called it *Sylvia's Request and William's Denial.* A version of the song had appeared under the title of the 'The Female Highwayman' in a Belfast chapbook in 1764. The heroine is usually named as Sylvia, or Sylvie. In some versions she makes it clear, in a final stanza, that if he had given her the ring she would have shot him.

The opening stanza here, introducing the butcher, seems disconnected from the rest of the song and most versions start with the young woman rather than the man she loves. It does, however, appear in the Disley broadside, and was also sung by Albert Doe for George Gardiner in Hampshire in 1909. It is conceivable that Alice Rowles and Albert Doe both got the song from the Disley broadside, either directly or indirectly.

108. The Maid and the Magpie

Roud 1532, Bathe Clissold Bk.3
Charles Hambridge, Buscot, Berkshire

A pleasant song, which I have heard in several quarters of the Vale. The copy I obtained of Charles Hambridge, Buscot, Berks.

There once was a maid kept an old magpie,
And the parson that prayed lived very close by;
Her lover was a sailor, and he sailed across the main,
She promised she would be his bride when he returned again,
But still she let the parson see her home from church,
Kissing, never thinking of the magpie on the perch.
  So the maid and the magpie would talk all the day.
  The maid would believe what the magpie did say –
  'But still I love the parson, but don't you tell the tar.'
  And the old magpie only said, 'Quaw, quaw.'

While stationed at Gibraltar the sailor, as it seems,
While sleeping in his cosy bunk had very funny dreams;
Then he took his passage homeward, as quickly as could be,
He landed safely at her house but no maiden could he see;
He then went to the magpie who was dancing on the perch,
So the magpie told him all about the parson at the church.
  So the maid and the magpie, *etc.*

Now when he met the maiden he passed her with disdain,
So she sued for breach of promise, five hundred to obtain;
He brought the magpie into court, who told a truthful tale,
And to get what she required the maiden did fail.
Then they went for the parson and in vain for him did search,
For when he heard about it he vanished from the church;
The lawyer couldn't find him, so the case went on the shelf,
And that pretty little maiden had to dwell by herself.
  So the maid and the magpie, *etc.*

Now the maiden and the magpie never talk all the day,
For that jolly little sailor took the knowing bird away;
And now, with all his shipmates, the jolly hearted tar,
  Will tell the truthful tale, while the magpie laughs – 'Quaw, Quaw.'

Part 21, Number 7, 4 March 1916

Written in 1879 by W. H. Phillips, this song was familiar enough to inspire a parody, 'The Maid and the Dustman'. It was heard by a few collectors in the second half of the twentieth century, notably from Cyril Poacher in Suffolk, and the Australian song collector John Meredith heard it from a shearer, Jack 'Hoopiron' Lee, in 1965.

109. Aaron's Lovely Home

Roud 1427, Bathe-Clissold Wt.349
Henry Harvey, Cricklade, Wiltshire

A general favourite, commonly sung by both sexes, which is the highest proof of a song's popularity. The tune was pleasant and perhaps this had something to do with its success among the villages. The title, probably should be 'Erin's lovely home', since this song deals with the 'Emerald Isle', though since I have heard it so often, and every singer of it says 'Aaron' I have kept to that rendering. The copy I obtained of the late Wassail Harvey of Cricklade.

When I was young and in my prime –
My age was twenty one,
Then I became a servant
Unto a gentleman;
I served him true and honest,
And that it is well known,
Till cruelly they banished me
From Aaron's lovely home.

'Twas in her father's garden,
All in the month of June,
His daughter she came to me,
In youth and beauty's bloom;
She says – 'My dearest William,
If along with me you'll roam,
I will not grieve for those I leave,
At Aaron's lovely home.'

'Twas on that night I gave consent,
Which proved my overthrow,
To leave her father's garden
And with the maid to go;
The moon was shining bright and fair,
From the garden we did roam,
And we thought that we had got safe away
From Aaron's lovely home.

But to my great misfortune,
As you shall quickly hear,
In two or three days after,
Her father did appear;
They marched me off to Warwick gaol,
In the county of Tyrone,
And there I was transported
From Aaron's lovely home.

The prison van came to the gate,
To take us all away,
My true love she came up to me,
And unto me did say -
'Cheer up your heart, be not dismayed,
For you I'll ne'er disown,
So do not grieve for those you leave,
In Aaron's lovely home.'

When I received my sentence,
It grieved my heart full sore,
But leaving my own true love then
It grieved me ten times more;
There are seven strong links all in this chain,
And seven years must I roam,
With the iron band upon my hand
From Aaron's lovely home.

Adieu unto old England,
For the space of seven long years,
And those I leave behind me,
Are wailing in their tears;
And if ever once I do return,
I never more will roam,
But bid adieu to all my friends
At Aaron's lovely home.

Part 21, Number 8, 4 March 1916

This tale of the consequences of parental disapproval and the trials of young love touched a chord with rural singers around the English-speaking world. The song is properly 'Erin's Lovely Home' and the change to 'Aaron' is either a mishearing by Williams of what Harvey sang, or else the change was made at an earlier point in the song's transmission. For a singer with a rural accent it would have been hard to recognize the difference between 'Erin' and 'Aaron' without foreknowledge of the song. Sabine Baring-Gould similarly noted the title of the song that he heard in Devon as 'Aaron's Lovely Home', but later corrected it. *Erin's Lovely Home* appeared on broadsides in the middle of the nineteenth century.

110. If You Will Walk with Me

Roud 573, Bathe-Clissold Wt.401
Elijah Iles, Inglesham, Wiltshire

For this copy I am indebted to Elijah Iles of Inglesham. Inglesham is but two and a half miles from Highworth, and it is singular the two versions should have been current side by side without the two singers knowing of the differences. I have many examples of the same kind of coincidence however.[40]

'Madam, I will give you a fine silver bell,
To ring unto your servants when you are not well,
If you will walk with me.'

'I will not accept of your fine silver bell,
To ring unto my servants when I am not well,
For never will I walk with thee.'

'Madam, I will send you a fine golden ball,
To toss and to tumble up against the wall,
If you will walk with me.'

'I will not accept of your fine golden ball,
To toss and to tumble up against the wall,
Nor never will I walk with thee.'

'Madam, I will give you the keys of my heart,
To lock us together that we never more shall part,
If you will walk with me.'

'O, I will accept of the keys of your heart,
To lock us together that we never more shall part,
And for ever I will walk with thee.'

Part 22, Number 2, 11 March 1916

This was another very popular song, with a number of different formats and a wide variety of gifts, which has been collected numerous times on both sides of the Atlantic. It does not seem to have been attractive to broadside printers, however. It was sometimes performed as a dialogue. The earliest version found so far is in the Crawfurd manuscript from 1826. Some versions add a postscript in which the singer reproves the woman for her venality, such as the example heard by Sabine Baring-Gould from John Woodridge in Devon:

---

[40] Here Williams is referring to the version he had given immediately before this one, 'If Thou Wilt Walk with Me' from Edmund Jefferies of Highworth, which he published in *FSUT*, pp. 81–82. He had also given a version from Mrs Russell of Tetbury in *Part 3*, which was published in *FSUT*, pp. 80–81.

When you might, you would not
Now you will, you shall not
So fare you well, my dark eyed Sue.[41]

111. Around the Grove as I Was Walking

Roud 218, Bathe-Clissold Gl.158
Mrs Russell, Tetbury, Gloucestershire

It will be noticed that many of the old songs began with the idea of someone overhearing another relating his or her misfortunes and sorrow. It is very naive though the scheme is not inartistic. Tedious, perhaps, it may appear now and then; but we must remember the nature of the materials we are dealing with, and not lose sight of the simplicity of those who sang the pieces. Copy obtained of Mrs Russell, Tetbury.

Around the grove as I was walking,
And in the fields, where all was green,
'Twas there I heard two damsels talking,
Which made the small birds whistle and sing.

He said – 'My dear, shall I enjoin you?
And for ever I'll prove true.
I hope a raging will destroy me,
If ever I should prove false to you.'

'Although my name it is Maria,
I am a girl of high degree;
He courted me both late and early,
Until he had his will of me.'

Although this fair and lovely creature,
She was invited to a ball,
Her jealous young man soon followed after,
It was to prove her overthrow.

He caught her dancing with another,
When jealousy fulfilled his mind;
And to destroy his own true lover,
This jealous young man he felt inclined.

A dose of poison he provided,
Mixed it with a glass of wine;

[41] Baring-Gould included the song 'Blue Muslin' as no. 22 in the first part of his *Songs and Ballads of the West* (1889).

He gave it to his own true lover,
She drank it up with a cheerful mind.

And when she had no sooner drank it –
'Pray, take me home, my dear,' said she;
'The glass of liquor you just gave me,
Has made me ill as ill can be.'

As they were walking home together,
This wicked young man unto her did say –
'I gave you poison all in your liquor,
To take your tender life away.'

'And I have drunk the same, my dearest,
I am as ill, as ill as thee' –
All in each other's arms they died,
Young girls, be aware of jealousy.

Part 22, Number 7, 11 March 1916

This tragic love story was printed by Catnach and others in the early nineteenth century, usually with the title *Oxford City* and, almost invariably, with the first line 'It's of a fair maid in Oxford City'. It was collected frequently in England and the tale was clearly popular with rural singers.

The opening conversation of Mrs Russell's version does not appear in any of the broadside versions that I have seen. It does, however, occur in a few West Country versions, though it is usually two lovers who are talking, and the young woman is named as 'Maria'. In the version collected by the Hammond brothers from Mrs Perry in Dorset there is a stanza:

Oh! When he had gained his will and pleasure
Oh! How he did laugh and scorn
And never again did I see that young man
Before my precious babe was born.

The story then goes on with the young man seeing her 'dancing with some other' and continues in the normal pattern. The fact that this version, which usually includes 'Grove' in its title, was found more than once suggests that there was another well-established song, which might have appeared on a locally printed, and so far undiscovered, broadside.

112. 'Twas Near Fleet-Street

Roud 218, Bathe-Clissold Bk.12
Elizabeth Bond, Faringdon, Berkshire

A second version of the above ['Around the Grove as I Was Walking']. *This was given me by a very dear and motherly old woman, named Bond, considerably over eighty years of age, living at Faringdon, Berkshire.*

'Twas near Fleet-Street, it was reported,
A fair young maiden there did dwell;
And by some servantman she was courted,
Who lovéd her exceeding well.

'Twas near that place there was some dancing,
When she unto the ball did go;
And this young man soon followed after,
All for to prove her overthrow.

He saw her dancing with some other,
Then he proved jealous in his mind;
And, to destroy his own true lover,
He gave her poison in a glass of wine.

She drank the poison, never thinking,
'Pray take me home, my dear,' said she -
'The glass of wine that you have given me
Makes me as ill as ill can be.'

He said – 'My dear, I've drunk another,
I am as ill as ill as thee;
Now in each other's arms we'll die together' –
So all young men never jealous be.

Part 22, Number 8, 11 March 1916

This is another version of 'The Oxford Tragedy' and is more closely related to the broadside versions since the young man is identified as a servant.

113. The Chain of Gold

Roud 1417, Bathe-Clissold Ox.206
Charles Tanner, Bampton, Oxfordshire

One of the songs of Charles Tanner, the old Morris dancer of Bampton, of whom we have already several times written. It is one of the original type of folk ballads of such as survive in the most remote villages.

Abroad as I was walking in the fields all alone,
I heard two lovers talking, telling tender tales of love;
They proved to be constant, and, forever to behold,
Before this couple parted they broke a chain of gold.

And when this chain was broken, all around her neck it twined;
Up stepped her aged father, who ofttimes walked behind:
And he flew in such a passion with his daughter and her swain,
And he swore by all who made them they would never meet again.

'For I'll send him to some Turkish seas, there for to roam,
He shall never come a-courting thee, nor to old England return;
And it's madam I'll confine thee to a closet in thy room,
I'll feed thee on bread and water once a day, and that's at noon.'

'I want none of thy bread and water, nor nothing will I take,
Since my true love has died for me, I'll perish for his sake:'
Friends and neighbours fell a-weeping, but her life they could not save,
And now she lies a-sleeping in yonder shady grave.

Part 22, Number 11, 11 March 1916

Another example of tragic jealousy on the part of a father who would rather see his daughter dead than married. The earliest known version of this song is *The Famous Town of Nottingham*, published by an unnamed London printer around 1800. Cecil Sharp also heard Charles Tanner sing the song in 1909, a few years before Williams, and he found another version in Cambridgeshire. A few other collectors, notably George Butterworth, collected it in southern England. In Australia it was collected from two singers as 'The Maid of Fainey'.

114. The Carpenter's Boy

Roud 971, Bathe-Clissold Gl.103
John Pillinger, Down Ampney, Gloucestershire

A very simple ditty. Words of John Pillinger, formerly of Lechlade.

It's of a carpenter's boy coming home from his work,
He hailed a most beautiful maid;
'O Betsy, love,' said he, 'Come sit down by me,
I'll tell you what I dreamed of last night.'

'Your dreams are no more than is fated, I know'.
'I dreamt, love, I was lying by your side,
And now I am going to fetch up the cows,
Which are down in the meadows below.'

They both went together to fetch up the cows,
Which were down in the meadows so green;
And what they said there, I'll leave you to guess,
He told her the contents of his dream.

He says – 'My dearest Betsy, yonder is a church across these fields,
Not scarcely now half a mile it seems;'
This couple they got married, and so happy they may be;
They often tell the tale of their dreams.

Part 22, Number 14, 11 March 1916

The earliest known version of this song is *The Stone Cutter Bold* published in Sheffield *c.*1840. Most other versions have the young man as a bricklayer and the issue is what they did 'down in the meadows so green', rather than what was said. A broadside version runs:

And what we did amiss, I shall leave you for to guess
For she wanted the contents of his dream.

In the version that Cecil Sharp heard from William Stokes at Chew Stoke this became 'And she *had* the contents of my dream' – but he never published it.

115. The Shannon Side

Roud 1453, Bathe-Clissold Wt.467
David Sawyer, Stratton St Margaret, Wiltshire

Evidently of Irish origin. I am not sure whether the English songs were as popular in the 'Emerald Isle', though doubtless they were so: many of the Irish were certainly highly acceptable to the villages on this side of St. George's Channel. Obtained of David Sawyer, Ogbourne and Bishopstone, Wilts.

As I walked out one morning,
To view the fields with pride,
I saw a comely damsel,
Down by the Shannon side.

I seemed to take no notice,
But still steered on my way,
Until she cried, with all her might,
And bid me for to stay.

Saying – 'Fifty guineas in bright gold O,
My father he will provide,
And fifty acres of bright land,
Down by the Shannon side.'

I said – 'My pretty, fair maid,
I love your offer well,
But I'm engaged already,
The truth I now will tell.

'There is some other fair damsel,
She'd wish to be my bride,
She's a wealthy grazier's daughter,
Down by the Shannon side.'

Part 22, Number 15, 11 March 1916

The ancestor of this song was *Captain Thunderbolt's Intrigue* published in 1799. The song was subsequently printed many times as *The Shannon Side*, but with wide variations in the text. It was collected throughout England and some versions have been found in Ireland and across the Atlantic.

David Sawyer's version has lost most of the original story. In *Captain Thunderbolt's Intrigue* we learn that the reason he tried to skulk past without her noticing was that they had met six months earlier and she was pregnant as a result. When asked his name (for the child's sake) he tells her that he is Captain Thunderbolt and that he lives with his gang on the mountain nearby. Most versions end with the customary warning against trusting young men.

116. The Rioting Blade

Roud 21216, Bathe-Clissold Wt.465
David Sawyer, Stratton St Margaret, Wiltshire

Most, if not all, the old the execution songs are about identical in style and sentiment, and repentance is always expressed in the last stanza or so. We wonder what they would have been like if they had actually been penned by the culprit? The difference in the point of view would have been striking no doubt. Obtained of David Sawyer.

Good people, pay attention to my unhappy lot,
I once was a good fellow, I loved my pipe and pot,
How I did rant and roar,
Till I'd spent all my store!
When I'd spent all I had I then could spend no more.

My wife a few relations had, and money they did raise,
They begged me both night and day to leave my wicked ways,
But being all in vain,
I turnéd back again,
Thieving, roaring, drinking, swearing, and so I did remain.

Now hanged I must be all on this gallows tree;
You married men and bachelors, a warning take by me.

Part 22, Number 16, 11 March 1916

This is a fragment of a longer song, *The Rakish Husband*, which appeared on broadsides in two different forms. In a version published by Pitts before 1819 it is given as a very long rhyming text which is not broken up into stanzas. The protagonist describes in detail how he managed to waste a fortune of £10,000, and tells of his appalling behaviour towards his wife and others with no more than a hint of remorse. A later version, published by Batchelar of London reduces the catalogue of bad behaviour to eight stanzas. Neither version, however, suggests that his behaviour resulted in his being hanged. It seems that the song was not heard by any other collectors.

117. The Indian Lass

Roud 2326, Bathe-Clissold Wt.502
Edwin Warren, South Marston, Wiltshire
Thomas Webb, Broadwell, Oxfordshire

An old ballad, one of those which originally emanated from seaport towns. I see Mr Frank Kidson has a copy in his 'Traditional Tunes' which was obtained in Yorkshire. I first heard of the song at South Marston and, later, at Broadwell, Oxfordshire. Words of Edwin Warren, South Marston and Thomas Webb, Broadwell, Oxfordshire.

As I was a-walking down by the seashore,
I called at an alehouse to spend half an hour,
And I sat drinking and taking my glass,
By chance there came in a young Indian lass.

This lovely young Indian, as you shall soon hear,
With her features of beauty none with her could compare;
She was tall and she was handsome, her age was sixteen,
She was born and brought up in a place near Orleans.

She came and sat by me, and squeezed my hand,
She says – 'You're a stranger, not one of this land.'
She says – 'I'll find lodgings, if with me you'll stay,
You shall have my portion without more delay.'

With a jug of good liquor she welcomed me in,
Now she says, – 'You are welcome to have anything,
And, besides, if you'll stay with me, never more to roam,
I know you're a stranger, and far from your home.'

Now the time being appointed for William to leave,
To leave this sweet damsel, the ocean to breathe;
She pulled out her handkerchief and wiped her bright eye –
'Oh, don't go and leave me, dear William,' she cried.

It was early the next morning we were going to set sail,
To cross the rolling ocean, boys, and leave her a while;
She says – 'When you are over in your own native land,
Remember the young Indian that squeezed your hand.'

We hoisted our anchor and away then we flew,
And a sweet pleasant breeze soon parted me from her view;
But now I am over, and taking my glass,
Here is a good health to the young Indian lass.

Part 23, Number 7, 18 March 1916

This male fantasy was first published on a broadside by Catnach at the beginning of the nineteenth century and was subsequently heard by many of the early collectors. It also made its way to eastern Canada, where it was called 'The Gallant Brigantine' and featured a young Spanish woman who was equally accommodating.

118. The Bold Privateer

Roud 1000, Bathe-Clissold Wt.501
Edwin Warren, South Marston, Wiltshire

This, too, figures in 'Traditional Tunes' by Mr Frank Kidson. Here it was a favourite song of Mr Warren's father, who was a thatcher, a very intelligent villager, and a fine singer. A few hours before the old man's death, a neighbour told him that he could not sing 'The Indian Lass' and, to the surprise of the those at hand, he sat up in his bed and sang it through perfectly, in a good tone of voice. He died the same night. Words obtained of Edwin Warren, South Marston.

It's farewell to my Polly, dear, since you and I must part!
In crossing of the wide seas, I'll pledge to you my heart;
Our ship she does lie waiting, it's farewell to my dear,
For I'm just a-going on board a bold privateer.

She says – 'My dearest Jimmy, I pray you to forbear,
And do not leave your Polly so deeply in despair;
I'd advise you stay at home with your true lover dear,
And not venture your life aboard a bold privateer.'

You know, my dearest Polly, your friends do me dislike,
Besides you have two brothers that have sworn to take my life;
It's from them I must wander, myself all to get clear,
So I am just a-going on board a bold privateer.

And when the war is over, if we do save our lives,
It's then we will return to our sweethearts and wives;
It's then I will get married to thee, my Polly dear,
And bid adieu for ever to the bold privateer.

Part 23, Number 8, 18 March 1916

The Bold Privateer was published on broadsides by Catnach and others in the early nineteenth century and is virtually identical to the text collected by Williams. That is also true of most versions heard by the Victorian and Edwardian collectors and of versions discovered in North America.

There is a different song, sometimes called 'The Bold Privateer', but often simply 'The Privateer', to which the same Roud number has been assigned. This I believe to have been derived from a broadside, *George and Nancy's*

Parting, published by Burbage and Stretton of Nottingham between 1791 and 1807. This has a first line 'Our anchor's a tript, and our ship's under way', but has many phrases in common with the Catnach version, though it refers to a man-of-war rather than a privateer. A later broadside, by Walker of Norwich, titled *The Bold Privateer*, similarly begins 'Our anchor is a peak my love, our ship is under way'. The only instance of this second version being collected in the field is that heard by the Rev. John Broadwood in Sussex *c.*1840.[42]

The true progenitor of the song that travelled through Britain and beyond to feature in the repertoire of so many rural singers was, I believe, the broadside published by Catnach. That the theme was successful is suggested by the fact that Catnach later published another broadside called *The New Privateer.*

119. Peggy in her Low-Backed Car

Roud 6954, Bathe-Clissold Wt.505
Edwin Warren, South Marston, Wiltshire

The old thatcher's wife, Martha, was also a good singer. Her chief favourites were 'The Outlandish Knight' and the following. This is of Irish origin, though it is old. Mrs Warren was over eighty when she died; her death took place about three years ago. Words obtained of her son, Edwin Warren.

When first I saw sweet Peggy,
'Twas on a market day,
In a low-backed car she used to ride,
Upon a truss of hay;
But when that hay was blooming grass,
And decked with flowers of spring,
No flower was there that could compare,
With the charming girl I sing.
As she sat in the low-backed car,
The man at the turnpike bar,
Never asked for the toll,
But just rubbed his old poll,
And looked after the low backed car.

Sweet Peggy round her car, sir,
Has strings of ducks and geese,

[42] John Broadwood, *Old English Songs, as Now Sung by the Peasantry of the Weald of Surrey and Sussex* (London: Balls, for private circulation, [1847]).

But the scores of hearts she slaughters,
By far out-number these;
While she among her poultry sits,
Just like a turtle dove,
Well worth the gage, I do engage,
Of the fair young god of love.
    While she sits in the low backed car,
    The lovers come near and far,
    And envy the chicken,
    That Peggy is picking,
    As she sits in the low backed car.

Oh, I'd rather own that car, sir,
With Peggy by my side,
Than a coach and four, and gold galore,
And a lady for my bride;
For the lady would sit forninst of me
On a cushion made with taste,
While Peggy would sit beside me,
With my arm around her waist.
    While we drove in the low backed car,
    To be married by Father Mahar,
    Oh, my heart would beat high,
    At her glance and her sigh,
    Though it beat in the low backed car.

Part 23, Number 8, 18 March 1916

'The Low Back'd Car' was written by the Irish songwriter Samuel Lover, *c.*1846. It appeared on several broadsides. The folk song collectors seem to have ignored it, apart from Williams and Clive Carey. The words recorded by Williams are remarkably faithful to Lover's original text, though his stanza two is omitted.

120. An Old Brass Locket

Roud 12888, Bathe-Clissold Wt.500
Albert Spackman, South Marston, Wiltshire

I cannot vouch for the age of the piece, though I am told it is an old folk song. It came from the neighbourhood of Didcot, Berkshire; at least that is where my informant learned the song some fifteen years ago. Words obtained of Albert Spackman, South Marston, Wiltshire.

While strolling by the margin of the sad sea waves,
Listening to the howling of those heartless waves;
Thinking of those souls at sea;
How they all might envy me –
As I paused and pondered on those storm-tossed ships,
With a prayer of mercy on my trembling lips;
Presently a billow cast upon the shore,
An old brass locket of one who is no more.
    It's an old brass locket washed up by the wave,
    It's an old brass locket from a sailor's grave;
    Inside there's a portrait, stained by ocean's foam,
    Of a sweetheart who is waiting in the distant home.

Twined round that portrait is a golden tress,
Hidden by sweet memories of happiness;
Truth and beauty here we trace,
In the maiden's fair young face;
Maybe she is waiting for him, day by day,
Little does she dream his soul has passed away;
But I will keep that locket, brazen stained and old,
As a precious emblem of love, unsoiled by gold.

Part 23, Number 10, 18 March 1916

This sentimental song was written by Harry Dacre in 1894. Dacre was a prolific songwriter who claimed to have sold over six hundred songs in the first two years of his writing career. His greatest hit was 'Daisy Bell' ('A Bicycle Made For Two'). Alfred Williams is the only folk song collector to have reported having heard this song.

121. It's Forty Long Miles I've Travelled this Day

Roud 608, Bathe-Clissold Wt.452
David Sawyer, Stratton St Margaret, Wiltshire

An old favourite, versions of which have been obtained – with variations, necessarily – in several parts of England, North and South. First copy obtained of David Sawyer, Ogbourne, Wiltshire.

It's forty long miles I've travelled this day,
And I saw a small cot by the way,
I never had seen before,
I never had seen before.

Then I stepped up and knocked at the door,
And a sweet pretty maid stepped over the floor,
And aloud she cried – 'Who's there?'
And aloud she cried – 'Who's there?'

'Why, it rains and it blows, it hails and snows,
And I shall be wet through all my clothes,
I pray love, let me in!
I pray love, let me in!'

'My daddy and mammy are fast asleep,
And my brother's away keeping his sheep,
So I dare not let you in,
So I dare not let you in.'

I turned my back round to go,
Some kind affection she did show,
She called me back again,
She called me back again.

Then she came out and let me in,
And I kissed her rosy cheeks and chin,
And I kissed them over again,
And I kissed them over again.

Part 23, Number 11, 18 March 1916

This song has been heard a number of times by collectors, with titles like 'Forty Long Miles' or 'The Cottage on the Hill'. Frank Kidson included three versions of it in *Traditional Tunes,* saying, 'I have never seen the words in print or elsewhere'.[43] He seems to be correct, as there is no printed version that matches this story, although there are broadsides for other night-visiting songs dating from the seventeenth century.

When I first encountered this song, I was sceptical about the distance said to have been travelled, but I later learned that forty miles was considered a normal day's walk for a journeyman moving between workplaces. The 'necessary variations' that Williams mentions relate, of course, to the activities that follow the young man's admission to the house.

[43] Frank Kidson (ed.), *Traditional Tunes: A Collection of Ballad Airs* (Oxford: Chas. Taphouse & Son, 1891), pp. 58–59.

122. Upon a Pleasant Hill I Stood

Roud 608, Bathe-Clissold Ox.237
William Faulkner, Taynton, Oxfordshire

This version of the above I obtained of William Falconer, Taynton, near Burford, and formerly of Brize Norton.

Upon a pleasant hill I stood,
A cottage in the vale I viewed,
Where I had never been,
Where I had never been.

I went up to that cottage door,
A pretty maid stepped over the floor,
And aloud she cried – 'Who's there?'
And aloud she cried – 'Who's there?'

It rained, it blowed, it hailed, it snowed,
And I was wet through all my clothes,
So I called to be let in,
So I called to be let in.

'Oh no, kind sir! That never can be,
There's no one in the house but me,
So I dare not let you in,
So I dare not let you in.'

When fond compassion touched her so,
She could no longer see me go,
So she called me back again,
So she called me back again.

We spent that night in sweet content,
And next morning to the church we went,
For I made her my lawful bride,
For I made her my lawful bride.

Part 23, Number 12, 18 March 1916

Another version of the same night-visiting song. Here, as in several of the other collected versions, the couple regularize matters by marrying the very next day.

123. All Through the Beer

Roud 475, Bathe-Clissold Ox.287
Ernest Adams, Shilton, Oxfordshire

An old song, though not a particularly inspiring one. Nevertheless, in spite of the poet's poverty, he could be optimistic, though I fear such optimism was rather feigned than real. This I discovered at Shilton near Burford, which was once famed for its song, though the old life has decayed now. Words obtained of Ernest Adams, shepherd, Shilton.

This old hat, this blessed old hat,
This old hat has seen better weather;
For the brim is wearing out,
And the crown is knocked about,
And my hair is poking through for better weather.
All through the beer, the jolly, jolly beer,
All through the beer and tobacco;
It was there I spent my tin,
With the lasses drinking gin,
Now across the briny ocean I must wander.

This old coat, this blessed old coat,
This old coat has seen better weather;
For the front is wearing out,
And the back is knocked about,
And my elbows are poking through for better weather.
All through the beer, *etc.*

These old trousers, these blessed old trousers,
These old trousers have seen better weather;
For the front is wearing out
And the behind is knocked about,
And my knees are poking through for better weather.
All through the beer, *etc.*

These old boots, these blessed old boots,
These old boots have seen better weather;
For the tops are wearing out,
And the soles are knocked about,
And my toes are poking through for better weather.
All through the beer, *etc.*

Part 23, Number 13, 18 March 1916

Williams published another version of this song in *Part 43* of this series with the title 'Good Brown Ale and Tobacco', which was included in *FSUT* (p. 296). In Allan Ramsay's *Tea-Table Miscellany* is a song called 'If E'er I Do Well, 'Tis a Wonder', which has been reworked many times over the years, though it does not seem ever to have appeared on broadsides.[44] It survives in the present day as 'All for my Grog'.

In the 1960s when John Baldwin was searching the Upper Thames area for remnants of the songs heard by Alfred Williams he heard 'All Through the Drunk' from Alfred Cobb of South Cerney.[45] Alf Cobb's father had been a member of the Sapperton mummers and this was one of the songs associated with their play. Alf himself provided the text of the play as he remembered it to Reginald Tiddy in 1914 and again to James Madison Carpenter in the 1930s.

124. Canada-i-O

Roud 309, Bathe-Clissold Wt.437
David Sawyer, Stratton St Margaret, Wiltshire
Henry Leach, Eynesham, Oxfordshire

This song has also given me some trouble, I had the first part of it at Stratton St. Margaret, and a little at Latton, and had almost given up hopes of completing the piece when I happened to stumble upon the remainder at Eynesham, near Oxford. The two halves suggest a slight difference of versions. The piece is as I received it. Obtained of David Sawyer, Ogbourne and Henry Leach, Eynesham, Oxfordshire.

It's of a young sea captain, who courted a lady fair,
He courted this fair lady all in her tender years,
But how to go to sea with him, I sure she did not know,
Yet she longed to see the pretty place, called Canada-i-o.

She dressed herself up like a duke, with a star upon her breast,
And swore she'd kill the captain, if he did her molest;
Just as the ship was sailing, she came down to the shore,
And said she'd see the pretty place called Canada-i-o.

Our officer stood, with cap in hand, a noble duke to see,
Expecting he was coming there commander for to be;
When she got into the ship, she saw her own true love there,
She quickly steppéd up to him and whispered in his ear.

---

[44] Allan Ramsay, *The Tea-Table Miscellany; or, A Collection of Choice Songs, Scots and English*, 10th edn (London: A. Millar, and J. Hodges, 1740), pp. 357–59.

[45] John R. Baldwin 'Song in the Upper Thames Valley, 1966–1969', *Folk Music Journal*, 1.5 (1969), 315–49 (pp. 340–42).

And when she'd got him safe away, she sat down in the shade,
And she began to ask him if he knew such a maid;
His eyes began to fill with tears on hearing of her name,
She said – 'My dear, don't troubled be, for I'm sure I am the same.'

Then she had him fettered, and handed him along,
She said – 'I'm going to confine you all in some prison strong;
You robbed me of my liberty, I'll have you tried for life.'
So she ventured fame and fortune all for to be his wife.

The sailors overheard, and in a passion flew –
'Not for all the ships that sail she shall persuade us to,
We'll bind her hand and foot, and overboard she'll go,
She shall never see the pretty town called Canada-i-o.'

Now the captain of the ship, he being not fast asleep,
Hearing this lovely damsel most bitterly to weep –
'Where is this lovely damsel you mean to make away,
That shall never see the pretty town called Canada-i-day?'

'She's bound both hand and foot, in irons very low,
She's bound hand and foot, and overboard she'll go' –
'You bring her unto me, and none shall ever know
She shall go and see the pretty place called Canada-i-o.'

They had not been in Canada not more than half a year,
Before the captain married her, and made her his lovely dear;
All in her silks and satins now she cuts a dashing show –
She's the grandest captain's lady in Canada-i-o.

Part 24, Number 3, 25 March 1916

The earliest known version of this ballad is a broadside of six stanzas published as *Kennady I-o* by Catnach at the beginning of the nineteenth century. Williams's version is longer and has a number of features that are not found in the broadside, such as the lady's dressing herself up like a duke. There is a lot of variation in the other collected versions of the song, but none have this idea in them.

125. Banks of Sweet Primroses

Roud 586, Bathe-Clissold Wt.387
Elijah Iles, Inglesham, Wiltshire

An old favourite, that used to figure largely on ballad sheets many years ago. Obtained of Elijah Iles, Inglesham, Wiltshire.

As I walked out one summer's morning,
To view the fields and to take the air,
Down by the banks of sweet primroses,
'Twas there I beheld a lady fair.

Three long steps I took up to her,
Not knowing her as she passed me by;
I stept up to her thinking to view her,
She appeared to be like some virtuous bride.

I said – 'Fair maid, where are you going?
Oh! What's the occasion of all your grief?
I'll make you as happy as any lady,
If you will grant me some small relief.'

'Stand off, stand off, you are deceitful!
You are a false deluding swain!
It's you that's caused my heart to wander,
To give me comfort is all in vain.

I will go down to some lonesome valley,
No man on earth there shall me find,
Where the pretty small birds shall change their voices,
And every moment blows blusterous wind.'

Come all young maids that go a-courting,
And give attention to what I say,
For there's many a dark and a cloudy morning,
Turns out to be a sunshiny day.

Part 24, Number 4, 25 March 1916

This very popular song, unlike the previous one, is remarkably consistent in its text, both in printed versions and in those heard from collectors. Once again, the earliest version came from the Catnach press in the early nineteenth century and it has remained a favourite with singers right through into the twentieth century. But why does the young woman react so angrily to their encounter? None of the early versions provides any further clue to the puzzle.

126. You Ask Me to Sing

Roud 2479, Bathe-Clissold Wt.416
Elijah Iles, Inglesham, Wiltshire

A curious song that used to be heard occasionally at the inns. To read the piece is to understand it. It was sung by one who had been asked for a song but who felt disinclined to oblige with a general specimen. At the same time, while excusing himself by offering reasons for keeping silence, he yielded to the request and sang the following. Obtained of Elijah Iles, Inglesham.

You ask me to sing, indeed! I'm quite sorry
That I cannot oblige this good company here;
But if I were to begin you'd find, in a hurry,
You soon would be gone and this room would be clear.

You would not sit still and have your ears pestered
With such horrid notes, but away you would run
To some hills or some valleys, remote and sequestered;
You wish, all kind sirs, I had never begun –

I once saw a shepherd kept sheep on a mountain –
Oh, that is too high for my voice by a tone;
Then I sat myself down by the side of a fountain –
Oh, that is too low, so I cannot get on.

But if it can be so, I'll try at another,
And with a shrill voice make the woodlands to ring;
But if it can be so, it's worse than the other,
Now I hope you'll excuse me, for indeed, I can't sing.

Part 24, Number 5, 25 March 1916

Frank Purslow described this clever song as 'the ultimate in non-songs'.[46] I have not found it anywhere other than in this version collected by Williams from Elijah Iles.

[46] Frank Purslow, 'The Williams Manuscripts', *Folk Music Journal*, 1.5 (1969), 301–15 (p. 314).

127. Where Cannons Loudly Roar

Roud 1539, Bathe-Clissold Ox.269
William Preston, Grafton, Oxfordshire

The Battle of Salamanca which is mentioned in this song, was fought July 22nd, 1812, between Wellington and the French troops under Marmont and resulted in a victory for the English after huge losses on each side. The age of the piece may therefore be conjectured. The last line but one of the song is rather hazy. For 'widows' I have heard 'villas', but I do not think either accord right. Obtained of William Preston, Grafton, near Clanfield.

'Twas early one morning in the springtime of the year,
I overheard a sailor bold, likewise a lady fair;
They sang a song together, which made the valleys ring,
'Twas birds and sprays, and meadows gay proclaimed a lovely spring.

Says Henry to young Nancy – 'Now I must sail away,
All on the lovely water to hear the music play;
For our King he does want seamen, and I'll not stay on shore,
I'll brave the wars for my country's sake, where the cannons loudly roar.'

Says Nancy to young Henry – 'Now you must stay with me,
Or I'll leave my home and parents to bear thee company;
I'll put on a pair of trousers, I'll leave my native shore,
If you'll let me go along with you, where the cannons loudly roar.'

Says Henry to young Nancy – 'Tis in vain for me to try,
All for to ship a female,' young Henry he did say;
'Besides your hands are very soft, and the ropes will make them sore,
'Twould be worse than all if you should fall, where the cannons loudly roar.

'There's a battle in Salamanca, they're fighting for proud Spain,
All in that dreadful battle there's thousands have been slain,
The hills they all are lined with widows to deplore,
Their sons are gone to meet the foes, where the cannons loudly roar.'

Part 24, Number 8, 25 March 1916

The story is a familiar one, but this particular working of it, sometimes known as 'Lovely on the Water', is comparatively rare. It is derived from a broadside, *The Lover's Separation*, which was printed by Catnach and others in the early part of the nineteenth century. William Preston's version is the only one I have found that mentions the battle of Salamanca, which took place in 1812. George Gardiner collected a tune with this title in Hampshire but did not note down the words. Williams's question about the penultimate line can be resolved by replacing 'widows' with 'mothers', as in the broadside.

128. All the Little Chickens in the Garden

Roud 2552, Bathe-Clissold Wt.337
Miss E. King, Castle Eaton, Wiltshire

This naive little ditty I obtained of Miss E King, Castle Eaton. It is of good age. I do not remember to have heard it elsewhere.

I once did know a farmer, a true and faithful soul,
He used to work upon his farm, down by his country home;
He had an only daughter, and to win her I did try,
And when I asked him for her hand, the old man would reply –
Treat my daughter kindly and say you'll do no harm,
And when I die I'll will to you my little stock and farm;
My horse, my cow, my sheep, my plough, my ox, my house, my barn,
And all the little chickens in the garden.

I love that young girl dearly, I know that she loves me,
And every night I go around her smiling face to see;
I watch her milk the old brown cow, and see it does no harm,
And many a cup of milk I drink before I leave the farm.
Treat my daughter kindly, *etc.*

The old man has consented and married we will be,
And own a little house ourselves, and live in harmony;
I'll try to keep the promise the old man asked of me,
I'll treat her well, his only child, I'll treat her kindly.
Treat my daughter kindly, *etc.*

Part 24, Number 9, 25 March 1916

'The Farmer's Daughter; or, the Little Chickens in the Garden' was written by the African-American songwriter James Bland, who was also responsible for 'Oh, Dem Golden Slippers' and 'Carry Me Back to Old Virginny'. He is said to have written seven hundred songs. Bland formed an all-black minstrel company, the Georgia Minstrels.[47] In 1881 he travelled to England with the Minstrel Carnival of Genuine Colored Minstrels and then remained in London for twenty years. 'All the Little Chickens in the Garden' was published in 1878, and subsequently on broadsides (without acknowledgement) on both sides of the Atlantic. It has been heard from a number of singers in this country. Miss King's version conforms closely to the original.

[47] The Georgia Minstrels blackened their faces, painted on red lips, and used exaggerated movements and dances in their shows in imitation of the white minstrel companies that were presenting a stereotypical version of the demeanour of African-Americans.

129. The Rich Merchant's Daughter

Roud 548, Bathe-Clissold Wt.515
Mary Simpson, Stratton St Margaret, Wiltshire

This is obviously imperfect; there is a gap after the second verse. Still, it is all I could find, and it will not matter much. The piece is old; we have heard several dealing with a similar subject. Obtained of Mrs Simpson, Stratton St. Margaret, Wiltshire.

It's of a rich merchant in London did dwell,
And he had a daughter, a beautiful girl;
She had a loving sweetheart, her parents much to blame –
Her own father's apprentice, young William by name.

As soon as her father he came for to know,
That he courted his daughter, and darling also;
He had her confined, locked up in her room,
With bread and cold water once a day was her doom.

The doctor was sent for without more delay,
To see this young damsel lay dying away –
'O doctor, dear doctor, my pain you can't move,
You see I am dying for the favour of love.'

Then William was sent for without more delay,
To see his young sweetheart lay dying away -
'O William, dear William, my pain you can't move,
It was my cruel father sent me to my doom.'

Part 24, Number 10, 25 March 1916

Another daughter learns the hard way that it is not a good idea to fall in love with one of your father's employees. As Williams says, the song is incomplete, and it is not the piece customarily known as 'The Rich Merchant's Daughter' or 'The London Merchant'. I cannot, as yet, offer any clues as to its true origin.

130. The Pleasant Month of May

Roud 1432, Bathe-Clissold Ox.198
Shadrach Haydon, Bampton, Oxfordshire

An old shepherd's song, common to Wiltshire and Berkshire. I have heard it near Malmesbury and Faringdon. Obtained of Shadrach Haydn, Bampton, Oxfordshire.

The pleasant month of May is now coming on,
The trees they are springing, and the fields are in full bloom;
The maidens and swains like lambkins do play,
To welcome the shepherd, singing – Tol a lol i day.

O when I am single I can take my ease,
All bound down to none, I can do as I please;
While maidens and swains like lambkins do play,
To welcome the shepherd, singing – Tol a lol i day.

O now I am married, I can take my rest,
All in my love's arms I can think myself blest;
For it's maidens and swains like lambkins do play,
To welcome the shepherd, singing – Tol a lol i day.

Part 24, Number 11, 25 March 1916

Sometimes described as a song for May Day, this was in print in the early nineteenth century and was heard by a few of the early song collectors, mostly from men. Cecil Sharp collected it from both Lucy White and Emma Overd, however, and they added a stanza:

Now I have a little one to dance on my knee
There's none like pretty Polly she's all the world to me
So young women and their sweethearts like lambkins they play
And its welcome young shepherds in the merry month of May.

131. My Blue-Eyed Nellie

Roud 2665, Bathe-Clissold Ox.230
John Faulkner, Black Bourton, Oxfordshire

A simple little song of slight pretensions but not on that account to be despised. I obtained the copy at Black Bourton, Oxfordshire, of John Falconer. I have not heard of it in Wiltshire or Gloucestershire.

The bird was on the bough retiring, love, to rest
And the sun was gently sinking down in yon beauteous west
'Twas there I roamed with Nellie, my own, my lovely bride
I blessed the hour of gladness when both our hearts were tied.
  Then O, my charming Nellie I will be true to thee
  My sweet, my blue eyed Nellie, Thou'rt all the world to me.

That blessed little church, down in yonder shady lane,
It's foremost in my sight, where Nellie changed her name;
We cannot boast of riches that others may possess,
But peace and happiness in all we wish them to be best.
  Then O, my charming Nellie I will be true to thee
  My sweet, my blue eyed Nellie, Thou'rt all the world to me.

Part 24, Number 13, 25 March 1916

The song 'Little Blue-Eyed Nellie' was included in the *Little Maggie May Songster* published in New York by Robert M. De Witt in 1869. Authorship has been attributed to Harry Luckstone, but he is not mentioned in the De Witt publication. It appeared on a few English broadsides late in the nineteenth century.

There are two manuscript copies in the Williams collection: Ox.230 corresponds to the text above and is marked as being from John Faulkner; Mi.642 is unattributed and there are a number of verbal differences. No other collector heard the song.

132. When Joan's Ale Was New

Roud 139, Bathe Clissold Ox.243
Frederick Webb, Broadwell, Oxfordshire

Version common to the northern division of the Thames Valley. Obtained of Frederick Webb, Broadwell, Oxfordshire.

There were five jolly fellows,
Came over the hills together,
Came over the hills together,
For they were a jovial crew;
They called for bottles of liquor and sherry,
To help them all over the hills so merry,
To help them all over the hills so merry,
When Joan's ale was new, my boys,
When Joan's ale was new.

The first to come in was a soldier,
With his firelock on his shoulder,
With his firelock on his shoulder,
To join the jovial crew;
The landlord's daughter she came in,
He kissed her rosy cheeks and chin,
The pots of purl came rolling in.
When Joan's ale was new, *etc.*

The next to come in was a carter,
He was none the smarter,
The next to come in was a carter,
To join the jovial crew;
He clanged his whip upon the ground,
And swore he'd spend just half a crown,
And Luke Forest's horses went round and round.
When Joan's ale was new, *etc.*

The next to come in was a dyer,
And he sat himself down by the fire,
He sat himself down by the fire,
To join the jovial crew;
The landlord told him to his face,
The chimney corner was his place,
And there to sit and dye his old face.
When Joan's ale was new, *etc.*

The next to come in was a mason,
Whose hammer wanted new facing,
The next to come in was a mason,
To join the jovial crew;
He flung his hammer against the wall,

And wished that churches and chapels would fall,
For that would make work for masons all,
When Joan's ale was new, *etc.*

The next to come in was a tinker,
Likewise no small beer drinker,
The next to come in was a tinker,
To join the jovial crew;
He says – 'Have you any old pots or kettles to fettle?
My solder is made of the very best metal.'
Good Lord! How his hammer and rivets did rattle,
When Joan's ale was new, *etc.*

Part 25, Number 3, 1 April 1916

This follows another version, included in *FSUT* (pp. 276–78), the eight stanzas of which introduce some other professions. We can say with confidence that this song is well over four hundred years old, since John Danter entered 'Jones Ale is Newe' in the Stationers' Register in 1594. No printed copies of that edition have been identified, however, and the earliest surviving version is in the Pepys broadside collection, from the 1680s. That version covers the activities of a dozen men of various occupations and nationalities. Later broadside printers reduced them to six, or even three. The song was reported by most of the Victorian and twentieth-century collectors. The 'purl' mentioned in Fred Webb's second stanza was a hot drink made with beer infused with wormwood and other ingredients.

133. My Love Is Gone

Roud 466, Bathe-Clissold Ox.296
Henry Potter, Standlake, Oxfordshire

An old curious song which I give in two versions, not because of any considerable differences of text, but in order to show the singular use of v for w made by many of the singers of folk songs in years past. I mentioned the matter in my introduction to the songs but I had not then seen any printed evidence of what I said. Upon finding the following versions I thought it worthwhile to produce both as an illustration of a peculiar and obsolete practice. First copy obtained of Henry Potter, Standlake, Oxfordshire.

As I walked out down by the sea shore,
Where the winds blow cold and the billows did roar,
I heard a fair maid make a sorrowful sound,
With the wind, and the wave, and the water all round.

Crying – 'O my love is gone, he's the lad I adore,
I never, no, never, shall see my love more.'

She'd a voice like a nightingale, and skin like a dove,
And the song that she sang was concerning her love;
I asked her to marry me, if that she would please,
But the answer she gave me – 'My love's in the seas.'
O my love is gone, *etc.*

I told her I'd silver, and much gold beside,
And a coach and six horses, and with me she could ride –
'No, I never will marry, nor be no man's wife,
But be true to my own love as long as I have life.'
O my love is gone, *etc.*

Then she opened her arms and took a long leap,
From the rock that was high, to the sea that was deep,
Saying – 'The shells of the oysters shall make me a bed,
And all the small fish shall swim over my head.'
O my love is gone, *etc.*

Now every night since, just at eight bells is seen -
When the moon that is white shines on the water that is green -
These two constant lovers, with all their young charms,
Rolling over and over, locked in each other's arms.
O my love is gone, *etc.*

Part 25, Number 4, 1 April 1916

The ancestry of this tragic, and therefore very popular, song can be traced back to *The Sorrowful Ladies Complaint*, published *c.*1673.[48] 'The Drowned Mariner', found in chapbooks from the late eighteenth century, follows the *Sorrowful Ladies Complaint* quite closely. Then, in the early nineteenth century, Catnach published two four-stanza versions under two different titles, *The Lover's Lament for her Sailor* and *O my Love is Dead*, each telling the same story in different words.

In the 1840s the music hall artist Sam Cowell performed a parody of the song and this version that appeared on some later broadsides as *Oh, my Love's Dead.* Cowell's song was a strong influence on later performances of the song. The second version that Williams collected (no. 134 below) is essentially Cowell's version.

The song has had a long career and has been collected widely, including in North America. There it made a successful transition from the folk to the country genre as 'I Never Will Marry'. Even here there are variations, as some versions stay at the seaside while others switch the action to the railroad.

---

48 It has been proposed that an earlier song, 'Captain Digby's Farewell', published in a songbook of 1672, is the 'original', but it contains none of the phrases that are common to the later broadside and collected versions. *The Sorrowful Ladies Complaint* has these in abundance.

134. My Love's Dead

Roud 466, Bathe Clissold Wt.489
Amelia Phillips, Purton, Wiltshire

This version of the above I copied from an old song book lent to me by Mrs Phillips, Purton, Wiltshire.

As I vas a-valking down by the seashore,
Vere the vinds, and the vaves, and the vaters did roar,
Vith the vinds, and the vaves, and the vaters all round,
I heard a young maid making sorrowful sounds.
Singing – 'Oh, oh, oh, my love is dead.
Him I adore. I shall never, no, never see my love more.'

She'd a voice like a nightingale, a skin like a dove,
And the song vat she sang it vas all about love;
I asked her to marry myself, could she please?
But her answer vas, 'No! My love's in the seas.'
Oh, oh, oh, my love is dead, *etc.*

I told her I'd silvier and gold, too beside,
And a coach and six horses, and vith me she could ride;
'No! I never vill marry, nor be any man's vife,
But be true to my love as long as I have life.'
Oh, oh, oh, my love is dead, *etc.*

Then she stretched forth her arms and gave a great leap,
From the rocks vat vas high, to the sea vat vas deep,
Saying – 'The shells of the oysters shall make me a bed,
And the shrimps of the sea shall viggle vaggle over my head.'
Oh, oh, oh, my love is dead, *etc.*

Now every night since, just at eight bells is seen -
Ven the moon vat is vite shines on the vaters vat is green,
These two constant lovyers with all their young charms,
Rolling over and over, locked in each other's arms.
Oh, oh, oh, my love is dead, *etc.*

Part 25, Number 5, 1 April 1916

As mentioned above, this is essentially Sam Cowell's treatment of the song, and demonstrates what Williams describes in the note to the previous song as the 'peculiar and obsolete practice' of the reversed pronunciation of 'v' and 'w', with the inclusion of words like 'silvier' and 'lovyer', which we know to have been used by some of the old singers and was a common way of representing Cockney speech in the mid-nineteenth century. It is frequently encountered in comic songs of the period.

135. The Bonny Blue Handkerchief Tucked under her Chin

Roud 378, Bathe-Clissold Wt.346
David Sawyer, Stratton St Margaret, Wiltshire

This is not so old as many in our list; I am told it dates from about the middle of the last century. I have seen a longer copy, but this is all that was used here, as I can with certainty speak. Obtained of David Sawyer, late of Ogbourne, Wiltshire.

'Twas early one morning I chanced for to stray,
I saw a lovely lassie come tripping that way;
With her cheeks red as roses, she gaily did sing,
With a bonny, blue handkerchief tied under her chin.

'Oh! Why is this handkerchief tied under your head?'
'It's our country fashion, kind sir,' she said.
'And the fashion, you know sir, I like to be in,
With the bonny, blue handkerchief tied under my chin.'

Then for to kiss her I tried to begin,
'Oh, stop, sir,' she said, 'While I tell you one thing.
He that kisses these lips must show a gold ring,
For the bonny, blue handkerchief tied under my chin.'

With gold and with silver I tried all in vain,
But she smiled in my face with scornful disdain –
'It is not your gold, sir, that one kiss shall win,
From this bonny, blue handkerchief tied under my chin.'

When I saw her so loyal I could not forbear,
I fell in her arms and called her my dear;
'Oh, my dearest jewel! Here is the gold ring,
For the bonny, blue handkerchief tied under your chin.'

Part 25, Number 6, 1 April 1916

This first appeared on broadsides from printers such as James Catnach in the first quarter of the nineteenth century, usually with nine stanzas. The song was heard by many of the early collectors and survived in the repertoire of rural singers into the late twentieth century. The broadside versions make it clearer that this is another young man returning from sea and that the blue handkerchief she is wearing was a gift from him.

136. Far from my Home

Roud 1081, Bathe-Clissold Ox.246
Frank Cook, Burford, Oxfordshire

I have heard of another song, similar, and also superior to this, but I have been unable to find it so far. It is old, perhaps not well known. The words obtained of Frank Cook, Burford.

I'm a stranger in this country, from America I came,
There is no one that knows me, nor can tell my name,
But if anyone should ask you why I am here alone,
You can tell them I am a poor girl and am far from my home.
Then why can't you be easy, and leave me alone,
And tell them I'm a poor girl, and am far from my home.

Now I will build me a mansion in the middle of this town,
Where lords, dukes nor squires don't dare to pull it down.
And if anyone should ask you why I live there alone,
You can tell them I am a poor girl and am far from my home.
Then why can't you be easy, *etc.*

Now the boys of Kilkenny they are sporting young lads,
And, like many others, go a-courting pretty maids;
They will kiss them, and cuddle them, and call them their own,
Whilst perhaps their own darling lies weeping at home.
Then why can't you be easy, *etc.*

So come all pretty fair maids, take a warning by me,
Never build your nest on the top of any tree;
For the green leaves will wither, and the roots will decay,
And the beauty of a fair maid will soon fade away.
Then why can't you be easy, *etc.*

Part 25, Number 7, 1 April 1916

This song is a mongrel pieced together with stanzas from four or five different songs. Stanza 1 is from 'Stranger from America' (Roud 136) and 'The Happy Stranger' (Roud 272), which also supplies the chorus. Stanza 2 is from 'The Jolly Miner' (Roud 2599). Stanza 3 is found in 'Boys of Kilkenny' (Roud 1451), although it also appears in the broadside version of 'The Happy Stranger' with Newry substituted for Kilkenny. Stanza 4 is a floater, found in many songs. No song quite like this was heard by other collectors.

137. Jack and Nancy

Roud 530, Bathe-Clissold Gl.71
William Morse, Coln St Aldwyns, Gloucestershire

A very old piece, of a type once highly popular. I have not met it south of the Thames. Words obtained of William Moss, Coln St. Aldwyn.

Jack went down to her parents' home,
Cried – Nancy, will you, Aye or No?
Or will you wed a jolly sailor?'
'Oh, no,' says Nancy.

Then John pulled out two handfuls of gold,
Cried, 'Nancy, will you, Aye or No?
'Oh, yes,' says Nancy, with a smile,
'I was only joking all the while.'

'If you are joking, I am not in jest.
That's not the question that I ask,
But if it's money that you love best,
You shall never wed your sailor.'

Then John set up in a public line,
Plenty of silver and plenty of coin;
It made young Nancy often pine,
Since she refused the sailor.

'There's no other girl that I can find,
That is so pleasing to my mind.
But I'll live single all my time,
Before she shall wed her sailor.'

Part 25, Number 10, 1 April 1916

This is *The Tarry Sailor* printed on broadsides in the first decade of the nineteenth century, when a lot of fortunate sailors were returning home from the wars with their share of prize money. William Morse's version has lost a few stanzas from the printed version, but the tale of the wealthy sailor returning and testing his lover is complete, although the outcome disappoints both.

138. William and Harriet

Roud 536, Bathe-Clissold Wt.477
David Sawyer, Stratton St Margaret, Wiltshire

One of the commoner folk ballads. It was widely distributed; I have many times heard it. Copy of David Sawyer.

It's of a rich merchant in Bristol did dwell,
And he had a daughter a sailor loved well;
Because he was handsome she lovéd him true,
And her father he wanted her to bid him adieu.

'Oh no, my dear father, I am not so inclined,
For to drive my young sailor quite out of my mind.'
'Then, unruly daughter, confined you shall be,
And I'll send your young sailor start over the sea.'

As she was a-sitting in her bower one day,
By chance her young Willie came walking that way;
She sang like a linnet and appeared like a dove,
The song that she sang was concerning her love.

She'd not been there long before young Willie passed by,
And on his dear Harriet cast a longing eye –
'If your cruel father with mine will agree,
They will send you a-sailing far over the sea.'

She says – 'My sweet William, with you I will go,
Since my cruel father has servéd me so;
I will pass for your shipmate and do all that I can,
With my Willie I'll venture like a jolly young man.'

So she dressed like a sailor, as near as could be,
They both went together across the salt sea;
They both went together to some foreign shore,
And never to old England returned any more.

As they were a-sailing by some foreign shore,
The wind from the ocean began for to roar;
The ship it went down to the bottom of the sea,
And cast on an island were William and she.

They wandered about some place for to spy,
They'd nothing to eat, and nowhere to lie;
So they sat down together upon the cold ground,
While the waves and the tempest made a terrible sound.

Sharp hunger came on them, and death it drew nigh,
They folded together, intending to die;
What pair could be bolder this world to bid adieu?
And now they must moulder like lovers so true.

Come all you true lovers that pass by this way,
Drop one tear of pity from your glittering eye;
Drop one tear of pity and point towards this way,
Where William and Harriet did slumber and die.

Part 26, Number 3, 8 April 1916

As has already been noted, rich merchants' daughters do not seem to have much luck in traditional songs. This over-sentimental piece was widely printed from around 1830 onwards and heard by collectors in Britain and North America, though not frequently.

139. William and Mary

Roud 348, Bathe-Clissold Gl.100
Mary Gosling, Lechlade, Gloucestershire

I have met with this only at Lechlade and Quenington, Gloucestershire. It is a simple old piece, and was the favourite of the dames and young women. Obtained of Mrs Gosling, Lechlade.

As William and Mary stood by the seashore,
Their last fond farewell to take –
'Should you never return,' little Mary she cried,
'My poor heart it surely will break;
For I love you so dear, so true and sincere,
And no other, I swear, beside,
If in riches I rolled, and was covered in gold,
You should make little Mary your bride.'

When three years were past without news, at last,
As Mary stood at her cottage door,
An old beggar came by with a patch on his eye,
Quite lame and did pity implore –
'Your charity bestow, and your fortune I'll tell.'
Says he, 'And this news beside –
The lad that you mourn will never return
To make little Mary his bride.'

'If he lives, Heaven knows the joys that I feel!
Still, for his misfortune I'll mourn.
But he's welcome to me in his poverty,
If his blue jacket's ragged and torn.
For I love him so dear, so true and sincere,
And no other, I swear, beside,

If in riches I rolled and were covered with gold,
He should make little Mary his bride.'

Then the patch from his eye this old beggar threw by,
His old coat and crutches beside,
His jacket so blue and cheeks like a rose,
It was William stood by Mary's side –
'Forgive me, my dear maid,' said he,
'I did it your love for to try;
Now to church we'll away by the break of the day,
And I'll make little Mary my bride.'

Part 26, Number 4, 8 April 1916

Another variation on the theme of the returning lover testing his sweetheart. The earliest version is said to have been printed by J. Evans of London in 1794.[49] It has been heard by collectors on both sides of the Atlantic. Mary Gosling's version has become somewhat corrupted in transmission.

140. The Whale Fishers

Roud 347, Bathe-Clissold Ox.200
Shadrach Haydon, Bampton, Oxfordshire

The Whale Fishers is interesting as showing the range of subject possessed by the old ballad writers. They had an eye for everything, and found means to compose a song upon every adventure of activity. Copy obtained of Shadrach Haydon, Bampton, Oxfordshire.

In eighteen hundred and twenty-one,
On the twenty-third of May,
We hoisted our colours to our topmast head,
And for Greenland bore away.

When we came unto Greenland,
Our ship we were forced to mend,
For the heavy waves fell on her side,
And stripped it from end to end.

'Here's a whale, here's a whale,' cries the bold fisherman,
As he glanced over the side,
And to catch that great whale, brave boys,
We instantly did try.

[49] Wm. Alexr. Barrett, *English Folk-Songs* (London: Novello, [1890]), p. 59.

Our captain stood on the quarterdeck –
A very good man was he:
'Overhaul, overhaul. Let your heavy tackle fall,
And launch your boats for sea.'

The boat was launched and the hands jumped in,
The whale fish appeared in view,
And it was resolved by the whole of us,
To steer where the whale fish blew.

The spear being launched, and the line paid out,
She gave a lash with her tail,
She capsized the boat and we lost five men,
And we did not catch that whale.

Now Greenland is a barren place,
Neither night nor day to be seen,
But cold ice and snow, and the whale fish to blow,
And daylight seldom seen.

Part 26, Number 5, 8 April 1916

The ballad starts with a very precise date, but this varies between different versions. The earliest printed copy of which we can be certain is *The Whale* in a garland of songs published in Glasgow around 1814. The song was very popular with rural singers in Britain, but was also found copied into the journals of American whaling ships – an indication, perhaps, that it was an accurate representation of the whaleman's life.

141. False-Hearted William

Roud 1414, Bathe Clissold Bk.469
Jonas Wheeler, Buscot, Berkshire

I have heard of this but once, viz., at Buscot on the banks of the Thames. The words were given me by Mr Jonas Wheeler. He tells me he learnt the song when he was a boy, at the wharf at New Bridge, where he was employed with the barges. A woman, one of the bargemen's wives, sang the piece.

In Brighton lived a fair young maid,
As fair as eyes could see,
'Till a young man came a-courting her,
And proved her destiny.

She came to him next morning,
And wept most bitterly,
Saying – 'Willie, dearest Willie,
When will you marry me?'

'To marry you, Miss Polly,
Is more than I can do,
For I never intend to wed a girl,
So easily led as you.

'Go home unto your parents,
And do the best you can,
And tell them your true love William,
Has proved a false young man.'

'I'll not go home to my parents,
Nor bring them to disgrace,
For I'd rather go and drown myself,
In some wild lonesome place.'

As Willie was a-walking,
Along the river side,
He saw his true love Polly,
Come floating on the tide.

He caught hold of her lily white hand,
And found that she was gone,
Saying – 'Lord have mercy on my soul,
I've proved a false young man.

'Let none of my friends or relations,
Come lounging after me,
For on these cold and sandy banks,
I'll die with my Pollee.'

Part 26, Number 6, 8 April 1916

This story of betrayal and suicide has been collected in Britain and Ireland and a couple of times in Canada. I have not seen a broadside that it replicates to any great degree, though there is some resemblance to *The Dublin Tragedy* printed by Mayne of Belfast, *c.*1860. Cecil Sharp and Henry Hammond collected several versions in the West Country. In 1968, during his sweep of the Upper Thames in Williams's cycle tracks, John Baldwin heard a version, 'Camden Town', from a woman in Oxfordshire. [50] That was also the title of a very complete version heard by Helen Creighton in New Brunswick, Canada.[51]

---

[50] John R. Baldwin 'Song in the Upper Thames Valley, 1966–1969', *Folk Music Journal*, 1.5 (1969), 315–49 (pp. 326–28).
[51] Helen Creighton (ed.), *Folk Songs from Southern New Brunswick* (Ottawa: National Museums of Canada, 1971), pp. 119–20.

142. The Broken Hearted Bride

Roud 567, Bathe-Clissold Ox.201
Sarah Martin, Bampton Buildings, Oxfordshire

This was formerly a favourite around Bampton; I have not heard it elsewhere. The copy I obtained of Mrs. Martin, Bampton Buildings

Last Friday night I was asked to a wedding,
It was to a young girl that proved so unkind;
And all the day long she was so discontented,
For her own former lover still rolled all in her mind.

Then supper being over, they all began for to sing,
It was a jolly song that of true love did tell;
And the one that was to sing it was her own former lover,
And the song that he sang she understood right well.

'Now there is one thing that I require of you,
And I hope it will be granted unto me –
That's one more night to sleep with my mother.
And for ever after to sleep along with thee.'

The question being asked, and already granted,
In sobbing and sighing they each went to bed;
He rose in the morning as daylight was dawning,
And he found that his new bride was dead.

You go down in the meadow, there grows a fine flower,
Which for to gather is everyone's desire,
Where young men and maidens pass many a happy hour,
In kissing and courting, but never come the nigher.

Part 26, Number 7, 8 April 1916

Another maudlin drama of the kind the rural singers revelled in. The earliest known publication is on a slip printed by Johnson of York, *c.*1800, but few other broadside versions were produced. The Hammond brothers collected a particularly fine version of this in Dorset, compared with which Sarah Martin's version is quite badly degraded.[52]

---

[52] 'The Nobleman's Wedding', sung by Mrs Crawford of West Milton, Dorset, in 1906, in Frank Purslow (ed.), *Marrow Bones: English Folk Songs from the Hammond and Gardiner Manuscripts*, rev. Malcolm Douglas and Steve Gardham (London: EFDSS, 2007), p. 74.

143. The British Man o' War

Roud 372, Bathe-Clissold Gl.145
James Mills, South Cerney, Gloucestershire

The date of this is probably that of the expedition to China in 1839. We are familiar with the style of the piece and also with its circumstances. It would be interesting to know how many ballads have been composed upon this and similar subjects. Words obtained of James Mills, South Cerney.

'Twas down in yonder meadows I carelessly did stray,
There I beheld a lady fair with some young sailor gay,
He said – 'My lovely Susan, I soon must leave the shore,
And cross the briny ocean in a British Man o' War.'

Pretty Susan fell a-weeping – 'Young sailor,' she did say,
'How can you be so venturesome, to throw your life away;
When I am twenty-one I shall receive my store,
Jolly sailor, do not venture in a British Man o' War.'

'Oh, Susan, lovely Susan, the truth to you I'll tell,
The British flag's insulted, old England knows it well;
I may be crowned with laurels, so, like a jolly tar,
I will face the wars of China in a British Man o' War.'

'Oh, sailor, do not venture to face the proud Chinese,
For they will prove more treacherous than any Portuguese,
All by some deadly dagger you may receive a scar,
So turn your inclination from a British Man o' War.'

'Oh, Susan, lovely Susan, the time will quickly pass,
Now come down to the ferry house and take a parting glass;
My shipmate is there waiting to row me from the shore,
And it's for old England's glory in a British Man o' War.'

The sailor took his handkerchief and cut it fair in two –
'Oh, Susan, keep one half for me, and I'll do the same for you;
Though bullets may surround me, and cannons loudly roar,
I will fight for fame and Susan in a British Man o' War.'

Part 26, Number 8, 8 April 1916

This song appeared on broadsides in the nineteenth century. It has been suggested that the mention of China in the song places it at the time of the Opium Wars. Since these started in 1839 the existence of a broadside by Catnach is slightly problematic since he died in 1838. A possible explanation is that his successors (Ryle and Paul) continued to use his imprint for a period after his death. Alternatively, the ballad refers to another adventure against the Chinese. The song was popular enough to require a sequel, *Susan's Adventures on Board of a Man of War: Answer to the British Man-of-War*, in which she disguises herself to join her lover's ship, then, as she faces 'the walls of China', is 'slightly wounded', before they return to England to get married. The earliest known version of this was published before 1841 by Birt of London, putting an upper limit on the earliest date for the 'parent' version. The song as collected by Williams is very similar to the broadside text but does not have its final stanza:

Then a few more words together when her love let go her hand
A jovial crew they launched the boat and merrily from land
The sailor waved his handkerchief when far away from shore
Pretty Susan blessed her sailor in a British Man o' War.

144. Farewell to Mary Ann

Roud 4388, Bathe-Clissold Gl.147
James Mills, South Cerney, Gloucestershire

For this I am also indebted to James Mills of South Cerney. It is short, if not sweet. Really it is not a bad little song, and the composer was not totally devoid of imagination as is evidenced by the last stanza.

Fare you well, my own Mary Ann!
Fare you well for a while!
For the ship's now ready, and the wind blows fair,
And I am bound for the sea, Mary Ann,
And I am bound, etc.

Don't you see the turtle dove,
Sitting on yonder stile,
Lamenting the loss of her true love?
And so am I for my Mary Ann,
And so am I, etc.

A lobster in a lobster pot,
A blue fish wriggling on a hook,
Can suffer, oh not half of that
Which I do feel for my Mary Ann,
Which I do feel, etc..

Part 26, Number 9, 8 April 1916

'My Mary Ann: The Yankee Girl's Song' was written by Barney Williams with music by M. Tyte. It was described as a comic song that was sung in a farce called *Our Gal* by Mrs Barney Williams, 'with immense applause, throughout the United States, Great Britain and Ireland'. It was published in various American songsters, such as *Mr. & Mrs. Barney Williams' Irish Boy and Yankee Gal Songster* in 1860.[53]

This is not the first reference to the song that I have found, though. An article in *Punch* in 1856 on 'The American Ballads' deplored, with tongue firmly in cheek, the way in which 'the Trans-Atlantic muse' was replacing songs like 'The Ratcatcher's Daughter' and 'Bonnie Annie Laurie' in the British audience's affections.[54] One of the examples quoted is 'My Mary Anne', and the writer ponders whether one of the American poets like Longfellow or Emerson had come up with the images of the lobster and the bluefish.

'My Mary Ann' was printed on a few broadsides at around the same time in the USA and Britain, but Williams is the only collector to have heard it sung. The original had a fourth stanza in which the narrator compared the size of his love for Mary Ann with a pumpkin.

The pride of all our produce rare
That in our kitchen garden grow
Was pumpkins, but none could compare
In angel form to my Mary Ann
In angel form, etc.

John Harrington Cox describes the song as the progenitor of the more serious 'True Lover's Farewell' (Roud 422).[55] The latter has been much more widely collected on both sides of the Atlantic.

---

[53] *Mr. & Mrs. Barney Williams' Irish Boy and Yankee Gal Songster* (Philadelphia: R. Simpson, 1860), pp. 46–47.

[54] 'The American Ballads', *Punch; or, The London Charivari*, 18 October 1856, p. 151.

[55] John Harrington Cox (ed.), *Folk Songs of the South* (Cambridge, MA: Harvard University Press, 1925), pp. 413–14.

145. Cupid's Garden

Roud 297, Bathe-Clissold Wt.487
Amelia Phillips, Purton, Wiltshire

A superior little piece. I have only heard it at Purton, though I dare say it was more widely known. Obtained of Mrs. Phillips, Purton, Wilts.

'Twas down in Cupid's Garden for pleasure I did go,
All for to view the flowers that in the garden grew;
The one it was a jasmine, sweet lilies, pinks, and roses,
They are the finest flowers that in the garden grow.
That in the garden grow.

I had not been in the garden passing half an hour,
Before I spied two maidens in a green and shady bower;
The one was lovely Nancy, so beautiful and fair,
The other was a virgin and did the laurel wear.
And did the laurel wear.

I boldly stepped up to her, to hear what she did say -
'Are you engaged to any young man? come tell to me I pray.'
'I am not engaged to any young man,' she solemnly did swear,
"But I mean to be a virgin, and still the laurel wear.
And still the laurel wear.

Part 26, Number 10, 8 April 1916

Another very popular song, frequently collected and often printed. The early broadside versions had seven stanzas, but later versions only four. The earliest printed version comes from the beginning of the nineteenth century but the song may be older than that. Writing in 1858, William Chappell asserted that this was one of the three most popular songs among the servant-maids of the time.[56] Williams's version loses the identification of the young man as a sailor about to return to his ship.

[56] William Chappell, *Popular Music of the Olden Time* (London: Chappell, 1855–56), p. 735.

146. Britons, Strike Home

Roud 1187, Bathe-Clissold Wt.481
William King, Purton, Wiltshire

Here again we have for a subject a maid's going to sea in order to be near her lover. The number of such songs is not exhausted yet; there are others to follow. Words obtained of William King, Purton, Wiltshire.

Come all you bold seamen, and see what is done,
See how a bold woman will fight for a man!
    So we'll cross the salt seas, let the wind blow so strong,
    While our rakish young heroes cry – 'Britons, strike home!'

My father was a squire and I was his heir,
And I fell in love with a sailor so rare.
    So we'll cross the salt seas, *etc.*

Our ship carried over nine hundred men,
And out of nine hundred, five hundred were slain.
    So we'll cross the salt seas, *etc.*

The sweet little bullets came flying apace,
I was shot in my right breast – how hard is my case!
    So we'll cross the salt seas, *etc.*

Come all you bold women, wherever you be,
And consider the hardships we suffer at sea.
    So we'll cross the salt seas, *etc.*

Part 26, Number 12, 8 April 1916

This unusual song has only been noted four times, the other collectors being Sabine Baring-Gould, the Hammond brothers, and William Barrett. It was published on broadsides by Catnach and Pitts, which are similar to the collected versions. All include the memorable line about the 'sweet little bullets'. The Bodleian Library holds an earlier broadside by Angus of Newcastle which is longer and more serious.[57] William Chappell describes having heard boys chanting the song in his school playground forty years earlier, that is *c.*1818.[58] The phrase 'Britons, Strike Home' is the title of a song from the opera *Bonduca* by Henry Purcell, but that is not the tune that was used for this song.

---

[57] It is difficult to date the output of the Angus family very accurately as, between Thomas, Margaret, and George, they operated between 1774 and 1825.

[58] William Chappell, *Popular Music of the Olden Time* (London: Chappell, 1855–56), p. 735.

147. Sweet Peggy O

Roud 545, Bathe-Clissold Wt.414
Elijah Iles, Inglesham, Wiltshire

A quaint and amusing piece of considerable age. It is doubtful whether the writer really knew anything of Killarney or not; perhaps he imagined the circumstances. The 'ocean' of the Irish Channel sounds something like Homer's Hellespont, that was usually spoken of as 'boundless'. The toast follows the song; that was spoken. Obtained of Elijah Iles, Inglesham.

There was once a captain in Derby O,
And he was come recruiting O,
But a pretty chamber maid.
His heart she betrayed,
And she was called sweet Peggy O.

But he had not been in Derby long,
Before sad news came to him very strong –
'You must come to Killarney and must not delay indeed.
You are wanted at Killarney with all speed.'

The captain went to the foot of the stairs -
'O come down with your golden hair!
Come down!' cried the captain O.
'For I to Killarney must now haste away,
Then bid me farewell, pretty Peggy O!'

Then over the ocean he soon sailed away,
And soon he arrived at Killarney O;
But so far, far away,
He was often heard to say –
'Here's a health to the pretty girl at Derby O.'

And at Killarney he got very helpless,
For his troubles he never would confess;
Love alone filled his breast,
He never could rest,
And he died for the pretty girl at Derby O.

Toast to Peggy.

The God of love his wanton power displays,
And oft torments us in a thousand ways;
And yet on Peggy none can lay the blame,
For not complying with the captain's flame.

Part 27, Number 1, 15 April 1916

This appeared as *Pretty Peggy of Derby* on broadsides printed by Pitts and Catnach early in the nineteenth century, but it was better known in Scotland as 'The Bonnie Lass o' Fyvie'.[59] It was widely collected in Britain, Ireland, and the USA. Fans of Joan Baez will remember her singing 'Fennario', which is an American version of the song.

148. As I Was Walking by Newgate One Day

Roud 552, Bathe-Clissold Ox.239
Job Phipps, Brize Norton, Oxfordshire

I have met with the following in two forms though the variations are not considerable. It was popular in many parts of the Thames Valley especially at Bishopstone, Wiltshire, and around Witney. The copy obtained of Job Phipps, Brize Norton, Oxfordshire.

As I was a walking by Newgate one day,
I heard a lady unto a judge did say –
'You banished my true love, you very well know,
And sent him to the salt seas where the stormy winds blow.

I'll give to each turnkey a bright sum of gold,
If they will contrive me to the arms of my love;
Now our ship it lies at Blackwall just ready to set sail,
So God bless you true lovers with a sweet pleasant gale.'

Now as they were a sailing at their own heart's content,
The ship sprang a leak, boys, to the bottom she went;
There were four and twenty of us jumped into a boat,
And on the wide ocean we were forced for to float.

Then hunger came on us and death drawing nigh,
We all did cast lots for to see which should die;
And this innocent virgin the shortest lot drew,
And she was to die for to feed the ship's crew.

'O hold your hand, butcher,' this young damsel replied,
'How can you destroy a poor innocent maid?
I'm a rich merchant's daughter, from London I be,
See what I'm brought to by loving thee!'

O, then the hot colour flew into his face,
With his eyes full of tears and his heart like to break,
The heart in his bosom was ready to burst –
'O now to preserve thee, love, I will die first.'

[59] Ian A. Olson, '"The Bonny Lass o' Fyvie" or "Pretty Peggy of Derby"?', *Review of Scottish Culture*, 22 (2010), 150–63.

Before the blow struck him, we all heard a gun -
'Tis hold your hand, butcher for help it is come;
'O hold your hand, butcher,' this damsel replied,
'There's some ship or some harbour that's near standing by.'

Now as we were a-sailing with a sweet pleasant tide,
We came to a village close by the sea side;
Said she – 'Brother shipmates, I bid you adieu,
That I have proved loyal you very well know.'

Now this couple got married, as I've heard them say,
The bells they did ring, and the music did play;
The birds made the valleys to echo and to ring,
The young men did dance, and the maidens did sing.

Part 27, Number 2, 15 April 1916

More usually called 'The Silk Merchant's Daughter', or 'New York Street', this dates back to the eighteenth century. The American prisoner of war Timothy Connor included it in his prison journal in 1777–79.[60] The central threat of cannibalism as a means of survival is still a favourite in today's media, but other versions added the themes of parental disapproval and cross-dressing, ensuring the song's popularity with rural singers. It was collected several times in Britain but even more frequently in the USA.

149. Arthur O'Bradley O

Roud 32441, Bathe-Clissold Wt.427
Walter Poole, Minety, Wiltshire

A very old song, dating at least from the sixteenth century, and it may have been earlier. There are, or were, several versions of the piece. I have heard of two, but have been unable to obtain both, this I have being, in my opinion, the inferior of the two. The following was sung around Aston and Minety; the other of which I have heard was popular at Bishopstone, Wilts. Obtained of Walter Poole, Minety.

'Twas on the twenty-ninth of May,
The pretty maidens they did say,
A Maypole they would have,
And one that was fine and brave;
So sallybub they brought up,

[60] George G. Carey (ed.), *A Sailor's Songbag: An American Rebel in an English Prison, 1777–1779* (Amherst: University of Massachusetts Press, 1976), p. 69.

That everyone might sup, –
'And I'll drink out of my cup,
For my name it is Arthur O'Bradley O.'

So Arthur a-courting went
Against his friends' consent,
And a sweetheart he would have,
And one that was fine and brave:
His sweetheart had one eye,
Her nose was all awry,
She'd a mouth from ear to ear,
And teeth as rotten as a pear,
And her name was draggle tailed Dorothy O.

The old woman squeaked and cried,
And called her daughter aside,
Saying – 'Daughter, you need not fear;
You are too young in years.'
'Peace, mother,' said she,
'Don't trouble your head about me,
I'll speak to a young man or two,
Besides my Arthur O'Bradley O.'

'Get out, old woman,' said he,
'I'll have as good as she.
When Death my father does call,
He straight will leave me all:
Barrels and bucket and broom,
A dozen of old wooden spoons,
Besides a rack and a reel,
And the rim of an old spinning wheel,
A cheese rat and a cheese ladder,
And two jem locks together,
A cart nail and a whimble,
A pack needle and a thimble,
And the last to fall to my lot,
A jolly old mustard pot;
A dozen of brassen buttons
Tied on a leather string,
Two left handed mills,
And a jolly old curtain ring.

Then a wedding we will have,
And one that is fine and brave;
We'll invite our neighbours round,
One out of every town.
There's old Mother Cobb in a cobble,
And old Mother Wobb in a wobble;
And in came neighbour Reef,
And he laid on upon beef;
And in came neighbour Sutton,
And he laid on upon mutton;
In come neighbour Stork,

And he laid on upon pork;
In came Stephen Ball,
With the round of his rump before,
And in came industrious Will,
Ready to eat his fill,
At the wedding of Arthur O'Bradley O.

Part 27, Number 3, 15 April 1916

The character Arthur of Bradley was already well known before the end of the sixteenth century and the song was familiar enough to be referred to in plays by Ben Jonson and Thomas Dekker. Francis Merbury in his play *Contract of a Marriage between Wit and Wisdom* (*c.*1571) quoted a passage that echoes the chorus of one of the later versions:

For the honour of Artrebradle
This age would make me swere madly!

We do not have a copy of that original song in print or manuscript and the earliest copies on paper are broadsides from the mid-seventeenth century. There is not, in fact, a single song but a family of songs based around the Arthur of Bradley character, the popularity of which endured for more than 450 years. This family has not been extensively researched but comprises at least five different songs, with interchangeable titles to add to the confusion. The songs themselves are, for the most part, nonsense.

Alfred Williams heard two versions while making his collection, this one, and a much longer song which he published in *FSUT* (pp. 271–74). The latter is a version of what is best known as 'Arthur O'Bradley's Wedding' (Roud 365). It was performed early in the nineteenth century by a Mr Taylor, a comic singer, who published it under his own name. James Dixon wrote: 'This Mr. Taylor was, however, only a low comedian of the day, and the ascribed authorship was a mere trick on the publisher's part to increase the sale of the song.'[61] The version that Dixon published is the same as that found on broadsides from Catnach and Pitts, and Williams's version in *FSUT* is essentially this text.

The version above, which we shall call simply 'Arthur O'Bradley' (Roud 32441) is harder to relate to previous songs, several of which begin with ''Twas in the month of May' or similar and then head off in different directions. The closest early edition that I have found is that in a chapbook called *The Diary* [*sic*] *Maid* published in 1774. This group of versions is characterized by the line 'The Syllabubs they brought up, that everyone might sup' in the first stanza – though the Somerset singer Jonathan Pearce sang it to Cecil Sharp as 'Silly Bob put off his hat for he be called a sup'. Sharp collected both versions of the song, and Sabine Baring-Gould heard 'Arthur

[61] James Henry Dixon (ed.), *Ancient Poems, Ballads, and Songs of the Peasantry of England* (London: Percy Society, 1846), p. 161.

O'Bradley' in the middle of Dartmoor. Harry Albino also heard a very complete version of 'The Wedding of Arthur O'Bradley', but no later collectors seem to have found it.

Newspaper searches show that the name of Arthur O'Bradley was ubiquitous in the nineteenth century, as the name for several racehorses, the cause of pub fights because of its perceived Irishness, as a nom de plume for writers to Irish newspapers, and as a character in pantomimes and a novel, *The History and Adventures of Arthur O'Bradley O.* The twentieth century seems to have had less taste for this particular brand of nonsense.

150. The Shepherd and the Hermit

Roud 2449, Bathe-Clissold Wt.412
Elijah Iles, Inglesham, Wiltshire

This looks more like a recitation than a song; it was sung, however, and was pleasing to the old folks of the last century. It was popular at Southrop and Lechlade, words obtained of Elijah Iles, Inglesham.'

The shepherd played his pipe so sweet,
And watched his lambs at play,
And there he saw a lady neat,
He stole her heart away.

She gave to him a diamond ring,
Into his arms she flew –
'Young man you stole my heart away,
In love I'll die for you.'

'If I have stole your heart away,
I'll give it you again.
My heart and all are thine, my love,
For ever to remain.

'To-morrow night, in yonder grove,
Under that well-known tree,
If you will meet me there, my love,
We'll name our wedding day.'

These words revived the lady's heart,
She smiled and dropped a tear –
'My heart and all are thine, my love,
I'll surely meet thee there.'

The shepherd penned his sheep, and went,
To meet his lady fair;
He never more his love did see,
The hermit killed him there.

Long time she wandered up and down,
Under that well known tree;
Long time she wandered up and down,
But no true love could see.

She wandered to that hermit's cave,
When dark was all the sky;
A thunderstorm did her oppress,
For her true love she cried.

'Walk in, fair maid,' this hermit said,
'Into my warm, sheltered cell;
Walk in, and rest your weary feet,
Here peace and safety dwell.'

But, seeing her love dead on the ground,
Lamenting she did cry;
Being tender-hearted like a dove,
She broke her heart and died.

The hermit he had got a cave,
Within that lonesome wood;
The shepherd he became his prey,
And served him for his food.

Part 27, Number 4, 15 April 1916

Cecil Sharp noted this song in 1913 from William Sparrow of Kemble, Gloucestershire, just inside Williams's Upper Thames region, though he only wrote down the first stanza, with the tune. I have not, so far, been able to find out anything more about the origin of this rather unpleasant song. Sharp's stanza and tune were printed in the *Journal of the Folk-Song Society* in 1927 in a section headed 'Love Songs'.[62] If Sharp had noted more than one stanza, it might have been categorized differently.

---

[62] *Journal of the Folk-Song Society*, 8.1 (no. 31) (1927), 19.

151. Pretty Susan, the Pride of Kildare

Roud 962, Bathe-Clissold Wt.343
Thomas King, Highworth, Wiltshire

A very old song, infrequently met with. It was first sung to me by the late Thomas King, of Castle Eaton, when he was in his ninety-eighth year. I have heard it but once since, i.e. at Highworth, Wiltshire.

When first from sea I landed, I had a roving mind,
Undaunted I rambled a true love to find;
When I met pretty Susan, with cheeks like a rose,
And her bosom was fairer than the lily that grows.

Her keen eyes did glitter like the bright stars at night,
The clothes that she was dressed in were costly and white;
Her bare neck was shaded with long raven hair,
And they called her, 'Pretty Susan, the Pride of Kildare.'

Long time I courted her till I'd wasted my store,
And her love turned to hatred because I was poor;
She said – 'I love another, whose fortunes I'll share,
So begone from pretty Susan, the Pride of Kildare.'

Sometimes I am jovial, sometimes I am sad,
Sometimes my love's courted by another lad;
But now we're at distance, no more I'll despair,
And blessings on pretty Susan, the Pride of Kildare.

Once more on the ocean I'm resolved to go,
I'm bound for the East with my heart full of woe;
And there I'll behold ladies with jewels so rare,
But none like pretty Susan, the Pride of Kildare.

Part 27, Number 5, 15 April 1916

This song was in circulation among American whalemen from the late 1840s. It may not be a coincidence, given Hull's connections with the whaling trade, that the earliest known version is on a broadside printed by Fordyce in Hull before 1837. Thomas King's text, like those from the many other singers from whom it was collected at various times, conforms closely with the broadsides printed in the mid-nineteenth century. It is probable, however, that the song originated in Ireland.

152. The Lady and her Apprentice Boy

Roud 903, Bathe-Clissold Wt.455
David Sawyer, Stratton St Margaret, Wiltshire

'Take love away and life would be defaced,' wrote one of our bards of Queen Elizabeth's time. At least literature would be defaced. And I do not know how the poets themselves, and especially the ballad writers, would have fared without it for a subject. We have met with the apprentice boy before. Here he obtained promotion, and for a guinea in a lottery, won £30,000. This opened the road to 'Cupid's Garden' but we knew beforehand that gold had power to break down the most formidable walls and barriers. Words of my old sheep shearing friend, David Sawyer, who has just celebrated his eighty fourth birthday.

While down in Cupid's Garden for pleasure I did walk,
I heard two loyal lovers, in secret they did talk;
The one she was a lady, and the other an apprentice boy,
And in secret they were talking, for he was all her joy.

She said to her apprentice, good-humoured, kind and free –
'If I should ever marry, love, 'twill be with none but thee.
Curse all the gold and silver, and riches I defy,
For my handsome young apprentice, a maid I'll live and die.'

As soon as her aged father came to understand,
He had her true love banished unto a foreign land;
Where she lay brokenhearted lamenting she did cry –
'For my handsome young apprentice, a maid I'll live and die,'

A servant to a merchant this young man he was bound,
And by his good behaviour a fortune there he found;
He soon became a butler, that promoted him much fame,
And by his good behaviour, a steward soon became.

For a fortune in a lottery, a guinea he paid down,
And there he drew a ticket worth thirty thousand pounds;
He had both gold and honour, and his coat was laced indeed,
And he returned from India to his true love with speed.

He went for to embrace her but she flew from his arms,
Saying – 'There's no lord, duke, nor nobleman shall ever enjoy my charms;
Curse all the gold and silver, and riches I'll defy,
For my handsome young apprentice, a maid I'll live and die.'

He said – 'Dear honoured lady, I have been in your arms!
And here's the ring you gave me for kissing of your charms;
You vowed if ever you married those charms I should enjoy,
Your father did me banish, and I am the apprentice boy.'

As soon as she heard these words and found that they were true,
With kisses out of measure into his arms she flew;

Then a road to Cupid's Garden these lovers quickly found,
And in everlasting pleasure, these lovers they were bound.

Part 27, Number 7, 15 April 1916

This charming song appeared in print as 'The Lady and the Prentice Boy' in *A New Garland, containing Three Excellent New Songs* published by George Swindells in Manchester before 1796. It was taken up by other printers soon afterwards. It was collected a few times, notably by Sabine Baring-Gould and Ralph Vaughan Williams, but it is often confused with 'Cupid's Garden' (no. 145). The song was also found in many versions throughout the USA and Canada. Here 'Cupid's Garden' serves as both the real place and as a metaphor for happiness. It is something of a relief to hear of a daughter who gains her apprentice, even if the route to her doing so involves a detour.

153. To Holland We Were Bound

Roud 811, Bathe-Clissold Gl.66
Charles Messenger, Cerney Wick, Gloucestershire

This dates from the eighteenth century, and refers to one of our Continental wars of the period. I obtained the words of Charles Messenger, Cerney Wick.

Come, all you wild young men, a warning take by me,
Never let your mind go astray into a far countree;
To Holland we were bound, to beat them was our intent,
Our officers were on board, and soon to sea we were sent.

As we were sailing along, the very first thing we did spy,
Was a bold seamen French ship of war, and they were our enemy;
Our decks were soon sprinkled with blood, and with vengeance loud cannons did roar,
And I wished myself back safe at home, with my own dearest Polly once more.

She's a tall and a clever youth, with a black and a rolling eye,
It's here I am bleeding on deck, all for her sweet sake I must die.
O had I wings like a dove, all up in the air I would steer!
I would search the wide world over until I'd found my Polly dear.

Part 27, Number 8, 15 April 1916

This was printed as 'The Valiant Sailor' in the *Irish Boy's Garland* published in Edinburgh in 1744, validating Williams's estimate of the age of the song. That version is longer and more detailed than the collected versions and it does not name Polly. Roy Palmer noted that there do not seem to have been any broadside versions printed in the nineteenth century.[63] Nonetheless, it survived in oral tradition and Polly acquired her name. She even appears in the only version of the song found in America, Lena Bourne Fish's 'The Press Gang Sailor'.[64] Versions were collected in England by Cecil Sharp, George Butterworth, and later collectors. The version of 'Polly on the Shore' that has become most familiar is that heard from the Sussex singer George Maynard.

154. The New Garden Fields

Roud 1054, Bathe-Clissold Wt.460
David Sawyer, Stratton St Margaret, Wiltshire

For this song and the following ['I Am a Pretty Wench', *FSUT*, pp. 122–23], *I am indebted to David Sawyer. He and Granny, who is aged eighty nine, live in a little cottage by the road side. David does all the work. He gets Granny's breakfast, cleans up, makes the bed, puts on the pot, cooks the dinner, washes the clothes once a week, and sees to everything else. He has travelled far in his time and is possessed of much useful knowledge, in addition to his songs, which are numerous. 'You never seed a better songbook than I be, I warn,' says David. And I admit that I never did.*

Come, all you young females, I pray, give attend,
Unto these few lines I am going to pen;
It is of lovely Mary I'm going to write,
She was all my day's study, and my dreams by night.

On the eighteenth of August, by the date of the year,
By these new garden fields, where I first met my dear;
She appeared like a goddess, or some young divine,
That was come for a torment, to torment my mind.

'Young man, I'm no torment,' these words she did say.
'I'm pulling these flowers, so fresh and so gay,
I'm pulling these flowers which nature does yield,
For I take great delight in the new garden fields.'

Then I said – 'Lovely Mary, dare I make so bold,
As your lily-white hand one moment to hold?

---

[63] Roy Palmer (ed.), *The Oxford Book of Sea Songs* (Oxford: Oxford University Press, 1986), p. 316.
[64] Anne Warner (ed.), *Traditional American Folk Songs from the Anne & Frank Warner Collection* (Syracuse, NY: Syracuse University Press, 1984), pp. 156–57.

It would give me more pleasure than this earthly store,
So grant me this favour, I'll ask you no more.'

'Oh, then,' she replied, 'I'm afraid you're in jest.
If I thought you in earnest, I'd count myself blest
For my father is coming.' These words she did say,
'So fare you well, young man, for I must away.'

'And now she has gone and left me all in the bonds of love;
King Cupid protect me, and you powers above!
King Cupid protect me, and now take my part,
For she's guilty of murder, she's broken my heart.'

She turned and she said, 'Young man, I pity your moan,
I will leave you no longer to sigh all alone;
And I will go with you to some foreign part,
For you are the first one to inflame my heart.'

Part 28, Number 2, 22 April 1916

The earliest version of this that has been found in print is on a slip from Armstrong of Liverpool in the 1820s, though Roy Palmer wrote, 'For my money it must date from the eighteenth century.'[65] The earlier versions have only six stanzas and the young man is left in despair. Later printers and singers were kinder to him, adding not only the stanza David Sawyer sang last, but also another in which the couple go off to be married:

We'll go to church on Sunday, and married we will be
We'll join our hands in wedlock, and sweet unity
We'll join our hands in wedlock and vow to be true
To father and mother we'll bid our adieu.

[65] Roy Palmer (ed.), *Folk Songs Collected by Ralph Vaughan Williams* (London: J. M. Dent, 1983), pp. 32–34.

155. William and Dinah

Roud 271, Bathe-Clissold Wt.345
Thomas King, Castle Eaton, Wiltshire

This was also entitled 'Villikins and Dinah', Villikins, it would seem, having formerly stood for William in certain localities. The song is very old. I first heard of it at Stanton Fitzwarren, Wiltshire; and later at Castle Eaton where it was sung by the very aged Thomas King, lately dead. I have met with it in several villages far remote from each other. Words of Thomas King, Castle Eaton, Wiltshire.

It's of a rich merchant in London did dwell,
He had but one daughter, a beautiful girl,
Her name it was Dinah, scarce sixteen years old,
And she had a large fortune of silver and gold.

Besides her large fortune, when her mother did die,
It caused many young men to love and draw nigh;
So coldly she viewed them – the truth I will tell,
For she loved her dear William and lovéd him well.

As Dinah was walking in the garden one day,
Her father came to her and this he did say -
'Go, dress thyself, Dinah, in gorgeous array,
For I've met with a young man both gallant and gay.

'I've met with a young man with five thousand a year,
And he says he will make you his bride and his dear;
He's houses and lands in three counties, I'm told,
And riches in plenty, with jewels and gold.'

'Oh, father, dear father, I've not made up my mind,
To marry just yet I don't feel inclined;
To you my large fortune I'll gladly give o'er,
If you'll let me live single some three years or more.'

'Get you gone, you bold strumpet,' her father replied,
'Since you have refuséd to be this man's bride,
I'll give away your portion to some of your kin,
You shall not reap the benefit of one single pin.'

Then Dinah wrote letters with all haste and speed,
And told her dear William what her father had said –
'Adieu, my sweet William. For ever, farewell!
How dearly I love you, there's no tongue can tell.'

As William was walking in the grove all alone,
He saw his dear Dinah laid dead on the ground;
With a cup of strong poison and a note lying by –
'It was my cruel father caused me this death to die.'

He kissed her cold lips as she lay on the floor,
And called her his jewel ten thousand times o'er;
He drank up the poison, like a lover so brave,
And now William and Dinah lie both in one grave.

Part 28, Number 4, 22 April 1916

A melodramatic song about the doings and double suicide of William and Dinah is said to have been written in the early nineteenth century by Harry Horton, a singer in the Birmingham music halls. This was published in about 1820 on a broadside as *The Cruel Father.* It was later recast into its better-known form as the parody 'Villikins and his Dinah'. It is unclear who did the rewriting or who composed the tune, but the song was certainly performed by Frederick Robson in a revival of Henry Mayhew's play *The Wandering Minstrel* at the Olympic Theatre in 1853. Mayhew later claimed to have created the piece himself, but it is more likely that it was the work of E. L. Blanchard. The song was taken up by the Anglo-American music hall entertainer Sam Cowell, to whom it owes its great popularity on both sides of the Atlantic. Most of the collected versions, including that above, owe more to the parody than to the original song.

156. The Green Bushes

Roud 1040, Bathe-Clissold Wt.397
Elijah Iles, Inglesham, Wiltshire
William Jeffries, Longcot, Berkshire

An old favourite, once popular throughout the Upper Thames Valley. It has many times been offered to me by the oldest men now living there, and it was equally pleasing to the women, who sang it in the fields. Words of Elijah Iles, and William Jeffries, Longcot, Berkshire

As I was a-walking one morning in spring,
To hear the birds whistle and the nightingale sing;
I heard a young damsel, most sweetly sang she –
'Down by the green bushes he thinks to meet me.'

'I'll buy you a beaver and a fine silken gown,
I'll buy you a petticoat flounced down to the ground,
If you will prove loyal and constant to me,
And forsake your own true love and be married to me.'

'I want none of your beavers nor fine silken gowns,
I want none of your petticoats flounced down to the ground,
But if you will prove loyal and constant to me,
I'll forsake my own true love and be married to thee.'

'Come, let us be going, kind sir, if you please;
Come, let us be going from under the those trees;
For yonder is coming my true love, I see,
Down by the green bushes where he thinks to meet me.'

And when that he came there and found she was gone,
He looked like a lambkin that was quite forlorn;
'She's gone with some other and forsaken me,
So adieu to the green bushes for ever,' said he.

'I'll be much like a schoolboy, and spend my time in play,
I will never so foolishly be deluded away.
A false hearted woman shall deceive me no more,
So adieu to the green bushes, 'tis time to give o'er.'

Part 28, Number 5, 22 April 1916

There is a great deal of confusion about the origins of this song as there are, actually, two separate songs, each of which has appeared under more than one name. The song heard by Alfred Williams from Elijah Iles was the one that we now know as 'Among the Green Bushes', or simply 'The Green Bushes', and it became one of the most popular of all English folk songs. It is characterized by the line 'I'll buy you fine beavers [hats, not animals] and fine silken gowns', which appears in nearly every later broadside and most collected versions, sometimes as the first stanza. Its popularity was further enhanced further when it was performed in John Baldwin Buckstone's play *Green Bushes; or, A Hundred Years Ago* (1845), and was shortly afterwards printed as sheet music. The 'fine beavers' stanza is sung in the first act. In the next generation it became known as an Irish song because it was performed frequently by the Irish tenor John McCormack.

157. Whisper, My Love, Do

Roud 672, Bathe-Clissold Wt.425
George Barrett, Marston Meysey, Wiltshire

This is older than the 'Green Bushes' though it is not so well known. I have met with it but once, entirely, viz at Marston Meysey where I obtained the words of George Barrett. It was his father's song. The old man has been dead for many years. A version is printed in 'The Scots Musical Museum', 1803, by which it would seem to be claimed as of Scots origin.

As I lay musing on my bed last night,
I dreamed of my own heart's delight;
I was so perplexed as I could take no rest,
Love did torment me so –
Then straight to my love's window I did go.

I went to my love's window with fame,
And gently called her all by her name;
My love arose, put on her clothes,
And to me she whispered low,
Saying – 'Go from my window, my love, do!'

'My mother and father they are both awake,
And they will surely hear you if you speak.
There'll be no excuse, but sad abuse,
Bad words and bitter blows –
So go from my window, my love, do!'

My love arose and tumbled over the chair,
Her father cries out, 'Who, who is there?'
'I am out of bed, I can take no rest,
The tiles they rattle so.
Hark! Father, hark! how the stormy winds blow!'

My love came down and opened the door,
Like an angel bright she stood all on the floor;
Her eyes shone bright, like the stars at night,
Like diamonds in the room,
But still she cried, 'Whisper, my love, do!'

Ten thousand times I kissed her sweet charms,
Ten thousand times I folded her in my arms;
But what I said there, I shall never declare,
No mortal man shall know –
But still she cried, 'Whisper, my love, do!'

Part 28, Number 6, 22 April 1916

This song has become very popular in the modern revival as a result of the inclusion of the version by Marina Russell of Dorset in the *Penguin Book of English Folk Songs* (1959) under the title 'One Night as I Lay on my Bed', which was collected by Henry Hammond in 1907. Williams's version and the other versions heard by the Victorian and Edwardian collectors are very similar to songs printed in the eighteenth century. The earliest found so far is in *The Buff's Garland*, from the second half of the eighteenth century, where it is called 'The Maid's Love to her Sweet-heart'. Surprisingly, there do not appear to have been any broadsides published in the intervening period and the song has survived only in oral tradition.

158. The Pitcher of Water

Roud 2671, Bathe-Clissold Wt.364
Henry Harvey, Cricklade, Wiltshire

This I have heard twice only, i.e. at Bishopstone and Cricklade where I obtained the words of the late Wassail Harvey. I think it must be well nigh a century old. The use of the word 'hind' for a female peasant in the second line, is unusual and indicate some age of composition.

'Oh, where are you going so fast, pretty maid?'
Said I to a hind the other day, now;
'For a pitcher of water, kind sir, to the well,
And so don't stop me, I pray, now.'
'For a pitcher of water,' said I, 'is that all?
Why, I am much stronger than you, now;
So give me the pitcher, I'll fetch it for you,
So dearly, indeed, I love you now.'

The well being not far, I ran to it straight,
I bade her to wait there close by, now,
But great the misfortune I have to relate,
For the spire of the church caught my eye now,
Not thinking of wedlock – 'twas something to tell –
Crying – 'Fanny! Oh what shall I do now?'
I slipped and the pitcher it dropped in the well,
And I was near falling in too, now.

In tears she replied, 'I am ruined indeed,
Oh, where shall I go, or what do now?
My mother I promised to be back with speed,
This came of my trusting to you, now.'
'Never mind, my dear Fanny, I'll risk my own life,

If you will consent to be my love.

Never mind the old pitcher! I'll make you my wife,
And blest I shall be with my true love.'

Part 29, Number 2, 29 April 1916

Also known as 'The Pitcher; or, Dearly I Love You' and 'True Love,' this song was published by Catnach and others early in the nineteenth century. The only other collector to have recorded that he heard the song was Percy Grainger who heard it in Surrey. Both collected versions correspond closely with the printed versions.

159. Down Ratcliffe Highway

Roud 598, Bathe-Clissold Wt.353
Henry Harvey, Cricklade, Wiltshire

This old piece I also obtained of the late 'Wassail' Harvey, of Cricklade. He died recently in his ninetieth year. I was a long time securing any of his songs; he appeared to have forgotten them and was very infirm. Happening to look in upon him in his tiny cottage one wet night in mid-winter, I found him possessed of a very severe cold, and gasping for breath. Thereupon I went to the inn, fetched a little rum and insisted upon his taking a glass hot immediately. The result was magical. After expressing gratitude he commenced to sing in a wonderfully deep tone of voice, that surprised me and quite startled his wife: she said he had not sung like it for fifty years. After that I saw the old man frequently till the time of his death, and we had many musical afternoons and evenings together. He was also possessed of much quaint lore and useful knowledge.

As I was walking one noon,
Down Ratcliffe Highway I did stray;
I chanced to call at an alehouse,
To spend the whole night and next day.

There was a young lass who sat by me,
She asked if I'd money to sport;
I called for some wine, changed one guinea,
And she quickly replied, 'That's the sort!'

The bottle was put on the table,
And glasses for everyone,
I asked for the change of my guinea,
And she tipped me the verse of a song.

'If that is your fashion to rob me,
Such a fashion I never could abide;
But tip me the change of my guinea,
Or else I will fire a broadside.

The bottle and glass I seizéd,
And soon at their heads I let fly –
To see how they instantly scattered,
Crying, 'Murder. Oh Lord, I shall die.'

Then the night being dark in my favour,
Up Ratcliffe Highway I did trip'
I got in a boat bound for Deptford,
And was soon safe aboard of my ship.

Part 29, Number 3, 29 April 1916

This appeared on broadsides in the early nineteenth century, the earliest of which was published in the 1820s by Armstrong of Liverpool, who called it *Change for a Guinea.* Other printers called it *Rolling Down Wapping.*

William Bolton, an old sailor who sang this song to Anne Gilchrist told her about the good times he had enjoyed on Ratcliffe Highway, saying that 'in his young days it was a favourite diversion among sailors ashore to take a walk down the Highway, and if their hearts were not cheered by the sight of some fight or disturbance already going on, to set about creating one without delay'.[66] Henry Harvey did not sing the moralizing stanzas that usually end the song.

160. The Banker

Roud 3321, Bathe-Clissold Gl.112
John Puffet, Lechlade, Gloucestershire

The Banker was popular around Lechlade and Buscot on the Upper Thames; I have heard it in other villages, but it was not widely known. Words of John Puffet, Lechlade.

As I walked out one morning fair,
To view the fields and to take the air;
'Twas there I saw a young banker alone,

[66] Roy Palmer (ed.), *The Oxford Book of Sea Songs* (Oxford: Oxford University Press, 1986), p. 198.

Leaving his true love to make her mourn.

He says – 'Pretty maid, will you come on deck,
For the chains of gold hanging round your neck?'
These words she says – 'You may prove true,'
The answer he made – 'I'll have none of you.'

The young banker turned to go away,
She followed after and bade him stay;
'Oh stay, oh stay, love, and I'll prove true.'
But the answer he made – 'I'll have none of you.'

Then this sweet, pretty maid her senses lost,
Ever since the day that her love was crost;
She sings and cries and longs for the day,
Cursing the hours she said – 'Nay, nay, nay.'

The young banker had such a handsome face,
Around his neck was a piece of lace;
And besides he had such lovely hair,
And cheeks as soft as a damsel fair.

Part 29, Number 4, 29 April 1916

In the rural economy of the past a 'banker' was someone who cleared and maintained ditches and stone 'hedges'. In a *Dialogue between a Brisk Young Farmer a Handsome Young Woman*, probably of the second half of the eighteenth century, the subject of the song is a farmer rather than a banker, but later broadsides recast it as *A New Song, called The Banking Boy*. The text of these later broadsides is essentially the same as John Puffet's song

It has been collected several times in northern England, but was encountered less frequently in the south.

161. The Gallant Hussar

Roud 1146, Bathe-Clissold Gl.115
James West, Quenington, Gloucestershire

Not one of the oldest folk songs. It is of some age however, dating probably from the opening of the nineteenth century, since it was sung at Quenington and Coln St. Aldwyn many years ago. Obtained of James West, Quenington.

A damsel possessed of great beauty,
She stood at her own father's gate,
The gallant Hussars were on duty,
To view them this maiden did wait;
Their horses were capering and prancing,
Their accoutrements shone like a star,
From the field they were nearest advancing,
She espied her young gallant Hussar.

Their fleeces were strung over their shoulder,
So careless they seemed, for to ride,
So warlike appeared these young soldiers,
With glittering swords by their side;
To the barracks so early next morning,
This damsel she went with her car,
Because she loved him sincerely –
Young Edwin, her gallant Hussar.

It was there she conversed with her soldier,
These words she was heard for to say;
Says Jane – 'I have seen none more bolder,
To follow my laddie away.'
'O, fie,' said young Edwin, 'Be steady,
And think of the dangers of war.
When the trumpet sounds I must be ready,
So wed not your gallant Hussar.'

Says Edwin – 'Your friends you must mind them,
Or else you're ever undone;
They'll leave you no portion behind them,
So pray! Do my company shun.'
She says – 'If you will be true hearted,
I've money of my own in store,
From this time no more we'll be parted,
I'll wed with my gallant Hussar.

'For twelve months on bread and cold water,
My parents confined me for you;
Oh, hard-hearted friends to their daughter,
Whose heart it was loyal and true!

Unless they confine me for ever,
Or banish me from you afar,
I'll follow my soldier so clever,
I'll wed with my gallant Hussar.'

As he gazed on each beautiful feature,
The tears they did stand in each eye –
'I'll wed with this beautiful creature
And forsake cruel war,' he did cry:
So now they're united together,
Friends, think of them now you're afar,
Saying – 'Heaven bless them now, and forever –
Young Jane and her gallant Hussar.'

Part 29, Number 5, 29 April 1916

This was published as *Young Edward, the Gallant Hussar* early in the nineteenth century and was heard by a number of song collectors. In the broadside the 'fleeces' on the shoulders of the Hussars in the second verse should have been given as 'pelisses', the fur semi-cape that was part of a hussar's uniform. Otherwise the song is close to the printed editions.

162. The Highwayman

Roud 2638, Bathe-Clissold Wt.448
David Sawyer, Stratton St Margaret, Wiltshire

We have had several highwayman songs, and I find there are several yet to come. I cannot pretend that they are in any way highly remarkable, but they appear to have served the purpose for which they were written and amused the rustics. Words of David Sawyer.

A nobleman lived in a city,
Whose daughter to market would go,
Thinking that nothing could harm her,
As she passed late to and fro.

Till a gentleman thief overtook her,
And the pistol he held to her breast,
Saying – 'Your money and clothes you surrender,
Or else you shall die, I protest.'

And then he stripped her stark naked,
And gave her the bridle to hold,
While she stood shivering and shaking,
Just ready to die with the cold.

Then from stirrup to saddle she mounted,
Saying – 'You are a hard hearted man,
And since that my coin you've accounted,
You follow me now, if you can.'

The highwayman rose in a passion,
And unto her did call aloud –
'O beautiful Nancy! stop, Nancy!
Your money and clothes are your own.'

'My money and clothes I don't value,
You can keep it all, if you please.'
He ran but he could not get to her,
For his boots they so hampered his knees.

Part 29, Number 6, 29 April 1916

Often called 'The Highwayman Outwitted' the clever young lady is usually a farmer's daughter from Cheshire (or Norfolk, or Leicester, or . . .). The song was in print towards the end of the eighteenth century as *The Maid of Rygate.* It has been widely collected.

163. Florence Nightingale

Roud 2655, Bathe-Clissold Ox.289
Job Gardner, Shilton, Oxfordshire

This is not a very old piece, as may be seen from the subject; nevertheless it is a folk song, and has some interest. Many rude, illiterate rustics have, by means of it, been made to know who was Florence Nightingale, and have come to admire her with as much sincerity as those who have been privileged to read the more magnificent 'Saint Philomena' by Longfellow. Words of Job Gardner, Shilton, near Burford.

On a dark, lonely night, on the Crimea's red shore,
There'd been bloodshed and strife the morning before;
The dead and the dying lay bleeding around,
Some crying for help, but there was none to be found.

Now God sent this woman to succour the brave,
And many she saved from an untimely grave;
Her eyes they beam with pleasure, she's bounteous and good,
The wants of the wounded by her were well understood.

Some with fever brought in, with life almost gone,
Some with mangled limbs, and some to fragments were torn;

But she cheers up their spirits, and their hearts never fail,
Now they're cheered by the presence of the sweet Nightingale.

Now God in his mercy He pitied their cries,
And the soldier so cheerful in the morn does arise;
For she cheers up their spirits, and their hearts never fail,
Now they're cheered by the presence of the sweet Nightingale.

Sing praise to this woman, deny it who can;
All women were sent for the comfort of man;
Who ever rail against them we hope to always fail;
Treat them well, then they'll prove like the sweet Nightingale.

Part 29, Number 7, 29 April 1916

Since Florence Nightingale had died only six years before he collected the song it is not surprising that Williams thought it 'not a very old piece'. Nightingale provided a good news story in a war that otherwise gave people at home little to celebrate and this song appeared on several broadsides. Williams seems to have been the only collector to have noted the song. Others might have said 'not a folk song'.

164. The Congreve Man

Roud 12880, Bathe-Clissold Gl.29
William Mills, Ablington, Gloucestershire

The three pieces immediately following I obtained of Mr William Mills, Ablington, Bibury, who sang them many years ago at harvest homes and other festivals. I am very pleased to be able to print them in our series since in addition to the interest of the songs themselves, is the interest attaching to the contributor. Mr Mills is the Tom Peregrine of that delightful book 'A Cotswold Village' written by the late Arthur Gibbs, who resided at Ablington Manor. The character, sayings and doings of Tom Peregrine, at home and abroad, represent a not inconsiderable feature of the charming volume. Since he was a gamekeeper to and also the intimate associate of the author, it may be taken for granted that he was directly and indirectly the source of some of the most pleasing pages of the work. To this knowledge must now be added the gratifying fact of his being a singer of folk songs and we welcome his inclusion in our list of collaborators.

Oh, I'm going to tell you a curious tale,
It happened of late, so it won't be stale;
A man went once to see a friend,
But little he thought how it would end.
    Ri tol the rol ol; fol the rol ol.

He reached the house, knocked once, or more,
His friend not appearing, he opened the door;
And, feeling thirsty, he thought it no sin,
To visit the shelf where his friend kept his gin.
Ri tol the rol ol; fol the rol ol.

A bottle he found, and to his gill
He put it, determined to have his fill;
But as he drank the contents his friend walked in,
Saying – 'What are you at?' 'Why, 'I've drunk your gin.'
Ri tol the rol ol; fol the rol ol.

'My gin?' says he, 'Why none I've got,
You've made a mistake, you foolish sot!
If you've drunk that stuff, it will burn you to ashes,
'Tis a liquid for dipping of Congreve matches.'
Ri tol the rol ol; fol the rol ol.

He'd no sooner heard it than off he went,
For a stomach pump was his intent;
But ere he reached the doctor's shop,
He was all in a blaze from bottom to top.
Ri tol the rol ol; fol the rol ol.

He ran with all his might and main,
Until a pond he chanced to gain;
He threw himself in – you may think it a lie –
But the heat of his body sucked up the pond dry.
Ri tol the rol ol; fol the rol ol.

He ran till he was dreadfully tired,
And every place he touched was fired;
He threw himself down in a wood for ease,
But his Congreve body burnt all the trees.
Ri tol the rol ol; fol the rol ol.

Now this man to London town he came,
He'd a fire-proof cloak made to keep in the flame;
But he so strong of the liquid did smell,
They all thought him a gentleman from h–ll.
Ri tol the rol ol; fol the rol ol.

Now this man he asked for lodgings bold,
And lucky for him the host had a cold;
So he nothing of the liquid did smell,
And the fire-proof cloak kept the flames in well.
Ri tol the rol ol; fol the rol ol.

Now he had not been to bed very long,
Before he found there was something wrong;
He awoke and was obliged to escape through the winder,
For the bed and the bedding were all burnt to a tinder.
Ri tol the rol ol; fol the rol ol.

Now this man he was in a terrible plight,
He was obliged to sleep in the fields all night;
And the people who saw him perceived, in a crack,
That he was none other than Spring Heel Jack.
    Ri tol the rol ol; fol the rol ol.

Now the people they were is such a stew,
He'd frightened to death no little few;
They swore, if they caught him, for causing such shocks,
They'd grind him and sell at a ha'penny a box.
    Ri tol the rol ol; fol the rol ol.

Now I'll tell you the last of this man's ills -
He went to Dartford Powder Mills;
He saw some powder and threw himself in it,
And blew up the place in less than a minute.
    Ri tol the rol ol; fol the rol ol.

The people surrounded the place next day,
I'm told that one of his legs ran away;
It turned round in a blaze, and went off in a hand-turn,
And 'tis called from that day the famed Jack and the Lantern.
    Ri tol the rol ol; fol the rol ol.

Now I've told you all, as near as I can,
About this dreadful Congreve man;
Be persuaded by me, whene'er you go in
To see a friend, don't steal his gin.
    Ri tol the rol ol; fol the rol ol.

Part 30, Number 1, 13 May 1916

Williams is the only collector to have noted this song, but it appears on a number of broadsides from the middle of the nineteenth century. Examples of songs that rely on fantastical science and technology for their plots are not common. Others include 'The Steam Arm' and 'The Cork Leg'. This was also the period when the story of 'Spring-Heeled Jack' was causing some alarm in credulous quarters.

The 'Congreve Match' was lit by being rubbed on sandpaper, but there was an earlier type of match that required it to be dipped into acid in order to light it. Williams's enthusiasm for Arthur Gibbs's book *A Cotswold Village* is something that I can endorse heartily.

165. The Mice and the Crumbs

Roud 21196, Bathe-Clissold Gl.31
William Mills, Ablington, Gloucestershire

Obtained of W. Mills, Ablington. The song was a favourite of his grandmother's.

A little old woman once lived in a house,
In a garret so monstrously high,
Each cupboard was lined, well stored was each shelf,
And in a sly pocket was plenty of pelf,
And a drop of good liquor when dry;
But the rats and the mice, through the holes,
Came into the cupboard in shoals,
So freely exercising their gums,
On cheese parings, candle ends, and crumbs;
A curious thing it may seem,
But they dipped their brown tails in the cream,
    Which was very bad manners you'll say,
    Alas and alack a day!
    A curious moral I'll make,
    So, listen, both great and small -
    You'd better have crumbs for the mice to eat,
    Than to have no crumbs at all.

Now this little old woman, plagued out of her life,
Collected of cats fifteen,
And went to bed with them all in her view;
There was black, white, tabby, and tortoiseshell, too,
But the candle was scarcely out,
When they made such a confounded rout,
Seizing the victuals, and tearing,
Clawing, spitting, and swearing,
Broke cups, plates, and dishes, all her store,
Lapped the cream up, and cried out for more,
    Which was shocking bad manners, *etc.*

Now this little old woman she awoke with a fright,
Not dreaming the cause of the din,
She groped out the tinder-box, and she struck a light,
And the very first object that came into her sight,
Was her bottle broke, and spilt all her gin;
She looked in the cupboard in despair,
But the d---l of anything was there,
Except plates and dishes broken small,
Cream jugs, saucers, cups and all;
Each cat looked as savage as a cur,
As if he could easily swallow her,

Which was shocking bad manners, *etc.*

Part 30, Number 2, 13 May 1916

I have not been able to find another version of this song anywhere, as yet, so must conclude that it is, again, unique to Williams's collection.

166. The Genius

Roud 12899, Bathe-Clissold Gl.30
William Mills, Ablington, Gloucestershire

Obtained of W. Mills, Ablington.

When once a very little boy,
My dad sent me to school;
The master said though least I was,
I was the biggest fool.
Such a genius I did grow, did grow, did grow,
Such a genius I did grow.

They tried, with cakes and cunning,
To put larning in my yead;
But I never knowed nor couldn't tell,
Girt A from crucked Z.
Such a genius I did grow, *etc.*

Arithmetic next puzzled me,
And, as my knowledge grew:
I soon found out that one and one,
When added up, made two.
Such a genius I did grow, *etc.*

They sent me to the barber's –
To shave, my Daddy's hope –
I took the lather for the milk,
And ate up all the soap.
Such a genius I did grow, *etc.*

They set me once to blow the fire,
Or out it would have gone;
And I ripped the billis open,
To see where the wind came from.
Such a genius I did grow, *etc.*

Upon my travels I set out,
The English folks to see;
I found that they had legs and arms,
And a yead the same as me.
    Such a genius I did grow, *etc.*

A great musician I became,
And, as the people say,
Upon the grinding organ,
I delightfully did play.
    Such a genius I did grow, *etc.*

I played before the Aldermen,
Also the great Lord Mayor;
And they sent me home, for fear that I,
Would set the Thames on fire.
    Such a genius I did grow, *etc.*

Part 30, Number 3, 13 May 1916

This song was performed as 'Such a Genius I Did Grow' at the Sans Pareil Theatre, London, in 1818. It was written and sung by Jane Scott, the co-founder and manager of the theatre, which later became the Adelphi. The song was printed in a number of songsters and on broadsides, but it was not heard by any collector other than Williams.

167. The Isle of France

Roud 1575, Bathe-Clissold Gl.28
Arthur Hawkins, Ablington, Gloucestershire

This song I also obtained at Ablington of Arthur Hawkins, a cottager, and it is interesting to learn that he too, contributed slightly to the making of 'A Cotswold Village'. Mr Hawkins knew two songs – the one here printed and 'Jim the Carter's Lad.' Mr Gibbs wrote the copy of the latter from his recital and included it in his book. The 'Isle of France' is much the older and better of the two songs, though the other was the more popular, and suited Mr Gibbs' purpose.

The sun was fair and the clouds advanced,
And the convict came to the Isle of France;
All around his legs were a ring and chain,
And his country was of the shamrock green.

The coastguard waited all on the beach,
While the convict's boat was about to reach;

The convict's chains did so shine and spark,
That it shook the veins of the coastguard's heart.

The convict launched his little boat,
Upon the ocean with him to float;
The birds at night took their silent rest,
But the convict here has a wounded breast.

Then the coastguard came to the Isle of France,
And towards the convict did advance;
The tears from his eyes did fall like rain –
'I hear young man, you're of the shamrock green.'

'I am a shamrock,' the convict cried,
'That has been tossed on the ocean wide;
For being unruly I do declare,
I'm condemned a transport for seven long years.'

When six of them were past and gone,
We were coming home to make up one,
When the stormy winds did so blow and roar,
That cast we were on a foreign shore.'

Then the coastguard played a noble part,
And with some brandy cheered the convict's heart;
Although this night being far advanced,
To find a friend in the Isle of France.

'God bless the coastguard,' the convict cried,
'He has saved my life from the ocean wide;
I'll drink his health in a flowing glass –
So here's success to the Isle of France.'

Part 30, Number 4, 13 May 1916

An Irish transportee on his way home from Australia after serving his sentence is wrecked on the coast of Mauritius (formerly known as the Île de France) and treated kindly by a coastguard. This song was printed on a number of broadsides in the mid-eighteenth century and was heard by most of the early song collectors. This is another song whose appeal lay in its sentiment. Ethel Kidson wrote about her uncle, Frank Kidson, collecting it from an old sailor named Dickenson, who said, 'I've seen the tears running from my captain's eyes when we sang that song.'

168. The Isle of Wight

Roud 32575, Bathe-Clissold Gl.153
Sarah Timbrell, Quenington, Gloucestershire
James Barnes, Quenington, Gloucestershire

I have met with this in two versions; the following is the better. It is old, as may be recognised from the style, and treatment of the subject. Obtained of Mrs S. Timbrel and James Barnes, Quenington.

Adieu, my lovely Nancy,
Ten thousand times adieu!
The rout is come this afternoon,
Good lass, what shall we do?
    Good lass, what shall we do?
    Good lass, what shall we do?
    The rout is come this afternoon,*
    Good lass, what shall we do?

I'll go unto the officer,
And unto him we'll say –
'I've brought a pretty fancy girl,
And I want to take her away.'
    And I want to take her away, *etc.*

'Oh, no,' replied the officer,
'Such things can never be;
There's not a lad in regiment,
That shall take a lass with he.'
    That shall take a lass with he, *etc.*

'If my orders you won't obey
I'll have you close confined:'
He says – 'My dearest Nancy girl,
I must leave you far behind.'
    I must leave you far behind, *etc.*

Then I took her round the turn,
Till we got out of sight –
'I'll send you letters plenty, love,
When I gain the Isle of Wight.'
    When I gain the Isle of Wight, *etc.*

For the drum and the trumpet they did sound,
The pipe did merrily play,
Right through the town called the Isle of Wight,
As we boldly marched away.
    Good lass, what shall we do? *etc.*

* The third line of each stanza should be inserted into its chorus.

Part 31, Number 2, 20 May 1916

This is a case where it is easier to say that it is not the well-known 'Adieu, My Lovely Nancy', which is concerned with a sailor leaving his true-love for a hard life on the sea from which he hopes to return. This piece shares only the first two lines of that song. Here, the young man is a soldier, chancing his arm by asking if he can take his girl on the march with him – a practice that was not unknown. I have not found anything similar in print or in a collected version; it seems unique to Williams.

169. The Boys of Kilkenny

Roud 1451, Bathe-Clissold Gl.47
John Sutton, Arlington, Bibury, Gloucestershire.

We have a verse of this song before, incorporated in something akin to it in sentiment. This is really the correct copy however, and is the original of the other song we printed. Obtained of John Sutton, Arlington, Bibury.

All the boys of Kilkenny are free and good lads,
And all their delight is in courting fair maids;
They kiss them, and court them, and spend their money free,
Of all the towns of Ireland, Kilkenny for me.

In the town of Kilkenny there runs a clear stream,
In the town of Kilkenny there lives a fair dame,
With her cheeks red as roses, and her lips much the same,
Like a bunch of fine strawberries so lovely they came.

Kilkenny is a pretty place, it shines as it stands,
The more I think of it the more my heart longs,
When I am at Kilkenny, there I am at home,
And there I have a sweetheart, but here I have none.

Now I'll build my love a castle on Kilkenny's free ground,
Where a duke nor a squire could not pull it down;
If any should ask you to know my name –
I'm an Irish excursion, from Kilkenny I came.

Part 31, Number 4, 20 May 1916

As Williams says, we encountered parts of this song above in 'Far from my Home' (no. 136). The original song is, of course, Irish, but it appeared on broadsides printed in London at the beginning of the nineteenth century. It has been heard by a number of English collectors, but not elsewhere.

170. The Cuckoo Is a Merry Bird

Roud 413, Bathe-Clissold Gl.127
Alice Barnett, Quenington, Gloucestershire

I have been waiting to hear a song about the cuckoo for a long while. I am certain it was sung about the Upper Thames. When I heard the opening of this piece I felt sure I had at least met with it, but I was disappointed. Nevertheless, the song is very quaint, and pretty and I am pleased with the words. Obtained of Mrs Alice Barnett, Quenington, late of Ablington.

The cuckoo is a merry bird,
He sings as he flies,
He brings us glad tidings,
And tells us no lies.

A-walking and a-talking,
And a-walking went I,
To meet my sweet William;
He'll come by and by.

To meet him it's a pleasure,
But to part it's a grief,
For an unconstant lover,
Is worse than a thief.

For a thief he will rob you,
Take all that you have,
But an unconstant lover
Will bring you to the grave.

The grave it will rot you,
And bring you to dust,
But an unconstant lover
No damsel can trust.

They will laugh under their hat, love,
As they see you pass by;
They'll bow with their body,
And wink with one eye.

They will kiss you and court you,
Poor girls to deceive,

There's not one in twenty,
A maid can believe.

They will kiss you and court you,
And swear to be true,
And the very next moment,
They'll bid you adieu.

Part 31, Number 5, 20 May 1916

The earliest version of this song is *The Forsaken Nymph*, which was printed in a Glasgow chapbook in 1802.

Both printed and collected versions are similar to the above, although the stanza order can vary. It was a very popular song on both sides of the Atlantic.

171. My Love Is like the Sun

Roud 583, Bathe-Clissold Gl.59
William Bradshaw, Bibury, Gloucestershire

For the three following songs I am indebted to William Bradshaw, Bibury, the 'Cotswold Village' depicted so admirably by the late J Arthur Gibb. I find, on examination, that Bibury was a highly musical village, and possessed many folk songs on times past. Most of these have disappeared now, since those who sang them are dead: it is good nevertheless, to encounter even the memory of such a state of things.

Cold winter's gone and past,
Pleasant summer's come at last,
The small birds are whistling on each tree;
Since misfortune proved unkind,
To the dearest love of mine,
And he's gone to the Isle of Kildare.

I will put on my suit of black,
With a fringe all around my back,
Gold rings on my fingers I will wear;
And straight away he'll appear,
From the Isle of Kildare,
And I soon shall set sight on him there.

My love is like the sun,
That through the firmament does run,
And always proves constant and true;
But I am like the moon,

Which does ramble round and round,
And every month it is new.

Part 31, Number 6, 20 May 1916

Though it is most usually known as 'The Curragh of Kildare', the earliest version of this song is *The Love-Sick Maid; or, Cordelia's Lamentation for the Absence of her Gerheard*, published in the 1760s. The 'Curragh' is a racecourse and in the original six-stanza version it is much clearer that she has gone to see her lover riding in a horserace. Sadly, he has gone to another meeting. The song was collected in only a handful of rather garbled versions, though widely printed.

172. Joe, the Collier's Son

Roud 1129, Bathe-Clissold Gl.58
William Bradshaw, Bibury, Gloucestershire

I do not think that the town of Marlborough in Wiltshire could have been intended in this song, as the local references do not agree with the neighbourhood. It is a very old piece, whatever its origin may have been. Words of William Bradshaw, Bibury.

I am Jolly Joe, the collier's son,
In Marlborough Town I dwell,
I courted lasses, many a one,
And I loved them all right well.

I courted Nancy, and young Kate,
And buxom Nelly too;
But Rachel's the girl that I adore,
And that you soon shall know.

I took a walk in Marlborough Town,
Down by the Bilstone Hill,
And who should I spy but my own true love,
With Jack from Ambrose Mill.

I hid myself behind the bush,
A-distant where they were,
He gave her kisses by one, two, and three,
Not knowing I was there.

I boldly steppéd up to him,
Saying – 'Rogue, what hast thou done?

I am Jolly Joe, the collier's son
Thou must either fight or run.'

And then to church young Rachel went,
A-sore against her will,
So maidens all, pity my downfall,
By Jack of Ambrose Mill.

Part 31, Number 7, 20 May 1916

This is 'Jack of Ambrose Mill' or, sometimes, 'Jolly Joe the Collier's Son'. Williams is correct to doubt the connection to Marlborough since the location varies in both printed and sung versions. It was, though, the habit of singers to insert the name of a place they knew, though not necessarily where they lived, since they might not want their own town associated with immoral behaviour. The earliest known version of this song is a broadside printed by James Catnach early in the nineteenth century and it appeared on several later broadsides. It was heard by most of the early collectors in southern England.

173. 'Twas on an Easter Monday

Roud 441, Bathe Clissold Gl.57
William Bradshaw, Bibury, Gloucestershire

Words of William Bradshaw, Bibury.

'Twas on an Easter Monday,
In the springtime of the year,
A mother and a daughter,
As you shall quickly hear.

Jane said, as they were walking,
'I'll tell you what I'll do:
I must and will have a husband,
For the fit comes on me now.'

'You say you will get married,
Where will you get a man?'
'Oh, then,' replies the daughter,
'I will have bouncing John.

'For he calls me his dear honey,
A milking of my cow,
And I know he loves me dearly,
For the fit comes on me now.'

'Suppose that he deceives you,
As he has done before?'
'Oh, then,' replies the daughter,
'I'll try a dozen more.

There's millers, brewers and bakers,
And men that follow the plough,
I will have a husband, mother,
For the fit comes on me now.'

'And now we have got married,
The truth to you I'll tell,
I have a handsome young man,
And he does love me well.

'We never have any words,
Or blows in any degree,
But we live quite contented,
In peace and unity.'

Part 31, Number 8, 20 May 1916

Usually called 'The Fit's Come on Me Now', this was published on a broadside by Catnach early in the nineteenth century. It is much earlier, though, as it is mentioned in Beaumont and Fletcher's play *Wit without Money* from *c.*1614. It has been collected a number of times on both sides of the Atlantic.

174. Ferry Hinksey Town

Roud 263, Bathe-Clissold Gl.44
George Hicks, Ablington, Gloucestershire

Again I have to refer to having obtained a song in two localities of the Vale. The first part of this was told to me by an old woman near Bampton, the second by George Hicks of Arlington, above mentioned ['Shepherd, Come Home to thy Breakfast', *FSUT*, pp. 176–77]. *The song had its origin near Oxford according to references to the river, and to Ferry Hinksey Town.*

I fell in love with a pretty girl,
With a black and a rolling eye;
I told her that I loved her,
And that most tenderly.

I promised for to marry her,
Upon a certain day;
But instead of that I was resolved,
To take her life away.

He went unto her uncle's house,
At ten o'clock at night;
And little did that poor girl think
He owed her any spite.

'Come, take a walk along with me,
Across the meadows gay,
There we will walk, and chat and talk,
And fix our wedding day.'

He drew a stake out of the hedge,
And beat her to the ground;
The blood from that young innocent
Came trickling slowly down.

Down on her bended knees she fell,
And aloud for mercy cried –
'Pray, Jimmy, dear, don't murder me,
For I am not fit to die.'

He took hold her curly locks,
And dragged her along the green,
Until he came to some river-side,
And there he threw her in.

She floated high, she floated low,
She floated there I spied –
'Instead of being a corpse, my love,
You should have been my bride.'

When he went home late at night,
No rest could he find,
Thinking of that pretty girl,
He'd killed and left behind.

And in a few days after,
Her body it was found,
A-floating down the river,
By Ferry Hinksey Town.

They took me up on suspicion,
My trial for to take,
For murdering of my own true love,
All by that cruel stake.

The judges and the jurymen,
They all did agree,
For murdering of my own true love,
It's hangéd I must be.

Part 32, Number 5, 3 June 1916

This song had enormous appeal to the old rural singers and has been collected many times on both sides of the Atlantic. In Britain it is often called 'The Berkshire Tragedy' and in America 'The Knoxville Girl'.

A broadside printed in 1744 supplies an important detail in its title that was missing from the Victorian versions: *The Berkshire Tragedy; or, the Whitham Miller, Who Most Barbarously Murdered his Sweet-Heart Big with Child.* Another clue to the killer's motive is given in other versions such as Harry Cox's 'Ekefield Town' in which he is identified as an apprentice. As such he would not have been allowed to marry, and the young woman's family would have ensured that he was not allowed to do so. An impossible dilemma – but the murder still seems extremely cold-hearted.

It is possible that the song is even older, as a ballad in Samuel Pepys's collection, *The Bloody Miller* (1684), has many of the features of the murder, with the added virtue of being 'A True and Just Account'.

175. The Bonny Labouring Boy

Roud 1162, Bathe-Clissold Gl.49
John Webley, Arlington, Bibury, Gloucestershire

'The Bonny Labouring Boy' is a ballad of a type that was commonly sung at the fairs, and was popular in many parts of the Thames Valley. I often heard of it, but failed to obtain the words till recently, when they were related to me by John Webley, Arlington, Bibury.

As I walked out one morning, 'twas in the blooming spring,
I heard a lonely maid complain, and grievously did sing,
Saying – 'Cruel were my parents that did me so annoy,
And would not let me marry my bonny labouring boy.'

Young Johnny was my true love's name, as you shall plainly see,
My father he employed him his labouring boy to be,
To harrow, reap, and sow the seed, and plough my father's land,
But soon I fell in love with him, as you shall understand.

'His cheeks were like the roses red, his eyes as black as sloes,
He's mild in his behaviour, wherever he does go;
He's manly, neat, and handsome, his skin is white as snow,
And in spite of both my parents, with my labouring boy I'll go.

'My parents thought to have me wed unto some lord or peer –
I being the only heiress to ten thousand pounds a year –

I fixed my heart on one true love, and him I'll ne'er deny;
Through the nation I will ramble with my bonny labouring boy.

'My father he came to me, and took me by the hand,
And he swore he'd send young Johnny unto a foreign land;
He locked me in my bedroom, my comforts to annoy,
And left me there to weep and mourn my bonny labouring boy.'

Said the daughter to her father – 'Your wish is all in vain,
Lords, dukes, earls and riches, I ever will disdain;
I'd rather live a humble life, my time I would employ,
Increasing in life's prospects with my bonny labouring boy.

My mother she came to me and unto me did say –
'Your father has appointed to fix your wedding day.'
I nobly made her answer – 'With him I'll ne'er comply,
For a single life I will remain for my bonny labouring boy.'

So it's fill your glasses to the brim, and let the toast go round,
Here's health to every labouring boy that ploughs and tills the ground;
For when his work is over his home he will enjoy,
So happy is the girl that gets a bonny labouring boy.

Part 32, Number 6, 3 June 1916

Here we have another daughter who makes what her parents consider an unsuitable match. The outcome is not spelled out clearly in John Webley's song, but there are longer, twelve-stanza versions, such as one printed by Pratt of Birmingham, in which the young woman shows her mettle:

Nine hundred pounds and all my clothes I took that very night,
And with the lad that I adored to Plymouth did take flight,
His love it has entangled me and that I can't deny,
So to a foreign land I'll go with my bonny labouring boy.[67]

Although the song has been widely printed and collected, the majority of versions do not contain the couple's escape and subsequent marriage.

[67] *Bonny Laboring Boy* (Wm. Pratt, printer, Digbeth, Birmingham) [London, British Library, L.R.271.a.2/7.(131.)].

176. The Unfortunate Tailor

Roud 1614, Bathe-Clissold Gl.50
John Webley, Arlington, Bibury, Gloucestershire

This, too, I obtained of John Webley, Arlington. I have not heard it elsewhere.

O list, O list to my sorrowful lay,
Attention give to my song, I pray;
And when you've heard it all, you will say,
That I'm an unfortunate tailor.
O, why did my Sarah serve me so?
No more will I stitch, no more will I sew;
My thimble and my needle to the winds I will throw,
I'll go and enlist for a sailor.

I once was as happy as a bird on a tree,
My Sarah was all in the world to me,
But I am cut out by a son of the sea,
And now I'm left to bewail her.
O, why did my Sarah serve me so, *etc.*

My days were happy, and my nights the same,
Till a man named Cobb from the ocean came,
With a big black beard and a muscular frame –
A captain on board of a whaler.
O, why did my Sarah serve me so, *etc.*

He spent his money so frank and free,
With his tales of the land, and songs of the sea;
He stole my Sarah's heart from me,
And blighted the hopes of the tailor.
O, why did my Sarah serve me so, *etc.*

I went to plead, but she did refuse;
She loved another, so we must excuse
Her candour, for it was no use,
She never would marry a tailor.
O, why did my Sarah serve me so, *etc.*

I felt it hard, and it made me sob,
He says – 'Get out, you blubbering swab,
If you don't begone I'll scuddle your nob';
And Sarah smiled at the sailor.
O, why did my Sarah serve me so, *etc.*

My Sarah was as tall as a young fir tree,
Fair as a lily, and brisk as a bee,
And many were the smiles that she smiled on me,
But now I'm left to bewail her.
O, why did my Sarah serve me so, *etc.*

My Sarah was the daughter of a publican –
A generous, kind, good sort of a man –
Who spoke very plain what he thought of a man,
But he never looked cross at the tailor.
O, why did my Sarah serve me so, *etc.*

So, now I'll cross the raging sea,
Since Sarah is untrue to me;
My heart's locked up and she has the key –
A very unfeeling jailer.
O, why did my Sarah serve me so, *etc.*

So now, my friends, at last, adieu!
No more my woes shall trouble you,
This world I'll ramble through and through,
I'll go and enlist for a sailor.
O, why did my Sarah serve me so, *etc.*

Part 32, Number 7, 3 June 1916

This song was written and composed by the music hall performer Harry Clifton who first advertised it in 1867. It was also collected by George Gardiner in Hampshire.

177. The Leather Breeches

Roud 12739, Bathe-Clissold Gl.34
William Avery, Aldsworth, Gloucestershire

This old song was popular in Gloucestershire, between Tetbury and Burford. I have not heard it south of the Thames though no doubt it was sung there formerly. Words of William Avery, Aldsworth, Gloucester.

When I was quite a little boy
My life passed sweet as honey,
Until my old grandfather died
And left me all his money;
It's twenty pounds and more
With harrows, ploughs and riches,
Of grunters half a score,
And a pair of leather breeches.
Rumpsey, bumpsey hey,
Rumpsey, bumpsey hey do.

One night as I went to woo
A damsel fine and dapper,
She looked at me so black,
And ding dong went her clapper;
Says she – 'I hate your plan,
My heart's against your riches,
And I'll never wed a man
That wears those leather breeches.'
    Rumpsey, bumpsey hey,
    Rumpsey, bumpsey hey do.

Then to town I did set off
My spirits for to rally,
And each one there did scoff,
In court and street, and alley;
Against me they did conspire
Threw me in ponds and ditches,
Slouched me in mud and mire,
And bebamsed my leather breeches [*besmeared*]
    Rumpsey, bumpsey hey,
    Rumpsey, bumpsey hey do.

Part 33, Number 1, 17 June 1916

This appeared on broadsides as *Hodge and his Leather Breeches*, with nine stanzas. In the nineteenth century 'Hodge' was a nickname for a simple countryman and there are many songs about countrymen's struggles in London. Hodge's adventures in the broadside versions include losing his prized trousers to a lady who has invited him to spend the night with her.

178. The Girls of Gloucestershire

Roud 12727, Bathe-Clissold Ox.261
Charles Hope, Filkins, Oxfordshire

This was popular in Gloucestershire and Oxfordshire, in which latter county Oxfordshire was substituted for Gloucestershire in the song. No doubt it was popular in other parts where the name of the county fitted in with the rhyme. Words of Charles Hope, Filkins.

Attend, you lads and lasses, a story you shall hear,
Concerning of the pretty girls who dwell in Gloucestershire;
They are handsome, they are charming, they're blooming and they're fair,
For there are no girls in England like the girls of Gloucestershire.

For they're handsome and they're charming, they're blooming and they're fair,
You'll find all over Britain's isles no lasses can compare
With the buxom pretty girls who reside in Gloucestershire.

Through England and Ireland, and Scotland I have been,
And over the Welsh mountains where beauty I have seen;
But of all the lasses in the land, I solemnly declare,
There's none that take my fancy like the girls of Gloucestershire.
For they're handsome and they're charming, *etc.*

There's Jane and Sal, and lovely Ann, and pretty Mary, too,
There's Betty and Amelia, and bonny black eyed Sue,
There's Martha and Eliza, and Kitty, too, so fair;
May happiness attend the pretty girls of Gloucestershire.
For they're handsome and they're charming, *etc.*

Some can brew, and some can bake, some can mend and sew,
Some can knit, some can spin, while some are plaiting straw,
Some can tie the velvet band all around their pretty hair;
Sure, you never saw such lasses as the girls of Gloucestershire.
For they're handsome and they're charming, *etc.*

Some can use the fork and rake, and some can drive the plough,
And some can sing like nightingales while milking of the cow,
Some can dance the hornpipe when they do go to the fair,
What sweet and lovely creatures are the girls of Gloucestershire.
For they're handsome and they're charming, *etc.*

Some can rock the cradle and sing lullaby all day –
'O John, false hearted Johnny, you've stole my heart away.'
Silk scarves and dandy ribbons to tie up their lovely hair,
What sweet and charming creatures are the girls of Gloucestershire!
For they're handsome and they're charming, *etc.*

Poor buxom blades of England, if you wish to change your life,
Pray, hasten unto Gloucestershire, and choose yourself a wife;
And when you're tired of wedlock's band, come bumpers full to share,
And drink a health unto the girls of Gloucestershire.
For they're handsome and they're charming, *etc.*

Part 33, Number 7, 17 June 1916

J. Livsey of Manchester published *The Girls of Lancashire* on a broadside in the first half of the nineteenth century, but most printers gave the title as *The Girls of ——shire*, so that customers could insert the place of their choosing. As a result it was collected by the Hammond brothers in Dorset as 'The Girls of Dorsetshire' and by Cecil Sharp as 'Somerset Lasses' and 'The Devonshire Girls'. Williams's headnote is a little confusing, but the surviving manuscript gives the title as 'The Girls of Gloucestershire' despite it having been heard in Oxfordshire.

179. Sarah Bloom

Roud 12611, Bathe-Clissold Gl.72
William Morse, Coln St Aldwyns, Gloucestershire

This piece was in frequent use around Fairford. It is not one of the best of songs, though it is of considerable age. Words obtained of William Moss, Coln St. Aldwyn.

A pretty girl came courting me,
Her name was Sarah Bloom,
She wanted me to marry her,
She said I was alone.
She said I was a nice young man,
And we may be well off soon –
But, I'll ask my mother and let you know,
Next Sunday afternoon.
    The kindness of that pretty girl,
    I never shall forget,
    She wanted me to marry her,
    But I cannot see that yet.

Now Sarah Bloom, one afternoon,
She took me for a walk,
She took my hand and pressed it very hard,
And lovingly did talk.
She wanted me to play with her,
At night by the light of the moon –
But, I'll ask my mother and let you know,
Next Sunday afternoon.
    The kindness of that pretty girl, *etc.*

She made me a present of a watch and chain,
Besides a brand new hat,
For Sundays when I walk with her
That I should cut a dash.
As soon as she found I would not play with her,
She wanted her presents back soon –
But, I'll ask my mother and let you know,
Next Sunday afternoon.
    The kindness of that pretty girl, *etc.*

If there's any young woman here tonight
Would like to be my wife,
Let her step forward and I'll do
The best I can through life.
And if she's in a hurry,
We may be married soon,
But, I'll ask my mother and let her know,
Next Sunday afternoon.
    The kindness of that pretty girl, *etc.*

Part 34, Number 2, 17 June 1916

This is 'I'll Ask my Mother and Let You Know Next Sunday Afternoon' written by Tom Bournley with music by George Ernshaw. It was published in St. Louis in 1868. In the original the name of the girl was 'Sarah Broome'. The song was published in a number of American songsters. Cecil Sharp also collected a version in Devon.[68]

180. Down in the Low Country

Roud 21213, Bathe-Clissold Ox.285
Ellen Trinder, West End, Northmoor, Oxfordshire

Words of Mrs Ellen Trinder, West End, Northmoor, Oxfordshire.

It was down in the low country,
A charming young damsel did dwell,
And she to the market went three times a week,
Her dairy goods there for to sell.

As she was a-rambling along one morning,
Before the break of day,
She had not been wandering, not past half a mile,
Before she had lost her sweet way.

She rambled all over the down,
And wandered it over again,
Till at length she spied a young shepherd boy,
Who was feeding his flock there with hay.

'Good morning, young maiden,' said he,
'Good morning, young fellow,' said she,
'I am a young maid and I have lost my way,
Except thou a friend prove to be.'

'Oh, sit thyself down on this stile,
Oh, sit thyself down for a while,
And I'll show thee the way, the very nearest way,
Within past one half a mile.'

[68] Sharp did not name place, singer, or date, but it can be inferred from the locations of the adjacent songs in his notebook that it was heard in north Devon.

'Good morning, young maiden,' said he,
'Good morning, young fellow,' said she,
'And if ever I should chance for to come this way again,
I surely will call upon thee.'

Part 35, Number 2, 1 July 1916

A simple telling of a familiar story – and yet I have not found this song anywhere else and must conclude that it is unique to this collection. It is, perhaps, surprising that having travelled to market three times a week she managed to lose her way.

181. When I Was a Maid, O Then

Roud 24144, Bathe-Clissold Ox.286
Ellen Trinder, West End, Northmoor, Oxfordshire.

Words of Mrs Ellen Trinder, West End, Northmoor, Oxfordshire.

When I was a maid, O then, O then,
When I was a maid, O then.
As many bright stars as there are in the sky,
As many young fellows I killed with my eye,
Wasn't I such a beauty then.

But now I am married, O then, O then,
But now I am married, O then,
I'm tied to this fantastical fop,
He goes with some other, and cares for me not,
How hard is my fortune, then!

But now he is married, O then, O then,
But now he is married, O then,
I'll make him remember in taking a wife,
I'll worrit and tease him quite out of his life,
And I'll be a widow, O then.

And when I'm a widow, O then, O then,
And when I'm a widow, O then,
I'll have a large house, and live at my ease,
I'll go out when I like, and come in when I please,
But I'll never get married again.

Part 35, Number 3, 1 July 1916

This is a reworking of the song 'I Wish I Was Single Again' (Roud 437) written from a female perspective. It is similar to a version in a cheap songster, *120 Comic Songs Sung by Sam Cowell*, published *c.*1850. Marianne Mason published a version that had come down through her family, the Mitfords, in her book *Nursery Rhymes and Country Songs* (1877). Mrs Trinder's version is different from both and the verse structure demands a different tune from the original. Though it is always a matter of regret that Williams did not note the tunes of his songs, it is particularly unfortunate in this case.

182. Never Cut your Toenails on a Sunday

Roud 20217, Bathe-Clissold Gl.136
James West, Quenington, Gloucestershire

This quaint and amusing song is to be met with very rarely, however – in Gloucestershire. I have not heard it south of the Thames. It used to be sung at least every year at the parish gathering at Quenington, by a woman of the village, usually in response to the request of the old Vicar, who was especially delighted with it. I have also quite recently heard the song mentioned at Ewen, near Cirencester. The copy was very kindly supplied me by James West, Quenington.

A spruce linen draper was Mr. John Low,
Walked the Custom House Quay on a Sunday,
He was dressed in the pink of the fashion and go,
When he met with the charming Miss Condy;
Her beautiful eyes took him all by surprise,
So queer was the state that he felt in,
He tried all in vain for to tell her his pain,
For his heart was really a-meltin'.
    But alas! Who could look into fate's book of laws?
    Mr Low would have married Miss Condy:
    He lost her, he lost her; and only because,
    He cut his toe nails on a Sunday.

The next time he met her, his love he made known,
Her person he thought all perfection,
He pressed her with speed to be bone of his bone,
She blushed, and had no objection;
So he gaily did sing, went and purchased the ring,
And the next Sunday was the bespeak day,
For that day would rhyme, and agree with his time,
Much better than having a week-day.
    But alas! Who could look, *etc.*

On the blest Sunday morning he got up with glee,
Little thinking that mischief was hatching,
Took out his penknife, his great toe to make free,
At night to prevent it from scratching;
But the knife slipped and gave his great toe such a wound!
Sweet wedlock there surely a fate in;
He could not put his foot at all to the ground,
Though he knew sweet Miss Condy was waiting.
    But alas! Who could look, *etc.*

Oh, words can't describe all his trouble and woe,
Only think if his sad situation,
A surgeon was sent for, who dressed his big toe,
And talked about amputation;
Laid up for a month, while Miss Condy so smart,
Disappointed at having this short knight,
Without delay got her another sweetheart,
And was married in less than a fortnight.
    So young men, if love has got into your head,
    Recollect Mr. Low and Miss Condy,
    And whatever you do, before you get wed,
    Never cut your toenails on a Sunday.

Part 35, Number 5, 1 July 1916

This is a song written by Thomas Hudson and published in 1824 under the title 'Cutting Toe-nails on a Sunday'. The tune was given as 'Michael Wiggins'. Williams's version is faithful to Hudson's original except that the location has been transferred from Hyde Park to Custom House Quay, which usually refers to Dublin. This might be explained by its having been included in the *Dublin Comic Songster* in 1841. Williams is the only collector to record having heard this song.

183. The Old Church Bells

Roud 9265, Bathe-Clissold Gl.53
Henry Temple, Barnsley, Gloucestershire

An old and amusing folk song, telling of a circumstance that is not unknown in our own times. I have myself been present at the ringing of the midnight peal, and can testify to the condition under which it used sometimes to be conducted. Copy obtained of Henry Temple, Barnsley, near Cirencester; it was also known at Shilton, near Burford.

O those old church bells! those merry bells!
Although they were but three,
A jolly set of ringers they,
As ringers ought to be.
It happened once upon a time,
How long I can't reveal,
Those old church ringers sallied forth,
To ring their midnight peal.
    O it really is a funny thing,
    The tales that I've been told,
    And plainly shows what ringers were,
    In the merry days of old.

They spent their evening hours before
In soaking well their clay,
And as they sallied forth at night,
Could scarcely find their way;
To hear them talk, and see them walk,
Along the road, 'twas rich,
The truth to tell, one old boy fell,
And tumbled in the ditch.
    O it really is a funny thing, *etc.*

The other two they got him out,
And to the church repaired,
Unlocked the door, and on their knees,
Went scrambling up the stairs;
Doffed off their coats, and seized the ropes,
But 'twas not long before,
The big bell ringer missed his pull,
And tumbled on the floor.
    O it really is a funny thing, *etc.*

Then, getting up he seized the rope,
But found 'twas all in vain,
For every time he tried to chime,
He would fall down again;
The other two their eyes were shut,
But still they went on ringing,
Till he cried – 'Stop! Let's have a drop,
And finish up with singing.'
    O it really is a funny thing, *etc.*

The bells went off with three, two, one,
And then with one, three, two,
For ring them right that very night,
Was more than they could do;
They blowed, they lugged, they pulled, they tugged,
But could not ring at all,
Until each man had made a stand,
With his back against the wall.
    O it really is a funny thing, *etc.*

The bells then stopped, and down they sat,
Upon the belfry floor,
They drank till all their beer was gone,
Of that you may be sure;
Then, groping back their way downstairs,
As homeward they did reel,
Each man declared he never heard,
A better midnight peal.
O it really is a funny thing, *etc.*

Part 36, Number 1, 8 July 1916

This song was published anonymously in a magazine for bell-ringers in 1888.[69] The actor and singer Bob Arnold, who lived in Burford, sang it for Peter Kennedy in 1952 and Francis Collinson also noted the song, although he did not say from whom he got it. Burford is 13 miles from Barnsley and (just) in Oxfordshire, but still within Williams's 'Upper Thames' area.

184. The Lover's Ghost

Roud 246, Bathe-Clissold Gl.272
Richard May, Fairford, Gloucestershire

This curious old piece I discovered at Fairford. I have nowhere else heard it. It is of great age, and I have no doubt that by reason of the nature of the narrative, it was welcomed by the rustics. Words of Richard May, Fairford.

It's of a farmer in our town,
His election goes the country round;
He had a daughter, a beauty bright,
In every place was her heart's delight.

Many a young man a-courting came,
But none of them would her favour gain,
Till a young man came, of low degree,
Came underhanded and she fancied he.

Soon as her father came this to hear,
He separated her from her dear;
For four score miles this maid was sent,
To her uncle's home for her discontent.

---

[69] 'Christmas Supplement' to *The Bell News and Ringers' Record*, 29 December 1888, p. viii.

Nine days after this young man died,
And his ghost appeared at her bedside –
'Rise, rise, my love and come with me,
And break these chains, and set me free.'

This maid arose and got up behind,
And he drove as swift as the very wind,
And not a word did this young man speak,
But – 'My dearest dear, how my head does ache!'

She had a handkerchief of the holland kind,
And around his head she did him bind;
She kissed his pale lips, and thus did say -
'My dearest dear, you're as cold as clay.'

He drove her up to her father's door,
And saw her father standing on the floor -
'O father dear, did you send for me
By such a kind messenger, kind sir?' said she.

He wrung his hands and tore his hair,
Much like a man in deep despair;
He tore the hair all from his head,
Crying – 'Daughter dear, the young man is dead.'

Early next morning this maid arose,
And straightaway to the churchyard goes,
She rose the corpse that was nine day's dead,
And found her handkerchief bound round his head.

O parents, parents, a warning take,
Don't chide your children, for heaven's sake!
Don't chide your children, for heaven's sake,
Or you'll repent when it is too late.

Part 36, Number 2, 8 July 1916

This is, indeed, an old ballad and a version of it, *The Suffolk Miracle*, printed in the 1670s, was on a broadside in Samuel Pepys's collection. Francis James Child included it in *The English and Scottish Popular Ballads* (Child 272), but it has been heard many times from traditional singers in Britain, Ireland, and North America.

185. The Gloucester Volunteers

Roud 21202, Bathe-Clissold Gl.91
William Simms, Fairford, Gloucestershire

It is not difficult to estimate the age of the following, since it evidently owes its origin to the formation of the County Militia. Most counties had such songs, though the compliments paid to the recruits may be characterised as rather doubtful. Copy obtained of W. Sims, Fairford.

Come all you brisk young fellows, that love your native land,
In honour of your country's cause, come join with heart and hand;
In forming the Militia, as plainly does appear,
No county can, I'm sure, surpass the Gloucester Volunteers.

We make no doubt, should honour call, they'll come, both bold and free,
And gladly too they may protect their Queen and Country;
Should anyone insult the land, I'll tell you without fear,
They'll be the first to fight their way – the Gloucester Volunteers.

You young and blooming females, in number may be seen,
A-viewing the Militia exercising for the Queen;
The marching was most excellent, as though they'd marched for years,
They knocked the brown beer about right well – the Gloucester Volunteers.

Now to conclude and make an end, may we live long to see,
Our native land protected by the friends of liberty!
So fill your glasses to the brim and drown all care and fear,
And drink a health to every man in the Gloucester Volunteers.

Part 36, Number 3, 8 July 1916

Militia and other bands of volunteer soldiers have been formed in Gloucestershire many times over the years. The volunteers being celebrated here were clearly from the reign of Queen Victoria, but despite Williams's confidence it is not possible, from the text alone, to assign a better date. This song is unique to Williams's collection.

186. The Jolly Miller

Roud 22067, Bathe-Clissold Gl.60
Raymond Smith, Bibury, Gloucester

Songs dealing with the miller and his trade were generally popular, though perhaps with those of higher intelligence and better education than with the bulk of the rustics. At the same time I have met with the two following songs [also 'The Miller of the Dee', *FSUT*, pp. 194–95] *in many villages and have heard them from farm labourers. Copy obtained of Raymond Smith, gamekeeper, Bibury.*

I live at the mill, at the foot of the hill,
Where the stream runs rippling by,
And for ten miles around, there cannot be found,
A merrier fellow than I;
For I laugh and I sing, and drive away care,
I've enough for my wants and a little spare;
And if any old friend should pass my way,
I'll make him as welcome as the flowers in May.

The jolly old mill, it stands there still,
As it did in my father's time,
Who often used to sing to me,
This little bit of rhyme.
'Remember my boy, don't turn up your nose,
At poorer people in plainer clothes,
But think, for the sake of your mind's repose,
That life's but a bubble that comes and goes.'

I have never seen the pleasure yet,
Of dressing very loud,
I think there's little good to be got,
In looking very proud,
Or passing over when you meet,
Some old acquaintance in the street,
I may be wrong, but then, you know,
It is always the style of the miller, just so.

You know I always think it best,
To pay your tailor's bill,
And pay your wrong and injury
With good instead of ill;
In fact, I think it best to do,
As you'd have others do to you,
I may be wrong, but then you know,
It is always the style of the miller, just so.

Part 36, Number 5, 8 July 1916

There are broadside versions of this, *As Welcome as the Flowers in May; or, The Jolly Miller*, published around the middle of the nineteenth century. It was, in fact, written, composed, and sung by the music hall performer Harry Clifton, who added it to his concert repertoire in 1870. It was noted by a few collectors, including Sabine Baring-Gould who heard it in Lydford, Devon, in 1892, and it was also collected as recently as 1970 by Ruairidh Greig in Derbyshire.

187. Tetbury Mop

Roud 21205, Bathe-Clissold Gl.123
Joseph Iles, Poulton, Gloucestershire

An old, local song, sung at the Michaelmas Fairs. Circencester, Highworth or Marlborough might have been substituted for Tetbury. Words of Joseph Iles, Poulton.

You young men and maidens, come listen to me,
I'll tell you a sight you never did see!
Oh, helter skelter, off you trot,
On the road to Tetbury Mop.

Oh, Michaelmas was drawing round,
And we poor slaves drawn off the ground;
There's many a farmer I'll be bound,
Will try to pull your wages down.

They'll say they cannot sell their grain,
To get the wages down again;
But of these men if you remark,
There's good and bad of every sort.

Now, when you come into the Mop,
There's fine fat sheep in every spot;
There's pigs upon crutches without any legs,
And two or three turkeys keep laying of eggs.

There are soldiers and sailors, and boys from the plough
A four-headed ox, and a two-headed cow;
I'll tell you the truth, and I don't care a pin,
There's a lot of old women get drunk with the gin.

There's old Farmer Waddle, so stout and so fat,
The nasty old rats ate the rim of his hat;
He's a nice little wife, as smart as a queen,
She has two wooden legs and a hooped crinoline.

The dames of the town get up for a spree,
They all get as lushy, as lushy could be;
They met an old smudge, and made him so drunk,
That he went for to light his short pipe at the pump.

Part 37, Number 4, 15 July 1916

This is another song that is unique to Alfred Williams's collection. The 'Mops', or statute fairs, were hiring fairs where men and women would go to seek employment for the year, bearing a tool or sign of their trade. The Cirencester event survives on two successive Mondays in October, but you will not see many mops being carried.

188. Rosy May

Roud 12890, Bathe-Clissold Gl.75
Joseph Bartlett, Down Ampney, Gloucestershire

I suppose these 'Darkie songs' as they are called, properly belong to America, though I have been led to entertain the idea that they may never have been sung there. They were certainly very popular here. I am sure that 'Rosy May' was sung in the Thames Valley as early as 1840, and it may be older than that. Copy obtained of Joseph Bartlett, Down Ampney.

Come darkies, listen unto me,
A story I will relate,
It happened in the valley
Of the Carolina State.
    O dearest Rosy May,
    You're as lovely as the day!
    Your eyes are bright, they shine at night,
    When the moon is far away.

It was down in the meadows,
Where I used to mow the hay,
And I always worked the harder,
When I thought of Rosy May.
    O dearest Rosy May, *etc.*

My master gave me a holiday,
He said he'd give me more,
I very kindly thanked him,
As I rowed my boat from shore.
    O dearest Rosy May, *etc.*

Then down the river I did go,
With my heart so light and gay,
To the cottage of my own true love,
My dearest Rosy May.
O dearest Rosy May, *etc.*

Part 37, Number 4, 15 July 1916

Williams's disdain for this song is evident and no singer nowadays would choose to sing it, yet minstrel songs were enormously popular with village singers. Most were imported ready-made from America, but I have not discovered an American edition of this song. It appeared as *Poor Rosa May* on British broadsides in the 1850s.

These four stanzas are the first two eight-line stanzas of the broadside version and miss out the part of the story in which Rosa May is carried away down river – 'The white man with his spreading sails, / Did bear my love away.' There are some other minstrel songs with the same name, one of which was collected by Sabine Baring-Gould. Williams is the only collector who heard the version above.

189. The Happy Country Lass

Roud 606, Bathe-Clissold Gl.120
W. Merritt, Meysey Hampton, Gloucestershire

For many years this song was the first to be sung at the general harvest home, observed at Meysey Hampton. It is of good age. I have seen the words on an old ballad sheet bought at Cirencester Mop. Copy of W. Merritt, Meysey Hampton.

I am a brisk and bonny lass
That's free from care and strife,
So sweetly I do my hours pass,
I love a county life;
At wake or fair I oft am there,
Where there's pleasure to be seen,
Though poor, I am contented,
And as happy as a queen.

I rise up in the morning,
My labour to pursue,
And with my yoke and milking pail
I trip the morning dew;
My cows I milk, and there I taste

The sweet that Nature yields,
And the lark is sure to welcome me
Into the flowery fields.

And when the meadows they are mown
My part I then do take,
And with the other village maids
I go the hay to make,
Where friendship, love and harmony
Amongst us there is seen,
And the swains invite the village maids
To dance upon the green.

Now in the time of harvest
So cheerfully we go,
Some our hooks and sickles,
And men with scythes to mow;
And when the corn is safe from harm,
We have not far to roam,
But all await to celebrate
And welcome harvest-home.

Now, in the winter, when the cattle
Are foddered with straw,
The cock he crows to wake me
My icy cream to thaw;
The western winds may whistle,
And northern winds may blow,
'Tis health and sweet contentment
The country lass doth know.

In winter or in summer
We are never known to grieve,
In time of need, each other
Will their neighbour relieve:
So I still think a country life
All others does surpass,
I sit me down contented,
I'm a happy country lass.

Part 38, Number 2, 22 July 1916

This song was printed as *The Country Lass* on a broadside by Evans of London in 1794 and later by others. Apart from Alfred Williams, it has been collected several times in Sussex. The Copper family sing 'The Brisk and Bonny Lad' (not to be confused with 'Brisk and Lively Lad'), which is based on this song, with the gender of the protagonist changed.

190. The Gossiping Wife

Roud 2658, Bathe-Clissold Gl.77
William Brown, Driffield, Gloucestershire

Songs satirising the weaker sex are rather abundant. If we had the views of the ladies concerning their tyrants and detractors they might have proved none the less sarcastic and damaging. It is possible too, that the castigations would have been equally well merited. Words of William Brown, Driffield. The song has been found in several parts of England.

Of all the wives that plague men's lives,
And keep them from their rest,
A gossiping wife or a passionate wife,
Pray which should you think best?
Why, a passionate wife give me for life,
She's never given to roam;
But a gossiping wife goes cadging about
She's got such a clacking tongue.
　　A gossiping wife goes cadging about,
　　Click-clack, but never at home;
　　She minds everybody else's business abroad,
　　But can never mind her own.

A gossiping wife I've got for my lot,
She is such a torment unto me,
She is never at home, I do declare,
But at breakfast, dinner and tea;
And as soon as ever my back is turned,
Away out of the house goes she
To a neighbour's house, with a dozen more,
With a child set on her knee.
　　A gossiping wife goes cadging about, *etc.*

Now, when that they are met and set,
If on them you should choose to pounce,
They out of the dozen you'll be sure to hear six
A-clacking all at once.
Click clack goes all their tongues,
They go just like whips all,
And when they have done not one half of them knows
What the others have been clacking about.
　　A gossiping wife goes cadging about, *etc.*

Now, if a man could but invent,
Such a thing as a gossip-spring,
For to stop all gossiping wives' tongues,
He would soon be rich as the king;
For there's many a man, I know full well,
Would employ that man, it is true,

For to stop his wife from going clacking about,
When she's got something else to do.
A gossiping wife goes cadging about, *etc.*

Part 38, Number 3, 22 July 1916

Although this appeared in the catalogues of broadside printers in the 1830s and in many subsequent editions, Alfred Williams is the only collector to have recorded hearing it. The manuscript page that he prepared to go to the printer has a stanza on it that has been heavily marked with blue crayon and was not included in the newspaper version:

When up steps one with a tongue a yard long,
Saying – 'What do you think I've heard?'
Your husband was with another woman last night,
'Tis true upon my word!
You know I always speak the truth,
Whenever we do meet.'
When all the people know full well,
She's the biggest liar in the street.
A gossiping wife goes cadging about, *etc.*

So why did Williams edit the song? Was it the third line that offended him? In the broadside versions it simply says, 'Your husband was seen last night.'

191. The Baker's Oven

Roud 12877, Bathe-Clissold Gl.52
James Trueman, Ampney St Mary, Gloucestershire

I have heard this but once, viz., at Ashbrook, near Cirencester. It is an old song, and the subject is ingenious, though it is doubtless founded on fact. Words of James Truman, Ashbrook.[70]

Job Jenkins was a baker, a very honest elf,
And by selling crust and crumb, he made a tidy crust himself,
But Job he lived in better days, when bills were freely paid,
And bakers were thought honest men, for bread was never weighed.
With a fol tol rol, ri ti fol the rido.

[70] Ampney St Mary was formerly known as Ashbrook.

As success creates ambition in this world, betwixt the poles,
Job thirsted after office, though a master of the rolls;
Job's patience it would not tire out, as quickly did appear,
And they very soon appointed him as Parish Overseer.
With a fol tol rol, ri ti fol the rido.

At length the tallow chandler the debt of nature paid,
And in his place, without delay, Job was churchwarden made,
Who soon declared that to his house a man must be a sinner,
To toil for parish work and go without his parish dinner.
With a fol tol rol, ri ti fol the rido.

While strolling through the churchyard he saw some old tombstones,
That long had marked the resting place of some poor neighbour's bones;
'These bodies have long gone to rest, the stone's no use,' he said,
'They'll make a bottom to my oven, and improve my next batch of bread.'
With a fol tol rol, ri ti fol the rido.

Tom Snooks, the parish mason, a very sportive blade,
Who in racehorses and the dead had done a decent trade;
To him Job gave his orders, regardless of amount,
And charged it to the parish in his next half year's account.
With a fol tol rol, ri ti fol the rido.

The job was done, the bread was baked, Job in his highest glee,
Got up at early morn that he might the improvement see;
But soon as drawn he dropped the peal, with horror on his looks,
And roared out like a madman, and knocked down Tommy Snooks.
With a fol tol rol, ri ti fol the rido.

'Get up, you wretch! and come and see the blunders you have made,
Your tombstone bottoms, sure, will prove a deathblow to my trade.'
He took him to the bake house, where a curious sight was seen,
The words on every loaf were marked that had on the tombstones been.
With a fol tol rol, ri ti fol the rido.

One quarter had 'In memory of,' and another, 'Here to pine,'
And a third, 'Departed from this life at the age of 99;'
A batch of rolls when they were done said this – 'Our time is past;'
'Thus day by day we pined away, and come to this at last.'
With a fol tol rol, ri ti fol the rido.

Next came the cottage loaves, and there, upon the bottoms plain –
'We trust in Him that made us and hope to rise again;'
On every loaf that they drew out all from that oven door,
There on the bread each one could read the letters on the floor.
With a fol tol rol, ri ti fol the rido.

Now, Snooks he turned away his head, his laughter to conceal,
Saying he thought it was a nobby way of making a bread seal;
Says Job – 'Thy seal has sealed my fate; how can I sell my bread
To feed the living, when it bears the memory of the dead?'
With a fol tol rol, ri ti fol the rido.

Part 38, Number 3, 22 July 1916

A version of this song was printed as 'Job Jenkins the Baker' in the *National Prize Medal Song Book* (no. 39) in 1874. A similar story was also told at Purton, Wiltshire, and was published in a local history book, although it lacks some of the early stanzas.[71]

192. Christmas Carol

Roud 1065, Bathe-Clissold Gl.124
Jane Ockwell, Poulton, Gloucestershire

As the communicator of the following carol is three score years and ten, and remembers to have heard the piece sung by her grandfather, it is evident that it is of considerable age. I have heard of several other very interesting carols in the neighbourhood of the Ampneys, though I was unable to obtain them. Copy of Mrs Jane Ockwell, Poulton.

God sent for us the Sunday,
All with his Holy hand;
He made the sun fair and the moon,
The waters and dry land.

There are six good days in the week,
All for a labouring man;
The seventh day to serve the Lord,
The Father, and the Son.

Now, when you go to church, dear man,
Down on your knees you fall;
And pay your worship to the Lord,
And on his mercy call.

For the saving of your soul, dear man,
Christ died upon the cross;
For the saving of your soul, dear man,
Christ's precious blood was lost.

Three drops of our sweet Saviour's blood,
Were shed and spilt for me;
We shall never do for our sweet Saviour,
As he has done for we.

[71] Ethel M. Richardson, *The Story of Purton* (Bristol: J. W. Arrowsmith, 1919), pp. 50–52.

My song is done, we must begone,
We stay no longer here;
As I wish you all a merry, merry Christmas,
And a happy New Year!

Part 38, Number 5, 22 July 1916

This is also known as 'The Christmas Mummers' Carol' and was published as such in the *Journal of the Folk-Song Society* in 1902. It was sent in by Godfrey Arkwright, who had heard it sung by the mummers at Kingsclere, Hampshire, in 1897. It was also found twice in Hampshire by George Gardiner, but Jane Ockwell's is the only version found outside that county.

193. Billy and Nancy

Roud 1643, Bathe-Clissold Gl.79
Jane Wall, Driffield, Gloucestershire

A plain old song, one of the simpler kind of ballads; it has been sung around Cirencester for more than a century. Obtained of Mrs Jane Wall, Driffield.

One day as I was walking
Down by the river side,
I heard a couple talking,
The damsel she replied –
'You most deceitful villain!
How could you serve me so,
When you promised me you would marry me,
About three years ago?'

'Now don't be discontented,
I never will break my vow,
For I've been disappointed,
And could not come till now.'
'If I'd all the gold and silver,
That lies by yonder sea,
I'd take more joy and pleasure,
In your sweet company.'

'As to what you say, my love,
I've heard you say before,
But you went from me these three years,
And never came nigh me more.
You went and courted Nancy,
The girl with the rolling eye,

It's she alone you fancy,
How can you this deny?'

'I hear to what you say, my love,
I own and swear it's true,
And as for Mistress Nancy,
She is no friend to you.
'She's often caused disturbance,
Betwixt my love and I,
With you I'll live for ever,
With you, I'll live and die.

'And as my name is Billy,
No longer will I tarry,
But to the church we'll go my love,
And surely we will marry.'
The weather being pleasant,
To church that couple passed,
And now they are got married,
Long looked for's come at last.

Part 39, Number 1, 29 July 1916

More often known as 'Long Looked For Come at Last' since most versions, while they have widely differing titles, conclude with this line. A similar song was published in *The Good Housewife's Garland*, *c.*1780. It was also collected by George Gardiner in Dorset and Cecil Sharp in Somerset and Gloucestershire.

194. Love Was Once a Little Boy

Roud 2664, Bathe-Clissold Wt.493
Annie Cross, South Marston, Wiltshire

This also is of great age. It is one of 'grandmother's' songs, which is sufficient evidence of its hoariness. It is not a common piece, though I believe it may rank as a folk song. Copy of Miss A Cross, South Marston, Wiltshire.

Love was once a little boy,
Heigho! Heigho!
Then with him 'twas sweet to toy,
Heigho! Heigho!
He was then so innocent,
Not, as now, on mischief bent;
Free he came and harmless went.
Heigho! Heigho!

Love is now a little man,
Heigho! Heigho!
And a very saucy one,
Heigho! Heigho!
He walks so stiff, and looks so smart,
As if he owned each maiden's heart;
I wish he felt his own keen dart.
Heigho! Heigho!

Love, they say, is growing old,
Heigho! Heigho!
Half his life's already told,
Heigho! Heigho!
When he's dead and buried too,
What shall we poor maidens do?
I'm sure I cannot tell, can you?
Heigho! Heigho!

Part 39, Number 4, 29 July 1916

This song was printed as 'Love Was Once a Little Boy' in *Fairburn's London Songster*, *c.*1823, and soon afterwards on broadsides. It was also published several times as sheet music in America later in the nineteenth century. Two singers sang the song to American collectors, but Alfred Williams is alone in having heard it in Britain. Annie Cross was the headteacher at South Marston School.

195. The Deserter

Roud 1655, Bathe-Clissold Gl.80
Jane Wall, Driffield, Gloucestershire

The following, if it has no special merits, may claim to be of great age. It was sung by the grandmother of my contributor, who is now an elderly woman. Words of Mrs Jane Wall, Driffield, Cirencester.

Once I thought I never should be,
In this dejected state,
A poor distracted effigy,
Exposed to hardships great;
The birds that flutter in the breeze,
Strike terror to my heart,
And every star alarmeth me,
Oh, why did I desert?

'Twas liquors caused me to go astray,
And from my colours fly,
What a poor coward I was that day!
The same I cannot deny,
'Twas liquors caused me to go astray,
And baffled every thought,
My life is now a scene of woe,
Oh, why did I desert?

'Twas under cover of a tree,
Where I was forced to lie,
To shelter from my enemies,
Although my friends were nigh,
Just like an owl that hides by day,
I dare not show my face,
But on my journey I will pursue,
And seek some friendly place.

My brother he came riding by,
Not knowing I was there,
My voice aloud to him did cry,
But me he could not hear,
His horse was borne from me away,
I could not bring him to,
And here distressed I must lie,
Not knowing what to do.

My sword and sack, and blue coat too,
To them I left behind,
The boots and spurs from off my feet,
For them I did not mind.
To the Light Horse I bade adieu,
It once was my delight
And on my journey I will pursue,
And travel through the night.

Part 39, Number 5, 29 July 1916

There are a number of songs about deserters, and the lofty text of this song is similar to a broadside printed by Catnach and listed in his 1832 catalogue. Some later editions came with an additional first stanza:

My parents reared me tenderly, I being their only son
But little thought it would be my fate to follow the fife and drum
The courting of a pretty maid until she won my heart
She first advised me for to list and afterwards desert.

This is actually borrowed from an earlier song, 'The Bold Deserter', which is more often found on Irish ballad sheets from the eighteenth century. The man also deserts from the Light Horse, but the song deals in more detail with his erstwhile sweetheart and, in one Irish edition he cries, 'The curse of the crows on you Cupid, it seems you can do what you please'.

The deserter that Jane Wall sang about was anything but bold and his desertion was due to liquor rather than a romantic attachment. In stanza five it should be his 'sword and sash' that he leaves behind, rather than 'sack'. Given that the song was reprinted frequently throughout the nineteenth century it has been collected surprisingly few times, mostly in central southern England.

196. To Beat the Drum Again

Roud 226, Bathe-Clissold Ox.248
Frank Cook, Burford, Oxfordshire

The circumstances of a young woman enlisting in the Army had a peculiar fascination for ballad-writers in the early part of the last century, and many pieces dealing with the theme are current. The one here given was popular at Filkins and South east Gloucestershire. Words of Frank Cook, Burford.

When I was a young girl, at the age of sixteen,
I from my parents ran away to go and serve the Queen,
I enlisted in the Army like another private man,
And very soon they taught me how to beat upon the drum.

My waist it being slender, and my fingers long and small,
Very soon I learned to beat the drum the best among them all;
The sergeant that enlisted me said I was a nice young man –
'And I'll think you'll make a drummer, so it's come along, my man.'

They sent me up to London to go and guard the Tower,
And there I might have been until this very day and hour,
But a young girl fell in love with me, and she proved I was a maid,
And straight unto my officer my secret she betrayed.

My officer then sent for me to know if it was true –
'For such a thing I can't believe, nor won't believe of you.'
'O yes it's true, dear officer,' she smiled and then he said –
'It's a pity we should lose you, such a drummer you have made.'

'So fare you well, dear officer! You have been kind to me,
And fare you well my comrades! You must sometimes think of me;
And should you be in want of men, why this I do attain –
I'll take off my hat and feathers and, I'll beat the drum again.

Part 39, Number 6, 29 July 1916

This was another very popular song among the old village singers. There are records of women who joined the army (or the navy) because they wanted to serve, rather than to follow a lover. Since boys much younger than sixteen served as drummers the story is not totally improbable. The earliest printed version is 'The Female Drummer' in a 1796 songbook called *The Blackbird.*

197. My Dashing Little Hunter

Roud 21206, Bathe-Clissold Gl.125
John Taylor, Poulton, Gloucestershire

We have already printed several fine hunting songs. Here we give several others that used to be popular in the Upper Thames region. There is something pleasantly human in the 'Dashing, little hunter'. The writer of the piece must have been tenderly fond of his horse to have spoken of it in such a charming manner. Words of John Taylor, Poulton.

I have as good a hunter as ever man did see,
So neat he picks his foot up, so well he bends his knee;
His shoulders good, his legs are strong, with such a depth of girth,
And what a pair of hocks he's got to help him through the dirt,
Has my dashing little hunter, has my gallant little grey.

His head's as fine as any fawn's, his neck is like a swan,
His haunches they are long and deep, his back is but a span;
His ribs are fine, his pluck is good, I never knew him flinch,
He's up exactly to my weight – that's fifteen hands, one inch,
Is my dashing little hunter, my gallant little grey.

When you see him by the cover side, with his snaffle bridle on,
While other horses prance and fret how quietly he'll stand;
When off the hounds, the fox is found, and settled on him steady,
He'll champ his bit, and toss his head, to let you know he's ready,
Does my dashing little hunter, does my gallant little grey

Now sly Reynard's broke and there's a Hallo! Gone away!
The scent is good, the country stiff, and there is no time to stay;
He's gone right up, upon a hill, and I'll venture any bet,
The long tail will be panting, and the knots all in a fret –
Is my dashing little hunter, is my gallant little grey.

Now along the vale we fly, while some begin to wane,
There's an awkward stiff stile in a bank, and a deep drop in a lane;
But my horse can stand and jump, that's often such a burst,
He's cleared it well, and landed safe, and now, my boys, who's first?
Why, my dashing, little hunter, why, my gallant, little grey.

Full fifty minutes then we ran, and only three the chase could stand,
And two of them were getting tired, but I was hand in hand;
Now they are gone and I'm alone, with rapture I am filled,
To think there were no other in with the hounds, boys, when they killed,
But my dashing, little hunter, but my gallant, little grey.

Part 40, Number 1, 5 August 1916

A song called 'My Gallant Little Hunter and my Charming Little Grey' was sung at a dinner for the Old Berkeley Hunt in August 1893.[72] A shorter version was published in Mrs Chatworth Musters, *Book of Hunting Songs and Sport* (private publication, 1885), p. 131. Francis Collinson collected a version from Brian Goodchild in Ely, Cambridgeshire, with some different stanzas.

198. Betsy of the Moor

Roud 21199, Bathe-Clissold Gl.40
Emily Freeman, Ampney Crucis, Gloucestershire

The following piece is not quite complete. It is very old and interesting, nevertheless. I have not heard it elsewhere. Words of Mrs E. Newman, Ampney Crucis.[73]

As I walked out one morning,
All for sweet recreation,
So happy in my station,
No care to trouble me;
To view the fruits of nature,
And every happy creature,
And all the gay amusements,
Before my eyes could see.

To watch fair flowers together
And the fruits among the heather,
The pretty little lambkins
How they did sport and play;
Bright shining came Aurora,
Accompanied by Flora,
And the bright rays of Phoebus
Began to feed the day.

72 'Chalfont St Peter, The Old Berkeley', *Uxbridge and West Drayton Gazette*, 8 August 1863, p. 5.

73 Chris Wildridge has identified the singer from census and other data as Emily Freeman, rather than 'Newman' as Williams named her.

High hills and lofty mountains,
Divided by small fountains,
Which run to join the ocean
All on that briny shore;
Through grief and sad vexation,
I lost all consolation,
My rule and habitation
Lies down this wintry moor.

[*Pair of lines missing*]

My parents they are aged
And them I will not leave;
For early they're repining
And daily are declining,
And hourly they are bowing
And bending to the grave.

As nature here don't bind me,
Since you are pleased to mind me,
Most dutiful you'll find me,
Until life is no more;
If you wait till they expire,
I will grant what you desire,
What more can you require,
Of sweet Betsy of the Moor.

Part 41, Number 4, 12 August 1916

This song seems to be unique to Williams's collection. From the style and language, it seems possible that it is Irish in origin.

199. Love It Is Easing

Roud 1075, Bathe-Clissold Wt.496
Lucy Lee, South Marston, Wiltshire

A simple ditty, with a pleasant air. It was very popular with the young ladies, and especially so in the neighbourhood of Burford. The copy I obtained of Mrs. Lee, South Marston, Wilts.

When I was young and well beloved,
'Twas by a man of this countree,
He courted me both late and early,
While he gained his free will of me.

Oh, love it is easing, and love it is teasing,
Love is a pleasure while it is new;
But when it grows older it still grows colder,
And fades away like the morning dew.

I never thought he was going to leave me,
Until one day as he came in;
He threw himself down and began to tell me,
And then my troubles they did begin.
Oh, love it is easing, *etc.*

'I left my father, I left my mother,
I left my brothers and sisters too;
I left my home and my relations,
I left them all for the sake of you.'
Oh, love it is easing, *etc.*

'Adieu, adieu, to all false lovers,
Adieu, adieu unto my dear;
You're like a star on a winter's morning,
You're far away when you ought to be near.'

Part 41, Number 6, 12 August 1916

This is 'The Wheel of Fortune', which was printed on broadsides in the mid-nineteenth century. That title comes from a stanza that Lucy Lee did not sing:

It's turn you round you wheel of fortune,
It's turn you round and smile on me,
For young man's words they're quite uncertain,
It's turn you round and smile on me.

Her song tells the story coherently, whereas many other collected versions have been reduced to a series of floating verses.

200. When I Wore my Apron Low

Roud 60, Bathe-Clissold Wt.424
George Barrett, Marston Meysey, Wiltshire

A variant of the old piece, 'There is a tavern in the town'. This may be prior to that, though one cannot speak with certainty. The copy was given to me by G. Barrett, Marston Meysey.

There is a flower, as I've heard say,
That blossoms by night and fades by day;
I wish I could that flower find,
To ease my heart, and cool my mind.

'Twas down in the meadows where she roamed,
Gathering flowers as they grew;
Some she gathered and some she pulled,
Until she gathered her apron full.

'When I wore my apron low,
He'd follow me through frost and snow;
But now my apron's to my chin,
He passes by and says nothing.

'There is an alehouse in the next town,
My love goes in and sits himself down;
He takes a strange girl on his knee,
He cares not for my company.

'I'll tell you the reason, I'll tell you the why,
Perhaps she's got more gold than I;
Her gold will fade, her beauty will blast,
And then she'll become like me at last.

'Pray dig me a grave that's long, wide and deep,
And strew it all over with flowers so sweet,
Write on my tombstone two turtle doves,
Let all the world see that I died for love.'

Part 11, Number 7, 12 August 1916

'When I Wore my Apron Low', like 'There is a Tavern in the Town' (no. 104), is a member of the extended family of songs known as 'Died for Love'. This cousin shares two stanzas with no. 104, but introduces the theme of her pregnancy, while losing that of suicide. In that, it shows kinship with an eighteenth-century broadside, *Lady's Lamentation for the Loss of her Sweetheart*, and the later 'The Brisk Young Sailor'. Versions of the song have been collected widely on both sides of the Atlantic and it remained a favourite with rural singers right through the twentieth century.

201. The Bold Champions

Roud 2411, Bathe-Clissold Gl.151
Eli Jasper Price, South Cerney, Gloucestershire

Not being particularly well read in the history of English sports I am unable to assign a date to the following though, perhaps some of our readers may recognise the circumstances related. It appears to be an old song; it has been sung around Cricklade for many years. Copy of Jasper Price, South Cerney.

Come, all you young men that delight in any game,
Come and listen to these few lines to you I will explain;
It's of two champions bold fought for a sum of gold,
And it was near London Town as I've been told.
  'Twas young Taylor, hurrah! 'Twas young Taylor, hurrah!
  Bold Robinson for ever, and young Taylor, hurrah!

Now the drums and the trumpets most sweetly did sound,
And the horsemen were mounted for to guard the ground;
The fight it was most noble, and young Taylor did say –
'It shall never be said that to thee I give the day.'
  'Twas young Taylor, hurrah! *Etc.*

Then up spoke bold Robinson, saying – 'The game it is my own,
I can find his heart does tremble at my every blow;
Come, all you understanding men, I'll have you for to know,
That I will be the champion, wherever I do go.'
  'Twas young Taylor, hurrah! *Etc.*

Then up spoke young Taylor, saying – 'I am just in my bloom,
I am willing for to fight thee from morning till noon.'
Young Taylor he then sprang, and gave bold Robinson a blow,
Saying – 'I will be the champion wherever I go.'
  'Twas young Taylor, hurrah! *Etc.*

At the end of six rounds these champions did meet,
With their bodies sorely wounded, and their hearts full of grief;
Bold Robinson he fell, without a sign or a groan,
That moment he died, and the battle it was won.
  'Twas young Taylor, hurrah! *Etc.*

And now to conclude, when this Young Taylor had won,
A rich lady fell in love with him for what he had done;
And if ever he recovers a grand wedding there shall be,
But young Taylor he died at the end of days three.
  'Twas young Taylor, hurrah! *Etc.*

Part 42, Number 2, 12 August 1916

I have found a newspaper article about the arrangements for a fight between Tyler and Robinson from November 1856, but not, so far, anything about the fight itself. The song was also collected by Cecil Sharp, George Gardiner, and Gatty and was printed on a number of broadsides.

202. Down in the Lowlands There Grew a Tree

Roud 129, Bathe-Clissold Wt.396
Elijah Iles, Inglesham, Wiltshire

An old and once popular song, that is to be met with in several forms, though I think the following is among the earliest versions. Words of Elijah Iles, Inglesham.

Down in the lowlands there grew a tree,
As fine a tree as you ever did see;
The tree was in the wood,
And the wood it was down in the lowlands low.

And on that tree there was a branch,
As fine a branch as ever you did see;
The branch was on the tree,
The tree was in the wood,
And the wood it was down in the lowlands low.

And on that branch there was a nest,
As fine a nest as ever you did see;
The nest was on the branch,
The branch was on the tree,
The tree was in the wood,
And the wood it was down in the lowlands low.

And in that nest there was an egg,
As fine an egg as ever you did see;
The egg was in the nest,
The nest was on the branch,
The branch was on the tree,
The tree was in the wood,
And the wood it was down in the lowlands low.

And in that egg there was a yolk,
As fine a yolk as ever you did see;
The yolk was in the egg,
The egg was in the nest,
The nest was on the branch,
The branch was on the tree,
The tree was in the wood,
And the wood it was down in the lowlands low.

And in that yolk there was a bird,
As fine a bird as ever you did see;
The bird was in the yolk,
The yolk was in the egg,
The egg was in the nest,
The nest was on the branch,
The branch was on the tree,
The tree was in the wood,
And the wood it was down in the lowlands low.

And on that bird there was a wing,
As fine a wing as ever you did see;
The wing was on the bird,
The bird was in the yolk,
The yolk was in the egg,
The egg was in the nest,
The nest was on the branch,
The branch was on the tree,
The tree was in the wood,
And the wood it was down in the lowlands low.

And on that wing there was a feather,
As fine a feather as ever you did see;
The feather was on the wing,
The wing was on the bird,
The bird was in the yolk,
The yolk was in the egg,
The egg was in the nest,
The nest was on the branch,
The branch was on the tree,
The tree was in the wood,
And the wood it was down in the lowlands low.

And on that feather there was some down,
As fine a down as ever you did see;
The song was of the down,
The down was on the feather,
The feather was on the wing,
The wing was on the bird,
The bird was in the yolk,
The yolk was in the egg,
The egg was in the nest,
The nest was on the branch,
The branch was on the tree,
The tree was in the wood,
And the wood it was down in the lowlands low.

Part 42, Number, 12 August 1916

This cumulative song, under various titles, can become very tedious – which is why it is frequently cut short. A broadside by Pitts from the early nineteenth century takes the story to its usual conclusion with a man lying with a maid on the bed that is made from the feather. Sabine Baring-Gould collected a version, 'The Everlasting Circle', in which the story (in fifteen stanzas) turns on itself with the man and maid producing a child, who plants an acorn that grows into a tree.

203. The Poor Fisherboy

Roud 912, Bathe-Clissold Mi.672
Jonathan Cole, Brinkworth, Wiltshire

The following interesting fragments of songs [the other is Jonathan and William, FSUT p.299] *I discovered at Brinkworth. They are all old, and have been popular in their time. Words supplied by Jonathon Cole, the aged gamekeeper.*

Down in the lowlands where the poor boy did wander,
Down in the lowlands where the poor boy did roam,
He looked so dejected, he was so much neglected,
The poor little fisherboy so far from his home.

Oh, where is my father? Oh, where is my mother?
My father's gone from me, which caused me to roam;
I have no relations, neither sister nor brother,
The poor little fisherboy so far away from home.

Part 42, Number 7, 19 August 1916

This is a fragment of another sentimental ballad, *The Poor Fisherman's Boy*, printed early in the nineteenth century. This song was mentioned in connection with 'The Poor Old Soldier's Boy' (no. 90) as part of a series of songs about orphaned children who are 'saved' by a wealthy benefactor.

204. We'll Chase the Buffalo

Roud 1026, Bathe-Clissold Wt 334
Allan Cutts, Brinkworth, Wiltshire

I too, have chased the buffalo, or at least the song; I have been at some pains to secure it. I first heard of it at Ogbourne; from there I traced it to Eynsham, near Oxford. Months of inquiry failed to elicit its exact whereabouts. By and by, however, I heard a little more at Aldsworth, and Bibury, and finally discovered it entire at Brinkworth near Malmesbury. Complete words of Allan Cutts, Brinkworth.

Come, all you bold fellows,
That have a mind to range,
Into some foreign country,
Your nation for to change!
Your nation for to change, my boys,
And from your homes to go,
We will lie down on the banks,
Of the pleasant Ohio.
    Through the wide woods we'll wander,
    And chase the buffalo.

Suppose some wild Indians,
Should chance to draw near!
We'll all unite together,
Our hearts free from fear.
We'll march into the town my boys,
And give them the fatal blow,
And lie down on the banks,
Of the pleasant Ohio.
    Through the wide woods, *etc.*

There are fishes in the river,
To render us good use,
And good and lofty sugar canes,
The finest produced;
There's all sorts of game, my boys,
Besides the buck and doe,
We can enjoy good sport
On the pleasant Ohio.
    Through the wide woods, *etc.*

Come all you pretty maidens,
And spin us up some yarn,
To make us some blankets,
To keep ourselves warm;
For you can card and spin, my girls,
While we can reap and sow,
And you can lie down on the banks,
Of the pleasant Ohio.
    Through the wide woods, *etc.*

Part 43, Number 2, 26 August 1916

The earliest known copy was printed by Evans around the beginning of the nineteenth century. Sabine Baring-Gould heard it in Devon and Cornwall, and Ralph Vaughan Williams in Salisbury, but it was not found widely.

205. Jack Hall

Roud 369, Bathe-Clissold Bk.18
William Jeffries, Longcot, Berkshire

An old song, dealing with the crimes and hinting at the execution of one Jack Hall. Chimney sweeping was not his sole occupation. Copy of William Jefferies, Longcot, Berkshire.

My name it is Jack Hall, chimney sweep,
Fifty long years in Cheapside dwelled I,
My name it is Jack Hall,
And I've robbed both great and small,
And my life must pay for all,
When I die.

I sold candles short of weight,
And they took me by the sleight,
And all rogues must have their right,
So must I;
They told me in the gaol
All my friends would not avail,
And my life must pay for all
When I die.

As I was going up Tyburn Hill,
In a cart,
At St. Giles Head I made my will,
That went hard;

Therefore all young men, take heed,
Of my most unworthy deed,
Or they'll hang you till you're dead,
And so must I.

Part 43, Number 3, 26 August 1916

Various claims have been made for the age of this song and the background to it. It is said to refer to a burglar executed in 1701, and Cecil Sharp made a claim for that being the date of the song, based on the existence of the tune around that time.[74] The earliest confirmed printing of the words was, however, on broadsides printed in the early nineteenth century. The song was popular with the village singers and was heard by most other English folk song collectors. Its popularity was reinforced by its reworking as the rather cruder 'Sam Hall', in the 1840s by the performer W. G. Ross.

[74] Cecil J. Sharp, *Folk Songs from Somerset*, Fourth Series (London, Simpkin; Schott, 1908), p. 77.

Folk Songs of the Upper Thames Conclusion

This is Alfred Williams's Conclusion to the series published in the *Wilts and Gloucestershire Standard* between October 1915 and September 1916. It was published as the final part (Part 44) in the series on 2 October 1916.

When we began the weekly publication of the folk songs I did not contemplate their continuance up to the present time. I considered about six months sufficient in which to show to the inhabitants of this locality the kind and quality of songs that had in times past been popular throughout the villages of the Upper Thames region. The materials I continued to collect proved so abundant, however, and the songs that had been printed gave pleasure to so many readers – as is evidenced by the number of letters I have received from various parts, and also by expressions of pleasure made to me personally – that, with the collaboration of the Editor, I thought it advisable to carry on the publication a few months longer, during such time, in fact, that I should still be engaged in examining the villages in the area south of Cirencester, in which the *Wilts and Gloucestershire Standard* circulates. This I have now about completed. What remains to be discovered in the extreme south and east of the Upper Thames Valley might not have a similar interest for our readers, so that it is fitting we should now conclude our weekly instalments of the songs. About four hundred pieces have been printed in the *Standard* since last October. They are not all I have, for I hold more than six hundred songs of my own collecting in this neighbourhood. I hope and expect to obtain an additional hundred or so before I have finished the work of examining all the villages, though that is a matter of some speculation. At any rate, we have done very well. One is first interested in a subject, and then bored with it. I do not want to be guilty of trespassing upon the patience of any. From what I have been told by enthusiastic readers of the songs I might find that difficult, in the present instance. Still, the danger is there; it remains a possibility.

I should like to point out that I had a special reason for wishing songs to be published in the *Wilts and Gloucestershire Standard.* The average collector of folk songs, I fear, is apt to take away from a locality. I will explain what I mean. If I had been induced to dispose of my materials to the Magazines I might still have performed a useful service, though I should certainly not have acted with the same disinterestedness to the localities from which I collected them. My duty from the first seemed to be to make efforts in order that the people of the Upper Thames Valley, as far as it lay in my power, should have the opportunity of an acquaintance with their own folk songs. I desired to make them as widely known as possible. With this object in view I approached the Editor of the *Standard*; he approved the idea – you have seen the result. I think we have been successful. In time – not till after the war, probably – the songs, with the notes, will be published in book form. It will not matter much then whether few or many in this locality obtain copies, since readers of the *Standard* will be in the favourable position of having already perused most of them. They have become common property, and some of the pleasure I have taken in collecting and preserving them has been shared by numerous others. That is my satisfaction and my chief reward. I hold it one of the most meritorious of things to have done, something worthy of serious public interest, and every good act requites itself.

The collecting of folk songs had been carried out in most of the counties of England before I began the work here two years ago. To tell the truth, it really wanted doing badly. Because no one had attempted to examine the locality methodically for folk songs it was assumed that none existed. The opinion was current that this was about the dullest part of England. We are an agricultural people here. What had we to do with music and merriment? Far from the large towns and cities, far from ship-bearing rivers and the sea, cut off, as it were, from the heart of the great world, its commerce and civilization, inhabiting a region calmly beautiful, but destitute of very stirring or striking scenery, engaged all their lives upon the soil, how could the hearts and feelings of the people be quickened? It was not to be expected that they should be so, much less that the village folks should discover any surprising and unusual propensity to and aptness for cultured and artistic sports and entertainments. It was not expected, and the natural inference was drawn. It was supposed that the people were stupid and ignorant, thick-headed, unmusical, and unimaginative – mere clowns and clod-hoppers. I hope that we have effectively shattered that illusion. Whatever other counties possess in the matter of folksongs they can scarcely claim to have more materials than have we of the Upper Thames. And the quality of the songs is good. I believe that versions of most, if not all, the best known folk songs are to be obtained in the villages around us, together with many that appear unfamiliar to residents in other quarters. The intensity of the life as it was in the villages is remarkable, and it would be inexplicable if we were to believe all that has been written concerning the 'misery, poverty, and starvation' rife among the agricultural populations a century, or three quarters of a century ago. If that had been true I should not be writing now. A proof of its falsity is in the abundance of evidence we have of the gaiety and optimism of the rustics, in the records of life remaining to us, not in books and histories, certainly, but in the aged surviving villagers themselves. One may doubt books, but he may not controvert living witnesses; and the evidence of the music, songs, pastimes, feasts, and games is final and conclusive. Whoever, in the future, pens a history of English rural life, and omits to take full cognisance of these, and the part they played, will have neglected half his subject; it is impossible to understand the actual life and conditions of the countryside without taking into consideration these highly important characteristics.

There is no need for me to write at length concerning the ground I have traversed in search of the folk songs, since I did that in my introductory chapter a year ago. Readers will remember that I defined my area as between Oxford and Malmesbury, the boundary on the north being a line drawn from Oxford through Witney, Burford, Bibury, Cirencester, and Tetbury. About half the ground lies north, and half south of the Thames, that of the former comprising portions of Gloucestershire and Oxfordshire, that of the latter parts of Wiltshire and Berkshire. A notable difference between the inhabitants of the two sections of the valley is to be observed. Those of Wiltshire and Berkshire are rather more boisterous and spontaneous, more hearty, hardy, strong, blunt, and vigorous, and a little less musical; those of Gloucestershire and Oxfordshire are gentler, easier, softer in manner, but weaker, more pliable, and less sturdy than the others. At the-same time, generally speaking, they have more refinement, and tastes more artistic than their neighbours of the southern half, though they have not quite the same tenacity and independence of spirit. This difference of character is very well illustrated by the diversity of pastimes in the two halves of the field; throughout Gloucestershire and Oxfordshire we had, as general sport, morris dancing; about Wiltshire and Berkshire the common amusements were back-swording and wrestling. While these were bedecking themselves with ribbons and tripping to the strains of the fiddle, those were breaking each other's heads with the single sticks, or strenuously engaged in casting their opponents in the ring. One may have his own opinion and predilection. The morris was exceedingly attractive, but there was something so stout, manly, and valiant about the back-sword play as to appeal to me with greater force than the music and rhythm of the dancers. Both were Greek – the one Lydian, the other Spartan; privately I should prefer the vigorousness of the latter to the softness, if not voluptuousness, of the former.

I have no evidence of morris-dancing in the villages south of the Thames. Step-dancing was common, but not morris-dancing. On the other hand, the morris was common in Gloucestershire and Oxfordshire. I find there were teams of morris-dancers at Eynsham, Southleigh, Standlake, Bampton, Filkins, Eastleach, Aldsworth, Sherborne, Fairford, Ampney Crucis, Latton, Cirencester, and, I have been told, though I am not entirely certain, at Southrop, Siddington, and South Cerney. All have disappeared now, except at Bampton, where, as tradition says, the annual morris games have been held in unbroken succession for 367 years. Other villages, wanting regular morris teams, were yet remarkable for music, games, and merry-making. Such especially were Aston, Brize Norton. Shilton, Langford, Coln St. Aldwyn, Quenington, Bibury, and Poulton. I must confess that I have a profound respect, almost a reverence, for these grand old villages. My blood quickens as I think of them. In my mind I invest them with a very great and true glory; there is a halo around them that is only to be compared with that about the classical towns of Greece and Italy. To me they stand as representations of a precious civilization, of the very best of the old English country life, vigorous, sane, and wholesome, unspoiled by the prejudice, affectation, and tasteless formalities in vogue in our own time.

The work of collecting the songs is laborious and tedious, though it is also highly interesting and pleasurable. I have everywhere met with much kindness and hospitality, especially among the cottagers, who possess real enthusiasm for songs and works of the intellect, and who usually discover more taste and humane feeling than those in a superior position and with better facilities of education. They are always anxious to provide me with hospitable entertainment. This one will have me stay to dinner or tea; that presses me to partake of supper, or offers me a night's lodging. Another invites me and my household to spend the week with him. One crams my pockets with fruits; this offers me a peck of potatoes. Another begs me to accept the gift of an overcoat. This has knitted me a pair of socks, or gloves, and that one would make me a present of a nice warm pair of trousers! Generally, I accept, for where gifts are offered with such kindness and simplicity it is cruel and boorish to inflict the pain of a refusal, and we are the greater friends afterwards. I have several times been taken for tramp, and also for a German spy. In the former case I had asked a very old lady, a cottager, that I might be directed to a certain house, and she, mistaking what I said, imagined I wanted food. Going inside, after a short delay, she came to the door holding in one hand a large crust of bread and cheese, and, in the other, a paper bag. 'Will you eat it now, or shall I put it in the bag?' inquired she.' I'd rather gie it, to you than to some o' they rough, dirty uns.' She had warm heart and was a kind, motherly creature. She has died recently.

The greater part of the work of collecting the songs must be done at night, and winter is the best time, as the men are then free from their labours after tea. This necessitates some amount of hardship, for one must be prepared to face all kinds of weather, and to go long distances. Some idea of the amount of travel necessary to the work may be gathered from the fact that, from where I am situated, I cannot complete the examination of the Upper Thames Valley without covering at least 25,000 miles; I have already traversed more than a half of this distance. In frost and snow, fogs, rain, and on sultry summer nights I have journeyed along the dark roads and climbed the steep hills bordering the valley, with the bats, the owls, the hares, and the foxes. I have faced the Thames' floods in almost inky blackness upon unknown roads and lanes, and shivered in the numbing cold of the damp mists exhaled by the river in the late autumn and winter months. Once, during a severe flood, following an extraordinarily rapid rise of water, I found myself immersed to the waist in Stygian darkness, and miles from any town or village: I have often scrambled along the banks in the blackness above the roaring brooks to escape a wetting. In the spring I have loitered on my return, evening after evening, till past midnight listening to the nightingale under the pure air and clear skies of the Cotswolds. Later in the summer, at the same hour, I have sat in the grass by the roadside amid the beautiful glow-worms while the air was warm and fragrant with the delicious scents of the newly-made hay. I have watched the late moon rise, now from behind the

Cotswolds, towards the north, and now, almost due south, above the rolling chalk downs of Berkshire and Wiltshire, west of the White Horse; and I have looked upon its reflection at midnight in the, calm river, now from Swinford, now from New Bridge, now from Radcot, and again from the Ha'penny Bridge at Lechlade or at Castle Eaton. At the end – though not yet at the end – I am happy, and happiest when I am on the road, having found, or hoping presently to find, another old song to add to our collection, at the same time not forgetting matters of graver import – the tragedies of life, the prolonged agonies and privations of this terrific war, and the greater and more glorious future that, is most certainly before us. Perhaps then our songs may be treasured with tenderness, and our labours kindly remembered; mine, who have toiled to save what is rare and valuable, yours – so many of you – who have assisted me and made my path easier, either by direct help, expressed pleasure, or sympathetic interest. I thank you all. A new world has dawned upon me since I undertook the collecting of the folk songs. If loved the countryside before, I do so far more dearly now. A new bond of friendship, that can never be broken, has been forged between it and me. I realise this as one of the most happy efforts of my life. The Upper Thames Valley is mine till I die.

Alfred Williams

Appendix A
The Kidson Letters

The *Wilts and Gloucestershire Standard* published six letters written to the Editor by Frank Kidson (described as the 'well-known authority on folk songs') in October and November 1915. These make a number of comments on the origins of the songs that Williams has offered for print, but the correspondence stopped after it became clear that the two men could not agree on what should and should not be described as a folk song. The letters are reproduced in full below. Many of the points made in them refer to songs that are not in the present collection, since they were included in the book *Folk Songs of the Upper Thames* (1923).

The first of these letters was printed on 23 October 1915, in the same issue as part four of the series and provides additional information about some of the first set of songs published a week earlier. That first selection did not contain any that Kidson could take issue with. In his second letter (30 October 1915), however, Kidson names three songs, 'Jeanette,' 'Maggie's Secret,' and 'I Don't Mean to Tell you her Name,' that he does not consider to be folk songs, as the composer was known and comparatively recent.

This prompted the first of three replies by Williams to Kidson's letters. His response was published in the *Standard* beneath Kidson's letter of 30 October and was brief and polite. He thanked Kidson for 'kindly providing the notes to our Folk Songs'. He went on, though, to firmly state his intention to print the songs that people in the locality actually sang, rather than attempting 'to deal exclusively with the purely Folk Song.'

Kidson opened his next letter (6 November 1915) with a sentence in which he congratulated Williams: 'Last week's instalment of Mr Williams's 'Folk Song of the Upper Thames' are all but one genuine productions of the rustic muse, and are true folk songs.' This was met with silence, as was the letter of the following week.

Williams did, however, respond to Kidson's fourth letter (20 November 1915). Here he is much more direct and rejects Kidson's comments on 'Sweet Molly O'Mog', saying that the fact that the song 'has been sung by the peasantry for the last hundred and fifty years might reasonably be sufficient, to entitle it to rank as a folk song, whatever its origin may have been.'

Kidson came back on this in a lengthy letter published on 27 November and provided an extract of the original text by John Gay as evidence for his assertion. In his reply, which terminated the newspaper correspondence, Williams robustly dismisses Kidson's definition of a folk song, saying that it is clearly wrong to insist that they evolved *from* the people, but rather that songs from the ballad-writers and sung by ballad singers were taken up, passed on, and adapted *by* the people. This is a definition that is accepted nowadays but was anathema to the Folk-Song Society.

He also repeated his view that 'Sweet Molly O'Mog' *could* have been a product of an old ballad writer that Gay reused. He may not have had a leg to stand on, but he was not going to give in to Kidson. His original point had been that the song was reported to have been printed on a broadside, sung at a Cirencester fair, and must have had some circulation more than a century earlier.

Apart from the letters directed to the Editor of the *Wilts and Gloucestershire Standard* there does appear to have been a direct contact between the two men, as there is one letter from Kidson to Williams that has survived, written in answer to a letter that Williams had written, but which has not been found among Kidson's papers.

The letter is undated but was certainly written in late 1915 or early 1916. It covers much of the same ground as those in the *Wilts and Gloucestershire Standard*, notably Williams's inclusion in his collection of drawing room and parlour songs that did not fit with Kidson's definition of a folk song and the disagreement over 'Sweet Molly O'Mog'. Kidson ends: 'All this I might have said in print to vindicate my original contention but I prefer to drop out of the whole affair and leave you a clear field unhampered by any of my notes and comments.'

And there matters rested.

Wilts and Gloucestershire Standard, 23 October 1915

FOLK SONGS OF THE UPPER THAMES

Mr. Frank Kidson, of Leeds, writes us as follows:

Mr Alfred Williams' selection of 'Folk Songs of the Upper Thames' is most interesting, as showing survivals and versions of folk songs which linger in the more obscure country places. Much corruption has, of course, taken place in the course of their traditionary existence. 'The Knight' is one of the large series of 'Riddle' songs, of which 'The Elfin Knight', 'The Courteous Knight', 'Captain Wedderburn's Courtship', 'Lay the bent to the bonny broom', and a host of others are examples. Mr Williams' version most nearly resembles the last-named, which will be found in full in D'Urfey's 'Wit and Mirth', vol. iv, 1719, p.130.

'The Ram' is also well known. It is generally named 'The Derbyshire Ram', and was set as a glee by J. W. Calcott. It is also to be seen in 'English County Songs' published in 1893. My copy of the 'Derbyshire Ram' with Calcott's music, occurs in 'The Harmonist', a book of glees in several volumes, in date about 1806. Strangely enough, my copy has at one time belonged to the 'Gloucester Vocal Harmonic Society.' 'If you will walk with me', is common in a full dozen poems; Versions will be found in Halliwell's 'Nursery Rhymes' and other nursery rhyme collections, and as 'The Keys of Heaven' in 'English County Songs'. The same may be said of the 'Carrion Crow'. It is certainly ancient, and copies will be found in Halliwell's 'Nursery Rhymes', 1853, and Bell's 'Ballads and Songs of the Peasantry of England', 1857. I myself published a traditional version in 'British Nursery Rhymes' (Augener and Co.)

'The Blue Cockade' is more properly known as 'The White Cockade'. The earliest and purest version I know is in Bell's 'Ballads and Songs of the Peasantry of England', 1857. It has been published many times, and it was well known in Lancashire and Yorkshire. I published a version with two sets of the air in my 'Traditional Tunes' in 1891. 'To Milk in the Valley Below' may be compared with Mr Baring Gould's version, 'The Sweet Nightingale', published in his 'Songs of the West'. 'Lord Lovel' was very popular in the fifties, when it was sung as a comic song on the concert hall platform; nevertheless, it is really an old ballad, I think.

If the tunes to which Mr Williams old songs were sung could be noted they would form an interesting collection

Frank Kidson

Wilts and Gloucestershire Standard, 30 October 1915

FOLK SONGS OF THE UPPER THAMES

Mr. Frank Kidson of Leeds, the well-known authority on Folk Songs, writes:

I am pleased to see a further instalment of Mr Williams's 'Folk Songs of the Upper Thames'. I notice many old favourites which are current in many places over the English counties. 'The Seeds of Love' and 'The Sprig of Thyme' are two songs which are inextricably mixed, and in all probability they have originally formed one song. A copy of 'The Seeds of Love' is in Bell's 'Songs of the Peasantry', 1857, and since then under either the title 'Sprig of Thyme' or 'Seeds of Love' has appeared with different airs in nearly every collection of folk songs published. See 'Songs of the West', 'English County Songs', Kidson's 'Traditional Tunes', Mr Sharp's 'Songs from Somerset', and different numbers of the 'Folk Song Journal'. 'Rosin the Beau' (or Bow) has, I fancy, an American origin. It is well known and has been published with its lively air. The author of the song 'Wrap me up in my old stable jacket' has been indebted to much of it for his verses; it is sung to the same tune. 'The Old Grey Man' is a version of the early Scottish song, 'The Carle he cam' o'er the Croft', which probably first appeared in Allen [*sic*] Ramsay's 'Tea Table Miscellany', 1724. 'The Spotted Cow' was common in Yorkshire and elsewhere; a version with two tunes appears in my 'Traditional Tunes', 1891. 'Paul Jones' is to be found in Dr Barrett's 'English Folk Songs' with the air which is current in Yorkshire, as well as in the South. 'High Germany' is in several modern folk-song collections. I noted a version down from a Worcestershire man. The three last-named are commonly met with on broadsides. 'Down in Covent Garden' is a version of 'Charley Reilley', a highwayman song. Under the name 'The Flash Lad' a copy with the air is in Dr Barrett's 'English Folk Songs'. 'Johnny the Ship's Carpenter' is commonly met with on broadsides as 'The Cruel Ship's Carpenter'. I noted a tune for it in Yorkshire.

I'm afraid that 'Jeanette', 'Maggie's Secret', and 'I don't mean to tell you her name', can scarcely claim to be folk songs. A folk song as generally understood to be, is a lyric with its music that has come from a non-professional class of musicians and verse writers. It is, in fact, a song evolved from the people; generally the rustic or more or less unlettered people. 'Jeanette and Jeannot' was a song published about 1848. It was written by Charles Jeffrys, and the pretty air was composed by C. W. Glover. It had at once immense popularity all over England, and an answer, 'Jeannot and Jeanette', was afterwards written to it. Its popularity lasted until well into the 60s. Jeffrey wrote, and Glover composed, many a dozen songs which attained the greatest favour in Victorian Drawing rooms. 'Maggie's Secret' is another professional drawing-room song that had some popularity in the 60s. 'I don't mean to tell you her name', was a little earlier. The music was composed by Robert Guylot, born 1794, died 1876. The words are attributed to Thomas Hudson, a well-known writer of comic songs in the 20s and 30s, but I have a suspicion they are by Thomas Haynes Bayly, author of 'I'd be a butterfly', and many other delightful songs that were in fashion in our grandfathers' days. The title generally assigned is 'My village fair'. The version given by Mr Williams is not quite verbally correct.

Frank Kidson

Mr. Williams, commenting on the foregoing, says:

We are all grateful to Mr. Kidson for so kindly providing the notes to our Folk Songs; they will throw an interesting light upon the minstrelsy of the Upper Thames district. Previous to this time certain counties had claimed to possess the majority of the Folk Songs and we of the middle South were represented as being dull, unmusical, and generally unintelligent. We hope that the publication of our songs will shatter that illusion effectively. As I pointed out in my introduction, we are principally concerned with our own locality, and not with the Folk Song in particular, or as it occurs in other parts of the country. I shall accordingly not attempt to deal exclusively with the purely Folk Song, but shall include any piece I think worthy of note, provided it ranked with the Folk Song, and stood in relation to the life of the people. I find that certain songs of Burns, and other choice pieces, were sung by the villagers, and it would be committing an injustice not to notice them. I shall also, later on, give specimens of local rhymes and mumming pieces, which were acted upon the Thames Banks.

Wilts and Gloucestershire Standard, 6 November 1915

FOLK SONGS OF THE UPPER THAMES

Mr. Frank Kidson writes:

Last week's instalment of Mr Williams's 'Folk Songs of the Upper Thames' is excellent, as the songs are all but one genuine productions of the rustic muse, and are true folk songs. 'Lord Bateman' is known in different versions throughout the three kingdoms. It has been said that this story is founded upon the adventures of Gilbert a Becket, the father of St. Thomas of Canterbury. Gilbert travelled in the East and is said to have been followed home by a Turkish lady who only knew two words of English, 'Gilbert' and 'London'. By using the last-named she arrived in the city, and by calling 'Gilbert' she found her lover. The absurd belief that the song was sung in Constantinople has evidently arisen in this wise. In 1830 George Cruikshank issued a version of the ballad in book form illustrated with delightful etchings. He jocosely put on the title page an intimation that it was published 'at Constantinople', giving a fictitious Turkish name as that of the booksellers. The booklet was revised in 1887; both editions are scarce, the first especially so. 'The Maids Wager' is an early ballad which is found under sundry titles. In Bell's 'Songs of the Peasantry', 1857, it is called 'The Merry Broomfield', or 'The West Country Wager'. I have a version also on a broadside. The tune with the words has been noted recently. 'Cold Blows the Wind' is well known, and frequent on broadsides. A copy will be found in 'English Country [*sic*] Songs', edited and collected by Miss Lucy Broadwood and J. A. Fuller Maitland. The song is sometimes called 'The Unquiet Grave'. 'Sheep, Crook and Black Dog' and 'The Faithful Plough' will also be found in 'English Country Songs'. 'The Painful Plough' is also found in Dr. Barrett's 'English Folk Songs. I have a copy of 'Sheep, Crook and Black Dog' in a 'Garland' printed about 1775. 'Now we are met let's merry, merry be' is as old as the 17th century; a copy will be found in Bell's 'Songs of the Peasantry', 1857. 'A-begging buttermilk I will go' is given as 'Buttermilk Jack' in 'The Scouring of the White Horse', by Thomas Hughes, 1859. 'Adieu my Lovely Nancy' is printed on broadsides and the tune has recently been collected. 'Shepherds are the best of men' is published in 'English Country Songs', and was obtained at Shipton-on-Stour. I do not think 'Come tell me when', etc., is a folksong.

Frank Kidson

Wilts and Gloucestershire Standard, 13 November 1915

FOLK SONGS OF THE UPPER THAMES

Mr. Frank Kidson writes:

The following notes regarding Mr Williams' last week's instalment may be of interest. 'The Outlandish Knight' is one among our most popular narrative ballads. It has been printed over and over again, and to a variety of tunes is to be seen in many collections of folk songs. The ballad is certainly of great antiquity. 'The Draggle-tailed Gypsies O'; a version of this has become popular from its being recently introduced in schools. A number of versions are to be seen in folksong collections and on broadsides. The best-known copy is named 'Johnny Faa or the Gipsy Laddie', which is often printed in Scotch collections of songs. This version appears first in Allan Ramsey's 'Tea Table Miscellany', 1724, and is said to chronicle an incident that occurred in the 16th or 17th century when Lady Cassillis ran away from her husband and followed the Gipsy laddie. Tradition says the gypsy was promptly captured and hanged on a tree facing the castle. 'The husbandman and servingman', 'The Duke of Marlbro', 'Bold General Wolfe', and 'William Taylor' are all folksongs fairly well-known; they are printed on ballad sheets and versions have been collected in different parts of the country. The last-named figured as 'Billy Taylor' in a comic version which was printed in song books nearly a hundred years ago. Even an opera was founded upon it and acted in the seventies or eighties of last century. 'Old Brown Ale' is really a fine song called 'O Good Ale thou art my darling!' It will be found in Chappell's 'Popular Music of the Olden Time', and in early song books. It used to be sung by Joseph Grimaldi the clown. I published a copy with the fine sturdy tune in 'Songs of the Georgian Period'. 'Joke and push about the pitcher' is rather curious. It appears to be founded on a once popular song called 'My friend and pitcher'. This was by John O'Keeffe and first was sung in his opera, 'The Poor Soldier', acted in 1783. Whether O'Keeffe's song was suggested by the lyric which Mr. Williams has discovered, or whether the reverse, I cannot tell.

Frank Kidson

Wilts and Gloucestershire Standard, 20 November 1915

FOLK SONGS OF THE UPPER THAMES

Regarding last week's instalment of Mr. Williams's 'Folk Songs of the Upper Thames', Mr. Frank Kidson writes:

Mr. Williams gives three variants of this well-known ballad, 'Barbara Allen'. This ballad seems to have had strange fascination for singers of folk songs, for versions are to be noted in every county in England. The earliest mention of the ballad occurs, I believe, in the 'Diary' of Samuel Pepys, under date January 2nd, 1665-6, when he speaks of the pleasure it gave him to hear Mrs. Knipp 'sing her little Scotch song of 'Barbary Allen'. Besides the little variations in versions there are two distinct sets of verses, Scotch and English. 'John Barleycorn' is also a fine old ballad to be found on early and late broadsides. In addition to many other printed ballad collections, it is to be found in Robert Jamieson's 'Popular Songs and Ballads', Vol. II, 1806. 'The Blind Beggar of Bethnal Green' is an old ballad still remembered in country districts. Its date is probably late 16th century. 'Auld Robin Gray' is, of course, well known, and how the authoress took the name of one of her father's farm servants and how she took the suggestion of the cow being stolen from her younger sister. The fine old tune, 'The Bridegroom greets when the sun gaes down', to which it was originally written, is never played now, this having been superseded by the popular tune by Rev. M. Leeves, who did not know of the original air. 'The Golden Vanitie' is found in most recent folk song collections; it is a curious and early ballad. Less known is 'The Banks of Green Willow', also early. 'The old woman tossed in a blanket', (should be 'basket') is an early nursery rhyme sung to the tune of 'Lilliburlero'. 'Sweet Molly Mog' can scarcely claim to be a folk song; it is by John Gay, and said to be written on an innkeeper's daughter at Oakingham, in Berkshire.[1] There are fifteen verses in the correct copy, and Dr. Maurice Greene set the song to music. It will be found with the air in John Watts' 'Musical Miscellany', Vol., II., 1729, and in many later collections. There is no reason in the world why the witty poem should be put into dialect form; there is nothing to justify such a thing.

Frank Kidson

Mr. Williams writes as follows with regard to Mr. Kidson's concluding remarks:

The fact that the song, 'Sweet Molly O' Mog', has been sung by the peasantry for the last hundred and fifty years might reasonably be sufficient to entitle it to rank as a folk song, whatever its origin may have been. It is quite possible that the dialect version is the older form and that it gave occasion to Gay's

[1] Kidson should have named the place where the song was written as Wokingham.

poem. We know that poets are notorious for their building upon others' foundations. Gay was more likely to change the dialect into pure English than was the later bard to turn his verses into local vernacular.

Wilts and Gloucestershire Standard, 27 Nov 1915

FOLK SONGS OF THE UPPER THAMES

Mr Frank Kidson writes traversing Mr. Williams's opinion that the dialect song 'Molly O' Mogg' may have given occasion to Gay's poem. He adds:

Mr Williams' verses are said to appear on a broadside bought at Cirencester fair in 1793. Gay, who died in 1732, printed his version at least as early as 1729, and from that day to this Gay's name as author has been associated with the song. Gay's verses could only have been produced by a polished wit, and extend to fifteen stanzas. Mr. Williams' traditional copy extends only to four, and are practically verbally the same, except that Z is used for S and V for F. Compare:

Says my uncle: 'I pray you discover
What hath been the cause of your woes,
That you pine and whine like a lover.'
I have seen Molly Mogg of the Rose.'

'Oh Nephew! Your grief is but folly
In town you may find better prog:
. . . . . . get you a Molly
A Molly much better than Mogg.'

I know that by wit's 'tis recited
That women at best are a clog
But I'm not so easily frighted
From loving of sweet Molly Mogg

. . . .

I feel I'm in love to distraction,
My senses are lost in a fog,
And nothing can give satisfaction
But thinking of sweet Molly Mogg

The only differences in Mr Williams' traditional copy, beside the mere change of letters I have indicated, are the words 'hakker' for 'pine' and 'zuit' for 'grief', and a quite necessary, though slight change, in the third line of the second verse. A further point in Mr Williams' letter may be noticed. He claims that 'Molly Mogg' having been sung by the peasantry for the last hundred and fifty years might reasonably be sufficient to entitle it to rank as a folk song'. In the first place, Mr. Williams tells us that he 'has not heard it elsewhere,' and only knows it as having been the favourite of a person's grandfather and father. That is not a proof of universal usage among the peasantry.

In the next place, it is not considered by most folk song collectors that an art song – that is, a song or melody written or composed by a professional writer or musician – is a folk song, however wide its usage. They limit a folk song, in the strictest sense, to the song born of or evolved by the unlettered people. Otherwise we should have to include the modern music hall ditty, and extend our range very much wider. The interest in folk song and folk melody lies in their spontaneity and freedom from external influence. Especially so in value are folk melodies which, in the best examples, owe nothing to composers outside the class among which the melody is produced. Folk song and folk melody have their limits – perhaps narrow limits – but they are valuable for keeping within those limits.

Regarding last week's instalment, 'Henry Martin', in two versions, was published in 1891 by myself in 'Traditional Tunes', from copies obtained in Yorkshire. Mr. Baring Gould obtained copies in Devonshire, and other versions have recently been published from different places in country districts. 'Dame Durden' is, of course, well known, and 'Old Dorrington' is a version, one of many, of the early Scottish ballad, or poem, 'The wife of Auchtirmuchty', which dates from the 16th century. 'John Grumlie' and 'The old man who lived in a wood' are also versions of the witty story. In the 50s of last century a farce called 'Domestic Economy', by Mark Lemon, having the same theme, was staged. 'The nobleman and thresher' is frequently found on broadsides. A copy appears in Johnson's 'Scots Musical Museum', Vol. IV., 1792, and in 'English County Songs', 1893.

Frank Kidson

Mr Williams replies as follows to the foregoing:

I made no claims whatever concerning the song 'Sweet Molly O'Mogg', simply stating the fact of its having been sung at Cirencester Mop in 1793, and adding that it was a favourite of the Baughans, of South Cerney. I suggested it might be the original of Gay's poem, and I still think it possible. At any rate, it is not an elegant piece, from the point of view of literature. I have not Gay's works by me and have not seen the poem, but I am disinclined to believe that he ever wrote 'From loving of sweet Molly Mogg'. The use of the objective genitive there is unpardonable in a writer with Gay's reputation; it is in the proper ballad-writer's style. The composition of the first stanza may not matter much, Though the line 'That ye hakker and pine like a lover', in the dialect version, is immeasurably better than the one given as Gay's authentic line. The fact that the longer piece has been attributed to Gay no more establishes his authorship of our short version than does Burns' faking of John Barleycorn entitled him to pose as the original author of that piece, which of course, he never did. The definition of the folk song is necessarily vague. It is obviously incorrect, however, to insist that it was evolved from the people, that is, from the unlettered. It was evolved *for* the people, not *from* the people. There is the difference. No person with a complete knowledge of the villagers, and knowing the difficulties of literary composition, would say that the rustics were capable of producing the words, much less the melodies, of the many hundreds of folk songs formerly in circulation. The great majority of the labouring classes could not read or write, and it would have been utterly impossible for them to make the songs. There was a school of ballad writers, who catered for the common taste. They lived in towns and cities and were professional men, if not artists in literature. They were, moreover, conversant with the affairs of the world, or they could not have incorporated and reflected them in their songs and ballads. The rustics learned the pieces from the ballad singers at the fairs, and passed them on by oral means. The fact that 'Sweet Molly O'Mogg', was printed on broadsides and sold at the fairs is proof indisputable of its comparative 'universal usage'. It matters nothing that one hundred and twenty years after it was known to be sung at Cirencester fair, I have only found one surviving singer of the piece. Not a quarter of the whole of the English Folk Songs were *everywhere* popular; I often find a person in possession of a particular song which would not be found in any other village in the Thames Valley, nor, perhaps, throughout the whole south of England. As for the 'art song', there is more pure art in many of the folk pieces than in a corresponding number of those penned by acknowledged professionals at the present time. The question is what one would call art. The differentiation between this and the folk song may be too strongly insisted upon; the most stupid rustic I have ever spoken to upon the matter could tell the difference between 'Henry Martin' and 'The Miner's Dream of Home', or even such a sweet old song as 'I don't mean to tell you her name', to say nothing of 'Yip i addy i day', and 'Everybody's doing it'.

Alfred Williams

Chippenham, Wiltshire and Swindon History Centre, 2598/60, manuscript letter from Frank Kidson to Alfred Williams, [n.d.].[2]

5 Hamilton Avenue
Leeds
Sunday

Dear Mr Williams

[2] This letter has, at some time, been transferred to an envelope with a date of 24 March 1924 with a London postmark. In collating, the letters have been placed in the archive folder in date order and so it is to be found by the date of the envelope. The letter must, in fact, have been written in late 1915 while the series was still running.

Excuse delay in replying to your letter. I have much sympathy with your task in noting the folksongs of your district & would help where I could; but I fear we are very much astray in elemental ideas on the subject & that some of my notes might appear as criticisms rather than as lights. You head your contributions "Folk Songs of the Upper Thames" but you include certain Victorian drawing room, or parlour lyrics by known writers & composers which may be found on contemporary sheet music. I don't know whether you rank these as "folk-songs" but certainly I do not, nor does any folk song expert that I have come across.

The folk song or ballad of which you have given so many examples are as distinct from this class of song as possible. It never appeared on the ordinary music sheet save on a very few special occasions, until the recent folk song movement. The words are found printed on the ballad sheet but the tune remained purely traditional.

As a matter of fact, I have (with few exceptions) all the songs you have given in ballad sheet form & the tunes of many have been noted by members of the Folk Song Society.

It is interesting to compare these versions.

With regard to Gay's song "Molly Mogg" I cannot understand your position. It has been accredited to Gay ever since its publication nearly two hundred years ago & you can bring forth no evidence save your own belief to the contrary. The song in its entirety is found in all reputable editions of Gay's poems & this fact has never been disputed. If you have read through the whole poem I cannot conceive you not seeing that it was written by an 18th century poet of Gay's standing. In regard to the line you object to, Gay might not have employed it in an elegant poem, but he puts it as a colloquialism in the mouth of one of his characters in the poem. Molly Mogg was an innkeeper's daughter who died in March 1766, apparently well known to Gay & his friends & there is no reason why Gay should not write a playful poem in her honour. All this I might have said in print to vindicate my original contention but I prefer to drop out of the whole affair & leave you a clear field unhampered by any of my notes and comments.

I am
yours truly
Frank Kidson

Appendix B
'Folk Songs of the Upper Thames Valley' by Alfred Williams (1926)

Published in *Word-Lore*, Vol. 1, No. 1 (January–February 1926), 12–16.

I hold it a pity, and I imagine most people would agree with me, that more districts, counties, and areas were not methodically examined at least half-a-century ago for the express purpose of ascertaining what relics of folk-lore remained, and thus making sure of their preservation. I say methodically examined, because extensive as the labour of folk song collectors has been, owing largely to its incoherence and the lack of a definitely worked out plan, only a few counties and localities have received anything like adequate attention. Out of this has arisen the idea that some counties and districts were very rich in folk songs and folk lore, and that others, though adjacent, possessed nothing, or but very little; whereas I have not the least doubt but that folk music, if not folk dancing, was general, at any rate, in the entire South of England. What was wanted was knowledge, and, of course, a proper amount of sympathy with local life, customs, and pastimes. But current fashion was against it. Literary taste ignored or condemned it. Complex and diversified as was the culture of the Victorian period, it was still incomplete, inasmuch as it was not able to appreciate the simplicity and artlessness of the folk performance, Nor yet its precious quality and definite value. That is why the recognition of the folk song and Morris dance was so long deferred. The delay was costly, because, in the meantime, much valuable material perished beyond recovery; than this nothing could be more safely established.

It was while writing prose chapters in the Upper Thames neighbourhood in 1913 that I first became aware of the large amount of folk lore relics and folk songs surviving in that district.

Of other collectors, or collections of folk songs, I knew nothing at that time. This was owing to my occupation at the Swindon Works, which left me but a few hours of leisure at the week-end. I had this advantage: I was born in, and I had slept in a village all my life. I remember hearing my mother sing 'Brennan on the Moor' when I was a child; and the village bands, at festival times, always played a certain amount of folk music. An old soldier, who had been in many wars, sang snatches of songs learned aboard ship, or at the ports; but, as was often the case with men of this type, he could not well be depended upon for versions, being defective in memory, and careless as to tunes. If I had been in the habit of attending the inns I should certainly have heard many old ballads. As it was, I missed them, and remained in profound ignorance of what was happening around me. It is the search that reveals. I was never more surprised than when, after I had shown myself interested in folk songs, a farm labourer who had lived near me for thirty years told me his favourite piece, which was 'The Prickly Bush'. I had never suspected him of singing anything; and this may be taken as an example of the peculiar elusiveness of the folk songs.

When the opportunity came for me to make a prolonged search for folk songs in this neighbourhood, I first sat down and mapped out a definite area. The occasion was provided by my being compelled, through ill-health, to leave the Swindon Works. This was in the spring of that fateful year, 1914. I decided on the ground lying north and south of the Thames, extending from Oxford to beyond the Thames Head – a distance of nearly fifty miles. From Oxford I drew a line past Wantage behind the White Horse to Marlborough and Malmesbury, and included, on the other side, Tetbury, Cirencester, Burford, and Witney, with the neighbouring Cotswold villages and Eynsham, as far as Wytham. Being situated in the centre of this area, I was able, by daily journeys, to visit every village and search out every family and individual who was known to sing folk songs, or who had any knowledge of the Morris.

The process was tedious, even arduous; and the countryside was stirred with the gigantic struggle that developed in France and elsewhere, and drew away so many of the youths of our local towns and villages. In eighteen months I had cycled 13,000 miles, without quite finishing the area; and the songs I collected of one sort and another in the time numbered about six hundred. Then I, too, joined the Army and went overseas. In 1920, when I returned (from India) I was able to realise how fortunate I had been in my haste to gather materials. Late as I had been in the field, I had saved much; now it would have been impossible. All my oldest and best singers were dead; their ages had ranged from eighty to one hundred years. We know that atmosphere of the early post-war days – the disappointment and despair of those whose interest lay in non-material things. To a great extent that has passed. We have time now to appreciate what has been done in this direction; but further collection is hopeless, because so many new interests have appeared on the scene, and the human repositories of the folk songs have died out.

I would here point out that my original purpose was not that which may have prompted other collectors of folk songs. It is fair to say this, because in the arrangement of my materials, as they stand in 'Folk Songs of the Upper Thames', I was at no particular pains to connote and classify; nor did I attempt to adhere to the accepted canon, which has always seemed to me too rigid as ordinarily applied to folk songs and ballads. My idea was to save whatever folk songs I could, not to add to existing collections, not merely in order to supplement the record of local life and activities undertaken in my prose volumes. In this sense I was not a specialist, but merely a labourer and an enthusiast. If the war had not broken out I should have achieved better results, because I should have had collaborators and obtained music as well as words. But under the circumstances that was not possible. Really, the work could not have been undertaken at a more inopportune moment; and the wonder is, not that I did not obtain better results, but that I succeeded in getting what materials I did.

In those silent and lonely villages, scattered along on both sides of the Upper Thames, when the war broke out, and for some time afterwards, I found aged men still singing songs connected with the Duke of Marlborough's campaign in the Netherlands and elsewhere, 1702–1704; and others dealing with the American War of Independence, and battles with the French towards the end of the eighteenth century. But a few miles from Oxford one sang 'Rodney so Bold', the hero of St. Lucia; another, not far from the Thames Head, sang of Captain Brooks, and the Chesapeake and the Shannon, in the celebrated engagement off Boston. Amid the solitude of Bradon Woods (North Wilts), the site of the once famous forest of Bradon, in which Fulk Fitzwarrene lay in wait for the King's merchant train, I found an old man singing such pieces as 'Bold Sir Rylas', 'Captain Grant', 'Widdicombe Fair', and 'The Parson and the Sucking Pig'. Other famous pieces, such as 'Arthur O' Bradley', 'Lord Thomas and Fair Eleanor', 'Lord Bateman', 'Holly and Ivy', 'Captain Barniwell', 'The Carrion Crow and the Tailor', 'The Husband Man and the Serving Man', and so on, were widely popular. Old catches, glees, convivial ditties, hunting songs, and other pieces were sung at almost every inn between Oxford and Malmesbury; and there is scarcely a village in the whole area that might not have put up a competent minstrel, or a choir of them, if necessary.

A feature of the locality was the annual singing contests at the inns, which took place during the autumn. At such times local 'champions' issued challenges, and, having fixed dates, supported by a crowd of followers, they assembled and entered the lists. The contest was to decide, not who could sing best, but who could sing most pieces. I knew several of these old men ; and they would unbutton their shirt-collar at six in the morning and sing for twelve, and even for eighteen hours, having a fresh piece each time, with the perspiration streaming down their cheeks. Obviously, such as these possessed a large stock of songs; I have personally proved several whom I knew to have had between two and three hundred, to say nothing of fragments. Of course, one heard the same familiar pieces again and again throughout the area ; but, in addition to them, one usually found, in each village of any consequence, at least one new song that was often held to belong to that village, or to an individual, or family, and which no-one else attempted to sing round about. And in the village itself individuals recognised a kind of right to sing a certain piece, and they seldom or never attempted to trespass upon the domain of another by singing that to which they were not accustomed.

In the area, which comprised parts of Wiltshire, Berkshire, Gloucestershire, and Oxfordshire, there was a pronounced difference of peoples and characteristics. The Thames proved a true dividing line, as it had done for centuries, and although river-traffic had been responsible for much folk activity and inter-association, the distinction, in some respects, was maintained with remarkable obstinacy. Where there was no bridge across the stream occupants of opposite banks looked upon each other as strangers, and even foreigners. Only at one place on the south side of the river did I find evidence of Morris-teams; i.e. at Buckland, near Faringdon. On the north side, right along the base of the Cotswolds, through Oxfordshire and Gloucestershire also, villages had their Morris-dancers. I found remains of teams at Eynsham, Southleigh, Standlake, Bampton, Filkins, Eastleach, Aldsworth, Sherborne, Fairford, Ampney Crucis, Latton, Cirencester, Southrop, Siddington, and South Cerney. Step-dancing was common in Wiltshire and Berkshire, but not Morris-dancing. People of the Downside had other recreations, which discover their robust nature and temperament. For physical sports they had wrestling and single-sticks, which drew even larger crowds than the Morris, but they might have been more rude and uncultured. At the same time, there was, perhaps, as much music, of a kind, in the southern half as in the northern ; and the villages along the Downside from Wantage to Marlborough, as well as those in the Vale, bordering the highways, were full of vigorous life and activity.

There were no, or very few, local songs, and no really meritorious dialect pieces. One of the outstanding features of the folk song, as it appears to me, is its ubiquitousness. It circulated everywhere, even amid the remote districts of North Wales. Ireland, we know, was alive with them; so was the North of England, and Scotland. I believe that if our seaport towns had been thoroughly examined, not later than the middle of last century, they would have yielded a rich crop of songs and ballads. Assemblage and intercourse were particularly favourable to the folk song. Indeed, in our own district, where there was none of this there was no music – no life and gaiety, For instance, you would find few songs or dances where there was no inn; but where there were many inns there would be many songs, and much music, There is no room here to dilate upon the reasons for this and that, or to explain away the disappearance of the folk song and dance. I perceive one very definite cause in my own locality, and that was the dispersing of the village bands, which synchronised with the general adoption of the church organ in the villages, This might not apply everywhere; but I have little doubt that it was an important factor in other districts besides this. The decay of local fairs, farm feasts, and festivals was another obvious factor; and besides, we have become less simple and less local in our tastes and experiences. I do not say that we are really happier and wiser, in the main, than the majority of our fore-runners. And I sometimes reflect that village life is becoming more languid, shallow, and uneventful than ever.

Bibliography

Works by Alfred Williams

The most important book about folk song written by Alfred Williams is *Folk-Songs of the Upper Thames* (London: Duckworth, 1923). He intended this to stand beside his other books about the people and culture of the Upper Thames Valley. These contain descriptions of people, including some of his singers, as well as items of folklore, song, and dance. They are:

A Wiltshire Village (London: Duckworth, 1912).
Villages of the White Horse (London, Duckworth, 1913).
Round About the Upper Thames (London: Duckworth, 1922).

While less relevant to his work on folk song, I also recommend reading *Life in a Railway Factory* (London: Duckworth, 1915), which gives a vivid description of the conditions in which he had formerly worked.

There are also number of articles about song written by Williams for various local newspapers between 1916 and 1929.

Biographies of Alfred Williams

The biography of Williams that is most easily available is Leonard Clark, *Alfred Williams: His Life and Work* (William George's Sons, 1945). This was reprinted by David and Charles in 1969 and in the introduction Clark wrote that if he were to do it again he would correct some of his youthful exuberances. The description of Williams's work on folk song is necessarily brief and not always accurate. No one has yet taken up the challenge of writing a better biography and, certainly, no one has written a biographical study of his work on folk song.

Another biography is by Williams's friend, Henry Byett, *Alfred Williams: Ploughboy, Hammerman, Poet, and Author* (Swindon: Swindon Press, 1933). This is based on a series of newspaper articles written by Byett for the *Swindon Advertiser*, with additional material. While it is not well written I believe this book gets closer to Williams as a person.

Other works consulted

Ashton, John, *Real Sailor Songs* (London: Leadenhall Press, 1891).
Atkinson, David, and Steve Roud (eds), *Street Ballads in Nineteenth-Century Britain, Ireland, and North America: The Interface between Print and Oral Tradition* (Farnham and Burlington, VT: Ashgate, 2014).

Atkinson, David, and Steve Roud (eds), *Printers, Pedlars, Sailors, Nuns: Aspects of Street Literature*, (London: Ballad Partners, 2020).

William Aytoun, *The Ballads of Scotland* (Edinburgh: William Blackwood, 1858).

Baring-Gould, Sabine, *Songs and Ballads of the West*, Part 1 (London: Patey and Willis, 1889).

Baring-Gould, Sabine, *English Minstrelsie*, 8 vols (Edinburgh: T. C. & E. C. Jack, 1895–97).

Bell, Robert (ed.), *Ancient Poems, Ballads and Songs of the Peasantry of England* (London: Parker, 1857).

Broadwood, Lucy, and J. A. Fuller Maitland, *English County Songs* (London: Leadenhall Press, 1893).

Carey, George G., *A Sailor's Songbag: An American Rebel in an English Prison, 1777–1779* (Amherst: University of Massachusetts Press, 1976).

Chappell, William, *Popular Music of the Olden Time* (London: Chappell, 1855–56).

Child, Francis James (ed.), *The English and Scottish Popular Ballads*, 5 vols (Boston: Houghton, Mifflin, 1882–98).

Creighton, Helen (ed.), *Folk Songs from Southern New Brunswick* (Ottawa: National Museums of Canada, 1971).

Cox, John Harrington (ed.), *Folk Songs of the South* (Cambridge, MA: Harvard University Press, 1925).

Frank, Stuart M., *Jolly Sailors Bold: Ballads and Songs of the American Sailor* (East Windsor, NJ: Camsco Music, 2010).

Hepburn, James, *A Book of Scattered Leaves: Poetry of Poverty in Broadside Ballads of Nineteenth-Century England*, 2 vols (Lewisburg: Bucknell University Press, 2000–01).

Hindley, Charles, *Life and Times of James Catnach* (London: Seven Dials Press, 1970).

Hobsbawm, Eric, and George Rudé, *Captain Swing* (London: Readers Union, 1970).

Hudson, Thomas, *Comic Songs* (London: T. Hudson, 1824).

Huntington, Gale, *Songs the Whalemen Sang* (New York: Dover, 1964).

Huntington, Gale, *The Gam; More Songs the Whalemen Sang* (Suffield, CT: Loomis House Press, 2014).

Karpeles, Maud (ed.), *Cecil Sharp's Collection of English Folk Songs*, 2 vols (Oxford: Oxford University Press, 1974).

Kidson, Frank, *Traditional Tunes: A Collection of Ballad Airs* (Oxford: Chas. Taphouse & Son, 1891).

Kilgariff, Michael, *Sing Us One of the Old Songs* (Oxford: Oxford University Press, 1998).

Long, W. H., *A Dictionary of the Isle of Wight Dialect* (London: Reeves and Turner, 1886).

Mason, Marianne H., *Nursery Rhymes and County Songs* (London: Metzler, 1877).

Ord, John, *Bothy Songs and Ballads of Aberdeen, Banff, and Moray, Angus, and the Mearns* (Paisley: Alexander Gardner, 1930).

Palmer, Roy (ed.), *Everyman's Book of English Country Songs* (London: J. M. Dent, 1979).

Palmer, Roy (ed.), *Folk Songs Collected by Ralph Vaughan Williams* (London: J. M. Dent, 1983).

Palmer, Roy (ed.), *The Oxford Book of Sea Songs* (Oxford: Oxford University Press, 1986).

Frank Purslow, *Marrow Bones: English Folk Songs from the Hammond and Gardiner Manuscripts*, rev. Malcolm Douglas and Steve Gardham (London: EFDSS, 2007).

The Quaver (London: Charles Jones, 1844).

Ramsay, Allan, *The Tea-Table Miscellany; or, A Collection of Scots Sangs*, 9th edn (London: A. Millar, 1733).

Richardson, Ethel M., *The Story of Purton* (Bristol: J. W. Arrowsmith, 1919).

Rogers, Charles, *The Modern Scottish Minstrel; The Songs of Scotland subsequent to Burns*, 2nd edn (London: Nimmo, 1876).

Roud, Steve, and Julia Bishop (eds), *The New Penguin Book of English Folk Songs* (London: Penguin Books, 2012).

Sharp, Cecil J., *Folk Songs from Somerset*, Fourth Series (London: Simpkin; Schott, 1908).

Thompson, Harold W., *A Pioneer Songster: Texts from the Stevens-Douglass Manuscripts of Western New York, 1841–1856* (Ithaca, NY: Cornell University Press, 1958).

The Universal Songster; or, Museum of Mirth, 3 vols (London: Jones, 1825–26).

Warner, Anne (ed.), *Traditional American Folk Songs from the Anne & Frank Warner Collection* (Syracuse, NY: Syracuse University Press, 1984).

Journal articles

A number of journal articles are mentioned in my notes to the songs and in the footnotes and I will not repeat them here. I will, though, draw your attention to the 1969 issue of *Folk Music Journal* (vol. 1, no. 5) which was given over to a 'Symposium' on 'Alfred Williams and the Folk Songs of the Upper Thames', comprising three papers:

Ivor Clissold, 'Alfred Williams, Song Collector'
Frank Purslow, 'The Williams Manuscripts'
John R. Baldwin, 'Songs in the Upper Thames Valley, 1966–1969'

While there are some factual errors in these articles, they were the first serious attempt to evaluate Williams as a folk song collector.

Online sources

Writing this book in a plague year meant that opportunities to visit libraries were rare and I was restricted to books on my own shelves, supplemented by the growing number of volumes available on the internet. The source that my keyboard can virtually find of its own accord is, of course, the Vaughan Williams Memorial Library's immensely valuable archive and database https://www.vwml.org.

Other sources of particular value and freely available are:

Bodleian Library Broadside Ballads Online: http://ballads.bodleian.ox.ac.uk.

English Broadside Ballad Archive (University of California, Santa Barbara): https://ebba.english.ucsb.edu/.

Internet Archive: https://archive.org. The Internet Archive contains several early folk song books, as well as three of Alfred Williams's books: *Round About the Upper Thames*, *Life in a Railway Factory*, and *Nature and Other Poems*.

Roud Folk Song and Broadside Indexes: https://www.vwml.org/.

Wiltshire Community History:
https://history.wiltshire.gov.uk/community/folkintro.php/.

Given that Williams collected many songs that were written in the latter part of the nineteenth century I have found very useful John Baxter's Folk Song and Music Hall website: https://folksongandmusichall.com/.

Finally, I should mention the magisterial PhD thesis written by Andrew Bathe, 'Pedalling in the Dark', a very comprehensive study of Williams's folk song activity. You can download a copy from https://etheses.whiterose.ac.uk/14510/.

Afred Williams with Elijah Iles at his home in Inglesham.
Courtesy of Paul Williams.

Index of Singers

Note: Index entries refer to song numbers (not page numbers).

Index of Songs

Note: Index entries refer to song numbers (not page numbers).